5ive minute consultant™

Solutions
to
Everyday
Business
Problems

by Paul Bieber

For additional copies, visit www.fiveminuteconsultant.com or contact:
Bieber Consulting Inc.
354 Upper Troy Road
Fitzwilliam, NH 03447
United States of America
Phone: 603-242-3521
Fax: 603-242-3527

Printer: Sheridan Books, Ann Arbor, MI
Editor: Penny A. Stacey
Art Director: Dawn E. Campbell
Illustrator: Christopher Bunn

Views and opinions expressed by the author are not necessarily those of the publisher.

Printed in the United States of America.
First Edition

ISBN 978-0-9896311-0-5

Dedication

This book is dedicated to my mother Ethel Bieber. When I was young she worked in a public library and brought home children's books every day, stretching my imagination and teaching me the beauty and importance of the written word.

—Paul

Contents

Contents Continued

Contents Continued

Introduction

Three years ago, Deb Levy of Key Communications asked my consulting partner, Stan Lane, and me to give a presentation at a glass industry convention on Long Island. We wrote four scenarios, created the requisite PowerPoint show, and suddenly I had the inspiration to expand that presentation to book-length.

I have worked in the architectural glass industry for 37 years, starting out as a salesman for C.R. Laurence Co. Inc. and then getting promoted to regional sales manager. My manager, Phil Siatta, taught me so much. Phil had the most beneficial talents: he was street-smart and then worked harder than most to learn new ideas and techniques, in order to become a superb teacher and friend.

C.R. Laurence was and still is a great company. My position required 40+ weeks of travel per year, and with our second child on the way, I joined Floral Glass and Mirror in Hauppauge, N.Y., as executive vice-president and general manager. It was there that I came to know and deeply respect Chuck Kaplanek, the president and owner of this family company. For the first couple of years there, Chuck was my boss. Sometime in the 1990s, we crossed a line and became brothers. Chuck helped me succeed in many of our crazy ideas, and, most importantly, he let me fail as well. Chuck taught me that the education from failures is just as important as the exhilaration of success. Most of the scenarios in this book come from our hands-on management of Floral Glass.

At Floral Glass we fabricated insulating glass, manufactured tempered and laminated safety glass, glass furniture and wholesaled glass throughout the New York City metropolitan area from our main plant in Hauppauge, NY, and new plants in northern New Jersey and southern Connecticut. The business tripled during my time there, mainly due to hard work by the entire company. I retired when we sold the company to an Ireland-based conglomerate in 2004.

Introduction Continued

Soon the phone began to ring, asking me for advice on a variety of business situations. I gladly answered my friends, but after a year off, I decided that consulting was viable. I joined with Stan Lane, a financial and personnel genius, and we started Bieber Consulting Group LLC, which helps all kinds of businesses in all kinds of situations.

Just as the consulting business was starting, Deb Levy, the publisher of *USGlass* magazine, asked me to create a bi-monthly column for her industry-leading magazine covering the architectural glass industry. The column still runs today. I am proud to give this magazine a mention and hope readers take a look at it on usglassmag.com. Additionally I write a weekly blog of business information and sometimes baseball, which can be accessed at http://usgpaul.usglassmag.com. Sincere thanks goes to the entire team at Key Communications and *USGlass* magazine. In addition to Deb's leadership, Penny Stacey, my editor, Chris Bunn, who did the cover art, and Dawn Campbell, who designed the layout of this book, deserve special mention.

Thanks to all of the people whose names I have slightly used. You know who you are.

Even more important than my business life, my wife of 39 years, Elaine, has taught me the most of any person I have ever met. Our two wonderful children, Jessica and Philip, are both pre-school teachers, following in Elaine's footsteps. All three have added to this book doing edits and offering suggestions.

Chapter 1

The Five-Minute Solution to Lost Paychecks

 Problem

You own Mickey's Mantle Company, which makes prefabricated fireplace mantles with 58 employees. On Thursday morning at 9:15, Molly, your bookkeeper, runs into your office and tells you that the company's payroll checks have not been received from ABC Payroll Company. She says she called the payroll company and was told the company would put a trace on the package with the checks.

You regularly give out paychecks on Thursday afternoon and know most employees are expecting a check, having already spent the money.

Possible Outcomes

- You promise your employees their checks will be here Friday. You listen to their problems and shrug your shoulders and say that it is not your fault the package was lost. Everyone at Mickey's looks angry.

- You ask Molly to call ABC Payroll Company and have a second set of checks cut. The company will do this, but you still can't get the checks until Friday morning.

- You decide to handwrite 58 paychecks, but realize that ABC has already debited your account for the payroll and you don't have enough funds to cover a "second" payroll.

- You realize that 23 employees have direct deposit—therefore no problems for them. You only need to write and cover 35 checks.

- You have an opportunity to be a hero or a bum. Choose wisely.

What to Do When Molly Runs into Your Office

1. Don't panic. Find out who Molly spoke with at ABC. Ask her to get the names of executives at ABC; call the highest-ranking person and find out what he will do; make him your partner in solving the problem. Don't place blame or get into a shouting contest.

2. Under no circumstances should you tell employees that they won't get their checks until the next day. Years of employee goodwill will disappear overnight. If the package is lost today, it still may be lost tomorrow. Do something now.

3. If ABC's printing office is within driving distance, send someone to pick up a second run of checks. If the roundtrip drive time is longer than ten hours, put two people in the car and have them alternate driving. ABC will honor this second printing request if the company gives a hoot about customer service. If ABC needs a second draw on your checking account, the company is pulling your chain; ABC can place stop orders on the missing checks.

4. The office is three states away. Have ABC wire the amount you need to cover the handwritten checks to your bank.

5. If ABC says the bank wire is not available, now is the time to start the shouting match. A reliable payroll company will place employer funds in an escrow account until the checks clear. If ABC has placed your company's funds in its general account, you should be wary of ABC's future.

6. Ask your bank for a seven-day loan to cover the extra payroll checks. A good relationship with your banker helps here. Even if you don't have a great credit history, most banks will use this opportunity to win more business and push their own payroll systems.

7. This must all take place within hours. Don't waste time planning for the future now. Have Molly write the checks. Use your credit cards for cash advances if you have to. Nothing is more important than covering these checks today.

8. If you still can't cover all of the checks, get as much cash as you can and give each employee what they need to cover their bills today. You will probably reduce your cash needs in half by asking the employees how much they actually need.

Preventing This Problem

Most companies outsource their payroll processing. Tax and withholding changes, federal and state regulations, IRS reporting and just the physical amount of time it takes your bookkeeper makes this outsourcing practical and cost-efficient. You have to assume that the lost check problem will happen and be ready for it.

1. When you sign the contract for the payroll service, make sure it includes a detailed description of what the company will do when a payroll is lost or delayed. Make sure it includes delivering your payroll via direct messenger in case of emergency. Give yourself an extra day on payroll. If payday is Thursday, have your contract specify that you receive the checks on Wednesday.

2. Your contract should state that your funds will be available for a second round of checks if the first printing is lost. If this vendor will not do this, shop for another company.

3. Make sure that your provider has a wire payment procedure in place if it needs to refund your payroll so you can write replacement checks.

4. Have the phone numbers and names of the key players at your payroll company handy. It is easier to start at the top than to call customer service and work your way up.

5. When you have been on your provider's plan for a short period of time, do a dry run of the problem of the lost paychecks.

6. Always set up a "payroll checking account" you can write checks from if an emergency occurs. Provide for a second signer who will be available when you are away. Know what your highest paycheck dollar value is and confirm with the bank that checks over this amount aren't valid.

7. For safety's sake, don't keep cash on hand to cover your payroll in an emergency.

8. Encourage as many of your employees as you can to go with direct deposit to their checking accounts or debit card. Some employees are hesitant at first. They may not have bank accounts or don't trust banks. Teach them the advantages:

   • No lost checks, by the company or the employee.

   • Employees gain immediate use of the deposited money—no waiting to clear.

   • No need to rush to the bank during lunch hour on Friday.

   • Employees still get their regular check stubs with all of the same information.

   • Many payroll services will give a prepaid Visa or MasterCard instead of a check or direct deposit. (Make sure there is no fee for using the card, or for leaving it dormant for a period of time.) This is perfect for people who don't have bank accounts. The direct deposit amount can be posted directly to the credit card account.

9. Some employees don't sign up for direct deposit because they don't want their spouses to see how much they are paid, especially when overtime is earned! In these cases, ask your payroll company for a split direct deposit. The basic payroll goes to one account, and any overage goes to a separate account. There may be a small charge for this, and your bookkeeper will have an extra couple of minutes of paperwork to complete when the payroll is submitted.

10. Not only will direct deposit save you money with your provider as creating a direct deposit is less expensive than creating a paper check, it will also reduce lost check problems.

11. Some payroll companies charge a reprint fee when an employee loses a paycheck and the company has to place a stop order. The bank makes money, you spend time, and the employee is upset at not getting his money quickly and having to pay the reprint fee. Usually, the employee will need cash quickly and ask you for an advance while waiting for the stop payment to be processed. Direct deposit prevents this.

12. Can you make direct deposit mandatory for your employees? A number of states allow you to make direct deposit mandatory:

Alabama;	Massachusetts;	South Carolina;
Georgia;	Mississippi;	Texas;
Hawaii;	Missouri;	Virginia;
Kansas;	Nebraska;	Washington; and
Louisiana;	Ohio;	West Virginia.

Visit www.fiveminuteconsultant.com for the current list.

Chapter 2

The Five-Minute Solution to Major Theft

5ive minute consultant™ · Problem

It's 9 o'clock Monday morning and Bill, the book-keeper, hasn't shown up for work yet. You don't think much of it until the bank calls at 10 a.m. and says company checks are bouncing. The bank tells you there was a check cashed late on Friday, made out to Bill, which took all of your working capital out of the business. You call Bill's home and cell; the numbers are disconnected.

Possible Outcomes

- You don't have too many options here. It could all be a big mistake by the bank. Don't count on this.

- Bill has done you a favor by moving the money out of your account so that computer hackers can't access it over the weekend. Keep dreaming.

- You have been taken to the cleaners. You sit down and cry as your long-term dreams evaporate.

What to Do After You Get the Phone Call from the Bank

1. Contact your bank(s) that handle your other account(s). Advise each bank that Bill no longer has authority over any transaction. After your verbal instructions, follow up with a fax, asking the bank(s) to confirm this in writing.

2. Call your credit card companies to change your numbers. Even though Bill might not have had a physical card, he will know the numbers and the expiration dates because he paid the bills.

3. Call the local police. If you think the Bill has crossed a state line, or if your bank is out-of-state, you can get the FBI involved. The FBI is very good at freezing any accounts to which Bill may have access. Cooperate with the police. Yes, it may be embarrassing to have this reported in the local paper. Live with it. Let the police work to their fullest capabilities. Tell them you will press charges.

4. Ask your bank which checks have bounced. Call the receivers of these checks and explain the situation. Be upfront and honest.

5. Visit your banker in person; ask for a short-term loan to cover your written checks. Set up an appointment with a loan officer to work out a longer-term financing plan.

6. Tell your employees. They will figure it out anyway. Most will work with you on solving this problem and some may have information

that could help you locate Bill! (Remember those who do help the company.)

7. Call your payroll company (if you have one) and explain the situation. Have your back-up person prepare the payroll. If you don't have a back-up person, and can't figure out what to do, tell the company to duplicate last week's payroll. It will be close enough. Train another person on the payroll as soon as possible.

8. Call your key vendors and advise them of the situation. They will hear the scuttlebutt in your industry and will be nervous. Keep them informed, and ask for some extra time on pay dates until you get organized.

9. Go home and pour yourself a glass of bourbon. Start tomorrow with all the effort that got you into business in the first place.

Preventing This Theft from Ever Occurring

1. Preventing employee fraud starts with the interview and hiring process. When hiring for a position that has any contact with funds, do a thorough job of checking references. Understand every gap in employment history. Confirm the educational portion of the resume for all people who access cash. If someone lies on a resume, he should not be trusted with your checkbook. Doing a personal credit check should be mandatory for all people in your financial department. Your state may require you to have written permission to do this; check with your attorney. Someone who owes considerable amounts of money, for whatever reason, should ring your alarm bell. Remember, nothing beats your gut feeling. If you are at all uncomfortable, don't make the hire.

2. Create an environment in your firm that does not tolerate theft of any sort. If you put a $5 bill in your pocket from company funds and your employees see you, it gives them tacit permission to do it too. If you run your personal mail through the office meter, pay

into petty cash. Let your employees see that honesty is your way of life.

3. In your employee manual state that you will fully prosecute employee fraud of any sort. Many employers do not want to complete the follow-up after a theft, and most thieves count on that. (What? You don't have an employee manual? Make this project a high priority.)

4. Set up an anonymous tip procedure so that employees may advise you of theft problems without being considered a rat. Create a reward system for a tip that results in a theft conviction.

5. Investigate every incident of cash shortage. A small discrepancy here and there may be just the tip of the iceberg.

6. If you have more than one person in your accounting department, have one do the cash intake and the other do the spending. Don't violate this. Have one do the payroll and the other the confirmation. This is the single most important thing you can do–separate responsibilities. You can also change your staff's responsibilities each year. Have the receivables clerk become the payables person. If you have only one person, then you have to be on your toes, randomly checking.

7. Your outside accountant should do regular audits, and, once a year, an unannounced one. Yes, it will cost you a couple of bucks, but it is cheap insurance.

8. Never give an employee a rubber stamp with your signature for writing checks. Get rid of other repetitive demands on your schedule and sign the checks yourself. Maybe there are just too many checks for you to sign; if so, set a dollar point at which all checks over this amount require a second signature.

9. A common service for business checking accounts requires an email or fax be sent daily to your bank listing all checks that have been written, and permitting only these checks to be cashed. This prevents a stolen check from clearing. A person other than the one who writes the checks should prepare this list. Take five minutes

yourself daily to review all written checks. Contact your bank for complete details on their services.

10. Do not let your accounting people skip their vacations. Make sure that others handle these jobs at least one week (five consecutive days) per year.

11. Keep the bulk of the company's money in an account that your employees cannot access. You can transfer funds once a week for your operating needs.

12. You can purchase insurance against employee fraud, but it is expensive and usually has a high deductible. Try your insurance agent, but don't count on this to prevent a problem.

Chapter 3

The Five-Minute Solution to Male Sexual Harassment

Problem

A gender discrimination suit is filed against your company—in a way you least expect: A male employee in your company complains to the Equal Employment Opportunity Commission (EEOC) about male-to-male harassment.

What you might take as an off-hand comment, another individual might see as disparaging. For instance, Fitz and his supervisor, William, are having a discussion. William light-heartedly calls Fitz "gay." The next week you receive a summons from the EEOC. William said it as a joke, Fitz took it seriously, and in his culture, it is considered an extreme insult.

Possible Outcomes

- You win the suit, pay your lawyer $5,000 and have an unhappy employee.
- The employee or the EEOC eventually drops the complaint and you still pay your lawyer $5,000.
- You and the employee agree to a settlement; you pay the employee $5,000, your lawyer $5,000 and all parties agree to keep the resolution private.
- You and the employee agree to a settlement; you pay the employee $5,000, your lawyer $5,000, and you go public with the problem and train your employees and managers to prevent this in the future.
- You lose the suit, pay your lawyer $10,000 to file at least one appeal, pay your employee a mandated $10,000 settlement and show other employees how easy it is to get $10,000.

What to Do When the Summons is Placed in Your Hand

1. Don't panic, but don't ignore it either. There is a date on the summons by which you have to respond. If you miss this date, open your checkbook.
2. Call your attorney. If Larry Lawyer doesn't have experience with discrimination cases, have him recommend someone who does. There will be negotiations before a judgment and someone with experience and contacts will benefit you.
3. Do not interview Fitz on your own and don't represent yourself at the hearing. Speak with William and with your new attorney, Donald, the discrimination specialist. You may not be allowed to speak with Fitz without a representative from the EEOC present.
4. Ask William if any other people were present to hear the alleged comment. Make them available to speak with Donald.

5. Listen to Donald's advice. Even if you disagree with Donald, the odds are he is right. Don't get stubborn and promise to fight all the way to the Supreme Court.

6. Of the 30,641 sexual harassment complaints filed in fiscal year 2009, 28,100 (91.7 percent) were resolved. A large number of these—21,714 (70.9 percent)—were closed because no reasonable cause was found or resulted in administrative closure, with no penalty or settlement payments. You stand a reasonable chance of winning if you play by the rules. If William's comment was a one-time event you may be in good shape. If such comments are pervasive in your employee lunchroom, or William has encouraged other employees to bother Fitz, open your checkbook.

7. Whatever the resolution, do what Donald says. Sure, you can argue and win the battle. But you will be paying a lot of money to Donald to prove you are right. A private settlement without admitting blame is cheaper than winning at a hearing.

8. Don't celebrate if you win. It shows disrespect for Fitz.

9. At this point, wishing that you had an effective and up-to-date employee manual and trained supervisors will do you no good.

Preventing This Problem

1. Accept that some people are narrow-minded. You might swear that your company is open and understanding, but don't believe it. Some people in your firm will make off-color jokes, use slang or utter insults based on stupid assumptions.

2. Think hard about your employees—specifically those with leadership positions. Listen carefully to what they say, look at posters in their offices or around their work areas, and view their screen savers—you will learn a lot.

3. Your attorney or a qualified consultant should go over harassment with your leaders annually. Make attendance mandatory. The

ones who complain about attending are the ones to coach during the year. Your supervisors are the most important link in this chain. They set the tone in day-to-day relationships in the company. Train them to respond to employee complaints properly. They should never toss aside a discrimination complaint under any circumstances.

4. Tolerance for harassing behavior starts at the top. If you make off-color jokes, your staff will consider this okay to do. If you comment on someone's appearance, the next person will do this, but probably more graphically. You will do yourself a favor if you don't gossip or laugh about:

- Age;
- Disability;
- Equal pay/compensation;
- Gender;
- Genetic information;
- National origin;
- Pregnancy;
- Race or ethnicity;
- Religion;
- Retaliation;
- Sexual preference; or
- Sexual harassment.

5. Learn your lesson. Make sure your employee handbook is current with a strongly worded anti-discrimination section. Quickly investigate the allegation(s) and give the employee an answer. He may not like your answer, but by talking first you will stop many problems from escalating.

6. Make sure you have a clearly defined program in place for every employee to speak directly with the head of human resources or with you when they feel there has been discrimination, with no exceptions. If Fitz comes to you, you may be able to resolve this with a sincere apology from William. If Fitz goes to his union or the EEOC before talking with you, open your checkbook. Emphasize to employees that there never will be retaliation for bringing up a problem!

7. When Fitz comes to you, treat it seriously. Don't tell him you will

have an answer next week. Do it now. Talk with William, get his side of the story, and explain to William that an off-hand comment can trigger a deep emotional response from Fitz.

8. Update your employee manual at least every other year. Make sure that the option to speak with human resources or with you is laid out clearly, is easy to do, and will be confidential. If you don't have an employee manual and scheduled leadership training sessions, get started now!

Chapter 4

The Five-Minute Solution to Selecting Good Vendors

5ive minute consultant™

Problem

You are new to the world of retail business. You have an idea: start a hardware store in your town. People drive 20 miles to the big-box home center but you feel customers would prefer the ease of dealing with your local business, Joe's Hardware. How do you pick your vendors?

Possible Outcomes

- **Price.** It is the easy answer, but is the lowest price the best answer? Should you buy from the cheapest vendors? What about quality and service?

- **Quality.** Of course, this is it. Sell the products from the top vendors in their field … but then you realize they are also the most expensive and your neighbors are thrifty folks. Will they spend more for your merchandise?

- **Service.** This must be the key. You'll give customers the best service around. But if your vendors don't service you properly, how can you service your customers? If a vendor sends a wrong part and upsets your customers, will the customers come back?

- Joe can buy 80 percent of his products from a super-distributor, but feels the extra cost isn't worth the service. He is comfortable dealing with all the vendors.

- You thought this would be easy. You have money to start Joe's and assumed vendors would be beating down the door to get involved. Now, you have to do your homework to pick the vendors that will help you succeed. What do you do?

What Can Joe Do to Pick the Best Vendors for His Business?

1. Joe has experience in hardware, having worked in the industry for 15 years as a manufacturing manager. He knows the names of the vendors, but doesn't really know the business end of the trade.

2. Joe has to decide his niche as he can't be everything to everybody. Joe should think about his customers, his location and his goals for Joe's American. He decides that service comes first, followed by quality, with price being the least important.

3. Let's pick one product line, power tools, and follow Joe's journey. There are a dozen manufacturers from which he can pick. Joe de-

cides to carry just three brands, basically a good, better and best in quality. He's comfortable with all the brands, so let's look at the fine points of Joe's negotiations.

4. What will be the vendor's service be for?

- **Returns.** Will they allow Joe to take back defective pieces or must the customer call an 800 number and wait a half-hour for a return authorization? Who pays the postage? How quickly is the tool repaired, replaced or refunded? A vendor that lets Joe service his customers gets a point;

- **Warranty repairs.** Will they give Joe a supply of loaners while repairs are being made? What are their statistics on the percentages of defective tools?;

- **Education.** Will they train Joe's staff? This is key for Joe's success. Will the vendor hold customer sales events to help sell products? Does it have a regional sales rep that will constantly update Joe's catalogs and give training on site? Will the vendor pay Joe's expenses to attend a sales seminar?; and

- **Referrals.** Does the vendor have a website that lists Joe as an authorized supplier? Does the vendor's 800 number give out Joe's company along with the big home center? Will the vendor allow Joe to sell to and service its national accounts?

5. Let's think about the business relationship for Joe and these vendors.

   a. **Pricing.** Is the vendor competitive for its price point? Does it offer periodic specials that allow Joe to stock up at discount pricing? Does it offer consumer rebates that will help Joe sell more tools? Will the vendor guarantee pricing for a fixed period of time?;

   b. **Terms.** A good vendor will offer extended terms to help Joe start his business. Expect 60 days with no interest for the first year, reverting to standard terms in the second year. There should be extended terms during peak holiday sales seasons along with an extended spring-time sales program. A two to three percent discount for ten days should be part of the package;

c. **Contracts.** Will Joe be required to buy a minimum amount? Can Joe buy from different divisions at the vendor, and can these purchases count towards your minimum? Is Joe allowed to sell at his own established pricing? Can he combine orders with other stores to achieve quantity discounts? Can Joe advertise in any area he wants? Will Joe get a protected geographic area?;

d. **Products.** Many companies make specific items for home centers, often of a lower quality to achieve low price points. Will they offer Joe competitive items? Will Joe get items the home center can't? Will he be able to access the vendor's full line or just hardware store products only? Can he serve the industrial and large contractor market? Will Joe have access to spare parts? How quickly will the company get Joe new items—the same time as the home center?;

e. **Returns.** Will the vendor take back slow-moving items at full value? Or with a minimum handling charge?;

f. **Shipping.** What is the minimum order for free freight? Will the vendor drop-ship special orders? How quickly does the vendor ship regular and custom orders?;

g. **Special events.** Will the vendor share the cost of a booth at a local contractor's show or home fair? Will it give Joe free stock to be used as door prizes at your grand opening or special events?;

h. **Advertising.** Will the company provide advertising artwork in digital and negative formats? Will it create a cooperative advertising fund for Joe? Will it share in the cost of developing Joe's website? Will it list Joe's in all of its regional advertising?; and

i. **Store Layout and Design.** Will the vendor provide displays, shelving, signage and promotional literature? Does it have a store designer on staff? Will the company help pay for high-quality lighting to display its products?

How Does Joe Get Them to Say Yes to All of These Points?

1. Well, you won't get all of them. Remember you said service and quality came first. Emphasize this in your negotiations with potential vendors. If there are four vendors in the "better" category, select your second choice and meet with this company first. See what the industry is offering. Use this information to help set the negotiations with your first choice.

2. What you need for start-up will be very different than your needs in your second and third year. Plan on renegotiating annually to meet your needs. If you don't survive the first year in business, you won't have to worry about the second year. Get the start-up help as your first priority rather than a bigger promise of help in your second year.

3. Here's a big surprise—you are not the first person to open a hardware store. The vendors have done this many times and should offer you advice and help. They may recommend a consultant with direct experience; if so get them to pay half the cost! (Remember—consultants whose last names begin with "B" are the best.)

4. Ask the vendors to set up a traveling tour for you to visit similar stores to yours. This will give you plenty of ideas and the vendor will set up people who will be glad to share ideas with you. When you are a seasoned veteran, be sure to offer this same thing to another newbie.

5. Is any vendor going to say "YES" to all of these points? Of course not. But the ones who are most helpful are the ones to consider. A couple of pages back we asked Joe to consider his niche and his

business plan. Let's remind him of the overarching business plan of every business:

a. Pay yourself the wages you need to live; and

b. Make enough profit to give yourself a return on investment better than other investment options.

6. A vendor who gives good service but doesn't give the products you can sell won't satisfy #5 above. A vendor who gives you second-tier products that won't sell in your marketplace is not your friend. This is a balancing act: the vendor with the best service and pricing on the quality items that will be your best-sellers will be your key vendor. And you thought opening your hardware store would be easy.

Chapter 5

The Five-Minute Solution to Small Claims Court

Problem

You own Dorothy's Doggie Day Care where people leave their dogs for the day or for extended stays. You've been in business four years, have six part-time helpers and are doing well enough to take a small salary. For the first three years you were cash or credit card only. This year, you started a monthly billing program; now you have your first dead-beat. Mr. Stewart Pidd didn't pay you for two months. He pulled out his dog, Ghost, owing you $900. When you finally worked up the nerve to ask him, he simply said, "Dorothy, I don't like your service anymore and I am not going to pay you." What do you do now?

Possible Outcomes

- Mr. Pidd reconsiders, sends you a check, and your faith in humanity is restored. Or not.

- You call Mr. Pidd five times; he doesn't return your calls. After eight weeks of waiting, you resign yourself to not receiving your money.

- The owner of Fred's Furries calls you and asks about Mr. Pidd, and says Mr. Pidd asked him to bill him monthly, avoiding the pay-every-day problems. You gladly tell Fred that Ghost was a great dog, but Mr. Pidd was a low-down mutt.

- You talk about Mr. Pidd with a friend and she tells you about small claims court, where it is easy, efficient and inexpensive to sue someone who owes you money. You decide to learn about going to small claims court.

What Did Dorothy Learn About Small Claims Court?

1. Small claims court is perfect for Dorothy's attempt to collect from Mr. Pidd. Although every state has its own rules and guidelines, there are many common aspects.

2. In Dorothy's state there is a $5,000 maximum. This varies by state with some as low as $2,500 and a high of $25,000. There may be other guidelines; for instance, some states allow a higher limit in real estate cases. To find out what the limits are for your state, Google "small claims court rules for _____" and add your state name. Every state will come up.

3. Small claims court is designed to be an informal opportunity for anyone to make a financial claim. These cases are called civil cases. You can't make claims for things like slander or libel, divorce or to get an order of protection. If this is a criminal case, go to the police or the local district attorney.

4. Small claims court is informal. The judge or arbitrator will ask you questions, listen to your witnesses and review your evidence without trying to intimidate you or make you wish you had a law degree. While the TV show judges like to bluster, that is all theater. I have never seen a real small claims court session with the intent to make a witness cry.

5. You never need a lawyer to go with you. In fact, it will usually cost you more than the case is worth. When you speak from your heart it will always be more convincing than using a paid professional. If you are suing a business, it may send a lawyer, especially if the business has a lawyer in-house or one on retainer. Don't be intimidated by this. I promise you that 99 percent of the judges will make it comfortable for you. You will always be speaking to the judge, except in the state of Washington, where you may request a jury.

6. There is no court reporter or recording. Don't worry about making mistakes in presentation. An informal and honest presentation will always beat a prepared "Perry Mason" style of stating your case.

7. Dress appropriately for a day at your business. Don't make yourself something you are not for your court date. Don't try to be overtly sexy. Don't try to look like you will be living on the street if you lose, unless that is a reality.

8. Every state will have a statute of limitations. In Dorothy's case, she will have to file within one year from her last transaction with Mr. Pidd. Some states go up to six years for commercial cases. As written above, to find info for your state, Google "small claims court rules for _____" and add your state name.

Let's Look at Dorothy's Preparation and Her Day in Court

1. Dorothy's phone calls to Mr. Pidd have not been returned. The bill is now 90 days old. Her next step is to write a polite demand letter containing the following parts:

    a. A history of their relationship and what has now caused the suit. Don't try to sound like a lawyer. Write this section as if you are speaking to someone.

    b. Tell Mr. Pidd what you are looking for, in this case, $900, and paid in full within ten days. Be specific here. Don't say you are willing to negotiate a final amount. Mr. Pidd gave up that option by not returning your phone calls.

    c. Advise Mr. Pidd that if he doesn't respond within ten days, your next step is to seek legal remedies. Don't threaten; simply state your intention if he doesn't settle his bill.

2. Send this letter via certified and regular mail to Mr. Pidd's address. What if you don't know his full legal name, or if you are suing another business? Use the name and address that you conducted business under. Bill's Dog Food Company may actually be a D/B/A, and the legal name might be Bill Smith's Foods. This rarely matters in small claims.

3. Mr. Pidd may now realize you are serious and offer to pay in full, or with a payment plan. Make a business decision here. Is half a dog bone better than none? If you don't hear from him, or his offer is ridiculous, then let's take the next step.

4. Dorothy should call the district court in her area or check its website to find out what the procedures are for filing a small claims court case. There will be some paperwork to fill out. In most states, this information is online as well. The court officer will advise her if she needs to file in a different district. In some states you have to file in the district where Mr. Pidd lives; in oth-

ers you file in the district where the financial transaction took place, which would be where Dorothy's Doggie is located.

5. The court system will assign a date and time for the appearance. There may be just a few trials or as many as 50 that day. There will be a first call, where your name and Mr. Pidd's name will be called. If you are both there, you will be assigned to a room or you may stay in the same court room. If Mr. Pidd still isn't there for the second call, you will still be assigned to explain your claim to a judge. If you have a good case, with evidence, you will probably be granted a judgment.

6. You may find out that Mr. Pidd has requested a time or date change, which will usually be granted for valid reasons, but usually not more often than once. If Mr. Pidd doesn't show up on the second date, you will probably be granted a summary judgment. If you don't show up, the case will be dropped.

7. Both of you are there. If the court is busy, you may wait hours. Bring a book to read; most courts don't allow cell phones or electronic readers. The judge will read your complaint and then ask you to concisely explain your reason for suing Mr. Pidd. Here is where the butterflies hit. Be calm; the judge knows you are not a pro at this. State your case; give the judge supporting documents you have. Dorothy brought along one of her dog handlers to testify that Ghost was there every day; you never had any problems with the dog or Mr. Pidd, and that Mr. Pidd just stopped dropping Ghost off one day. Don't bring all six of your assistants if they are going to say the same thing.

8. Mr. Pidd then will defend himself to the judge. Don't interrupt his testimony. The judge will ask you to rebut anything he says. Don't be argumentative either. The whole thing will probably last only about ten minutes. Mr. Pidd may make a counterclaim during his testimony and may state that you owe him rather than he owes you. Again, trust the judge. He will be a pro at seeing through this. He has seen it thousands of times and didn't

get to be a judge without lots of education and experience.

9. Most often, the facts will win the case. In some cases, where there is no evidence or witnesses, believability will carry the day with the judge. Never amplify the truth; never repeat third-party conversations; never withhold parts of the story. I cannot stress this strongly enough–trust the judge.

10. You win, you lose or the judge may grant a reduced amount from what you are claiming because of the counterclaim or your evidence doesn't totally support the amount you are asking for. In some states the judge may give you the answer right there. In others the results will be mailed to you and the defendant. Ask about this when you file the original papers. If you lose, go home, make a cup of hot tea and learn from the experience. In some states you can appeal a small claims court result. Very rarely will that work; it will cost you lawyers' fees and lots of time.

11. If you win in full or partial, you still have to collect the money. Most people will pay at this point. But, Mr. Pidd may not care if you have a judgment against him. Then you have to place a lien against his assets: his house, car or bank account. Get help with this. Call a collection attorney. She will probably charge you a third of your judgment. But now, if Mr. Pidd is still refusing to pay, it is okay to not be polite. Let the collection attorney loose.

12. By the way, at the small claims hearing, Dorothy finally found out why Mr. Pidd stopped coming to her daycare center. He felt he was insulted when one day as you saw him walking in, you yelled to your assistant, "Get Ghost ready; his owner, Stew Pidd is coming in." I guess it is all in how you say it.

Chapter 6

The Five-Minute Solution to Hundreds of Resumes

5ive minute consultant **Problem:**

You are the owner of Phil & Muttsey's Stuffed Animals, a New England company whose 18 employees make unique and expensive stuffed dogs. Your long-time production manager is moving and gives you three months' notice. Since you don't have an in-house candidate, you place ads in Boston newspapers, a couple of job-seeking websites, and five days later you have more than 400 resumes on your desk. How do you find the right candidates?

Possible Solutions

- It's easy. Throw all the resumes up in the air and the ones that land on edge are the ones to read. Or, maybe not.

- If it takes you three minutes to review each cover letter and resume, that's 20 hours, and you haven't yet spoken to a person. There has to be an easier way.

- You call a headhunter to do the work for you, but the fees scare you away.

- You decide on a list of important characteristics you want in the production manager. These include direct experience in managing a company your size, ability to communicate and reside within an hour's drive of your plant. You decide the applicant should have at least two of these points to go further.

- Okay, it's time to sit down with a blank sheet of paper and prepare a plan.

How Will Phil Narrow Down This Overwhelming Pile of Paper?

1. In a period of high unemployment Phil has the luxury of extra resumes, giving him a broader field of candidates. On the other hand, high unemployment means a weaker economy, which hurts all businesses, including Phil & Muttsey's.

2. Back to the resumes. Phil should peruse each resume and separate into hold or discard based on his three characteristics. How?

   a. No cover letter? These go into the discard pile. This shows poor communications skills, laziness and lack of business protocol.

   b. Phil has decided he doesn't want the expense and uncertainty of moving a manager from out of town. He also feels that someone who commutes more than an hour will quickly tire of this and when an opportunity closer to home appears, will jump to that. In winter, that hour-drive may become two. So, each resume where the address is farther than an hour's drive is discarded.

3. Phil eliminated about half of the resumes with these two checks. By the way, Phil has to hold on to these resumes for at least a year, due to federal regulations, in case Phil is involved in a discrimination complaint.

4. Deciding on what defines experience in a company like Phil's is not easy.

    a. If a manager ran a 75-person production group, but before he got that promotion he ran a 20-person department, should he go into the hold pile? My suggestion is yes, he should be further looked at.

    b. What if the applicant had not ever been a leader, but wrote a great cover letter? With plenty of applicants, this resume would be discarded.

    c. How about the guy that ran a large factory with hundreds of people, and wants to work for a small company? Discard, because there is a huge difference in running hundreds of people versus Phil's 18.

    d. Phil's workforce is 12 women and 6 men. He strongly believes that either a woman or a man with the right experience will work. If Phil's workforce all comes from one nationality, it would make sense to look for a leader that understands the needs of this group. Be careful: in advertising, Phil can't state the manager should be of one nationality or gender. If Phil's workforce's primary language is not English, he can list fluency in that language in his help-wanted ads.

5. Phil is down to about 100 resumes; it's time to read for content. Start with the cover letter, the main purpose of which is to get you interested enough to read the resume. If it is addressed: To Whom It May Concern, go directly to discard, do not pass go, do not read any further. The letter should be unique to Phil's, emphasizing

points contained in the help wanted ad. The letter should be one page, business-like and easy to read with one or two points drawing Phil's attention to specifics in the resume. Many cover letters just repeat the resume; this is poor communication.

6. Is communication important to the manager's job? If yes, the cover letter is important. If the job is on the shop floor all day, working on machinery and training employees, then written communication is not as important. Phil has to consider this when qualifying the cover letter. At Phil & Muttsey's, Phil does most of the selling and customer contact along with maintaining his very popular web site. So, the cover letter here is not as important, and could best be used to disqualify poor responses.

7. Phil is down to 75 resumes. These are ones that have passed the three initial requirements. Look at each one, changing from trying to disqualify to placing them in a pile of:

    a. Looks really good;

    b. Looks good; and

    c. Probably not.

8. How do we get to looks really good? Phil should look for experience really close to his company size. Next, is there experience in his industry, or something fairly related? Someone from an aircraft manufacturing background, where tolerances are a thousandth of an inch, might have a hard time in stuffed dogs. Phil has high-quality standards, but loose manufacturing regimens.

9. Phil is looking for someone with a creative side along with the ability to lead people. Leadership, there it is. This is what Phil is looking for. His manufacturing regimen is in place; he is not a startup. Phil has good employees. He needs someone to lead them.

10. The key thing to look for in the resumes: is the person a leader at and outside of work? Has she taken courses that point in this direction? A resume may describe her bottom line success stories or how she contributed by cutting costs, changing vendors or bring-

ing in new customers. More importantly, Phil should be seeing points covering how she taught new employees, helped solve people-related problems and kept turnover to a minimum.

11. If many of Phil's workers speak Spanish as their primary language, then the manager must be able to directly communicate with them.

12. Phil is down to 30 resumes. Now he calls each one, spending about ten minutes on the phone. The first two minutes are an introduction, thanking the candidate for sending a resume and describing Phil & Muttsey's and the job. Phil should practice this before his first phone call to get it down pat. The next question is simply: "Briefly, tell me about your work history." If the candidate says, "It's on my resume" or, "What do you want to know?" you can place this person in the probably not pile. He or she should be able to give you a two minute history of working, highlighting job history that would relate to Phil & Muttsey's.

13. How do they know what relates? Simple. Anyone who applies for a management job and has not gone to the company's web site before submitting the resume is not bright enough to work for you. To me, it's that basic.

14. You are now four or five minutes in. Your next question is: "Please, tell me a little bit about yourself." The most common answer Phil will hear, is, "What do you want to know?" Your reply, "Just tell me about you." You are listening to how they respond more than what they say. Is he confident? Is he self-assured? He should be telling you about his work ethics, his abilities in business that relate to Phil's and enough about his personal life so you can understand he is committed to hard work. All of this in three minutes. If the candidate can't do this, he is not really looking for a job; if he were, he would have practiced this many times.

15. Your last qualifying question, "Roughly, tell me about your earnings history, and what are you looking to earn this year?" This

should be a one minute answer, covering her last two jobs. The second part of the question is tougher. In slow economic times, people will take pay cuts. If times are good, they are looking to earn more. You want to hear if the applicant is within the pay range you are budgeting. One of my rules in hiring is that someone taking more than a 20-percent pay cut will keep looking for a job that will meet his financial needs. The exception to this is someone who is moving to a new area where the cost of living is much lower, or someone who has had a significant life-changing event, such as learning a new career, recovering from a long illness or returning to the workforce.

16. In any event, at the end of the call, thank the applicant for his time; tell him that you have more people to speak with and if there will be an in-person interview he will get a call within a couple of days. Say yes if he asks if he can call you with a follow-up question. Actually, you hope a good applicant will do just that. A short conversation reminding you about a particular skill will show you he is serious.

17. After the calls, Phil should have no more than eight to ten applicants. If he has less, he's been too tight in his requirements; more and he has been too loose.

18. By the way, why is Phil doing all the work? Where is his partner Muttsey? Actually, Muttsey has been by Phil's side the whole time, wagging his tail at the resumes he liked.

Chapter 7

The Five-Minute Solution to the Big Bounced Check

Problem

On Monday morning at 9:15, your bank calls to let you know a check you deposited has bounced. The bank is processing it for redeposit, but is not clearing your checks in the meantime. You find out the check in question was from Manny's Mighty Manufacturing, and it is equal to about 5 percent of your annual sales. You were so glad when you got the order from Manny's; after all, you had been calling on Manny for two years and this was your breakthrough order.

Possible Outcomes

- The check clears on Tuesday, and Manny's Mighty's bookkeeper apologizes. If you believe this, you'll believe that big league ballplayers are underpaid.
- The check doesn't clear on Tuesday. You go to Manny's office, wait for two hours for Manny to come out of a meeting, and he says you will have a replacement check by Friday.
- Friday comes along with a promise for Monday.
- On Monday, out of cash, you go to your bank for a short-term loan, and this helps, but not enough. Manny's check still does not appear.
- You have to rebuild your entire business on a shoestring.

What to Do When You Get the Phone Call from the Bank

1. Find out which of your checks are not clearing due to the bounced check. Call these people as soon as possible and tell them first, before your checks don't clear. Be honest with your explanation and tell them you will keep them abreast of the situation.

2. Stop manufacturing Manny's orders in house. Call Manny's other vendors and see what their status is with Manny's.

3. On Tuesday, if the check doesn't clear, call Manny's and ask the company for ten smaller checks all dated today, telling Manny you will deposit them a few days apart. Oftentimes a smaller check will clear while a large one will not.

4. Ask Manny for a credit card number you can use to cover the amount of the bounced check.

5. By Wednesday, call your lawyer, Leroy, telling him about the transaction and where you think the goods are now. Leroy should investigate whether you can get a lien on the goods or get an order of repossession. Do not threaten Manny, and don't threaten him

with police action either. In most states you cannot threaten someone by invoking the police. If this ultimately goes to court, your case may be tossed out.

6. If you know where Manny sold or used your goods, call Manny's customer(s) and ask if they have paid Manny. If not, ask them to make out a two-party check, payable to Manny's Mighty Manufacturing and you. This will make Manny angry. So what? He is no longer your friend.

7. In most states, where goods are delivered as a COD and the check bounces, you can go to the police and file a felony complaint. Many departments have a white-collar crime section that will be most helpful. If the check was an open account payment, your best route is to file a civil lawsuit. For a list of each state's laws, visit www.fiveminuteconsultant.com.

8. By this point, you no longer have a customer relationship with Manny. Have your lawyer write a pre-suit letter, giving the company seven days to make payment, and then follow through by filing the suit. Most states have a required format for notifying a person/company that you are trying to collect a bounced check. Your lawyer can give you the format. Under no circumstances should you wait 30 days to take this action.

Preventing This Problem

1. It all starts with a proper customer/credit application. Even if a customer asks to be on COD, the customer still should complete your application as COD checks can bounce or orders can be cancelled after you have invested in production. Here are the basics of a good application:

   a. Name, address, phone, fax, website, and email address;

   b. Names, home addresses and phones of owners and/or partners;

   c. A personal guarantee clause—ask Leroy the Lawyer for the right language in your state;

d. A release giving the customer's bank permission to give account details. Most banks will not respond to you without this. Your banker should help you with language here;

e. Four references in the customer's primary business. Ask for additional references if you receive utility companies, local stationary shops, hardware stores or gas company credit cards;

f. State that you impose a finance charge for past-due accounts and that customers are responsible for collection costs and fees; and

g. Ask your customers what they intend to spend each month and on what products. This helps your salespeople target their work and allows you to accurately set a credit limit.

2. If you are selling to General Electric, you won't get a personal guarantee. Most small- and medium-sized businesses will sign. If they don't sign, keep that in mind when giving a credit limit.

3. When you get that **big** order, ask "Why now?" Was it the result of your selling efforts or did someone else cut their credit off? Even if you checked their references in the past, do it again now.

4. Get a fresh bank reference and check the company's average daily cash balance and the number of non-sufficient fund checks. Find out if the company has a bank line of credit, and if it is maxed out.

5. If this is a big order, don't be afraid to discuss terms when you get the order. Most customers will work with you if they care about building a lasting business relationship with you. Try to work out progress payments as you go along or obtain a deposit for your material costs.

6. Ask your bank to call or email you when a check bounces the first time. Most banks will automatically redeposit a bounced check and only tell you when the check doesn't clear the second time. Banks can only present checks through the national clearinghouse twice. After that, they return the check to you.

Here's a tip: you can take the twice-bounced check to the bank on which the check was written. If there are funds in the bank, you can cash the check right there. Call the bank everyday asking if the check is good at present. If so, run down there right away.

7. Find out if you are in a pre-lien state, meaning you can file a lien before the goods are shipped. If so, do this as a matter of routine on big, new orders.

8. Never sell to an international account without an iron-clad bank letter of credit. Talk to your local banker to learn more about this, or visit www.export.gov/salesandmarketing/eg_main_018203.asp. This website, powered by the U.S. Department of Commerce, is the best I have seen to help a company learn to sell in the international marketplace.

9. When you get the big order, ask yourself: If this order goes sour, what will be the impact to my company? If it will significantly hurt you, think hard. This is a bet-the-company decision. If you decide the order is too big for you, ask if you can supply it over a period of time rather than in one large shipment. This will spread out your cash needs. Ask if you can share this order with a trusted secondary source, so that you can spread the risk. If Wal-Mart is giving you a big first order, credit is not the problem, but cash flow is.

10. Receiving post-dated checks is better than not receiving a check at all, but be aware that post-dated checks that bounce cannot be considered fraud or carry a criminal sentence. Your only recourse in the case of a bounced, post-dated check is a civil suit. If a customer wants to give you post-dated checks, ask him to make all of the checks with today's date, and promise you will only deposit them according to an agreed-upon schedule.

11. Since Manny's check is a big one, work with your lawyer. For small checks, your best bet is small claims court. (*See Chapter 5 for more on this.*)

12. Some states make the signer of a bounced check personally responsible, even on a company check. Your lawyer will help you understand this very effective tool for collection.

Chapter 8

The Five-Minute Solution to Preventing Workers' Comp Fraud

5ive minute consultant™

Problem

You are a partner in Tom and Larry's Auto Body. You and Larry have been friends for decades and split the workload. Larry does all the customer stuff, works with the insurance companies and handles the books. You manage the shop and the employees. Life has been good, and you both make a nice living … until this year. Your workers' comp insurance went up $150K over last year. This cost can sink Tom and Larry's. You had one serious accident last year, but are sure that two other claims are fraudulent. What do you do now?

Possible Solutions

- You raise prices to cover the increased costs, $450,000 over three years. You start losing some bids and one fleet customer switches.

- You complain to your insurance carrier and threaten to switch. Your agent tells you that no carrier will quote based on your record of three major claims last year.

- You call the Acme Detective Agency to spy on the two suspected fraudsters and tell them to spend a full day watching. Their report is inconclusive and disappointing.

- You call the local police and ask them to investigate the fraud. Since you have no real proof, you're told they don't have the manpower for your case.

- This cost can sink Tom and Larry's. Out of desperation, you call your buddy, Paul, the Five-Minute Consultant. He takes ten minutes; this is what you learn.

What Can Tom and Larry Do to Reduce or Eliminate This Bill?

1. Tom and Larry's is not the first company to have this problem. In fact, just about every company has one comp exaggeration or fraudulent claim. The guys need to listen to folks with experience. (*See Chapter 54 for more details.*)

2. The three workers on comp (let's call them Al, Bill and Carl) each have a $50,000 reserve on their case. Carl really did break his leg when he tripped on a carelessly positioned car jack. You suspect Al and Bill of fraud for a couple of reasons:

   a. Carl has returned to work on crutches to help with estimates and answer the phone and is helpful in any way he can. Al and Bill can't be found, except by the mailman who delivers their weekly insurance company checks.

   b. On your first conversation with Carl's medical case manager you explain that Carl is back to work on a limited basis, but you are paying his full salary. The medical case manager drops his reserve to $25K, which saves you $75K over three years. The manager can't move on Al and Bill as he has no new information.

c. Al and Bill are good friends and their back injuries happened within a week of each other. Each complained after they lifted something and then didn't come to work the next day. Both are going to the same clinic, a 45-minute drive from their homes, when there are many closer. Al and Bill were only employed at the shop for a year. This points to malingering or outright fraud.

3. Paul throws a scenario to Larry: "If you could buy a machine for $20K that has a 50/50 chance of decreasing your costs by $200K over three years, would you do it?" Larry doesn't hesitate to say yes. "So," says Paul, "would you spend $20K on a top-to-bottom investigation of Al and Bill, which, if successful, would save you a couple of hundred grand?" Larry hesitates, at first thinking he is throwing good money after bad, but then the bulb lights over Larry's head.

4. Paul also says, "Place pressure on the insurance carrier to start a fraud investigation. The company should do it if you give a good starting point. You are not trying to make the carrier your best friend … be forceful!"

5. Maybe the carrier says it can start an investigation in two months because of its backlog; then it is time for Larry to start the ball rolling on his own. The private investigator spends one day watching Al and Bill's houses and sees nothing that would help the case. At $500 per day, Larry doesn't want to go further. Larry should go back to the agency and lay out a better surveillance plan. Forget rainy days as most people stay home. The agency following Al's car should take videos of him shopping or doing any movement. You will hit the jackpot if he plays a round of golf or goes bowling.

6. In approximately half of the states you can decide which doctors your employees see. Check with your attorney for your state regulations. If you do have this capability make sure your chosen doctor knows about your light-duty program. If he clears Al and Bill for light duty and they don't show up, you will get the wage portion of their comp reserves cleared out, but you will still have the medical claims.

7. Your insurance carrier will have a nurse case manager for Al and Bill. It is appropriate for the nurse to review the case with Al's doctor. The nurse may, in some states, go on the doctor's visit with Bill. This definitely reduces fraud.

8. If Al hired an attorney within a couple of weeks of his initial claim, this is a sure-fire indicator of problems to come. Your carrier will assign an attorney to work the case along with the medical team. Communicate with this attorney and let him know your position on fraud and why you think Al is committing fraud.

9. Some insurance carriers are not motivated to save money, as they just increase premiums to cover their costs. Their motivation is to close the case. What can you do? If you have the ability to shop for a carrier, talk with their loss control groups and get a firm understanding of their goals and methods. This is way more important than the salesperson leaving a calendar on your desk. If you are in a state that mandates you work with a state insurance fund (North Dakota, Ohio, Washington and Wyoming), or your record is so bad that nary a private carrier will write you, you have to take the lead in the fraud investigation. State-funded carriers are overwhelmed with cases and there will be long waits to get your cases looked at.

10. Many companies hire third-party administrators (TPAs) to manage their claims. This often helps reduce fraud. The TPA group will be on top of every claim from the first day, know the laws and regulations in your state and has your best interests as its only goal. TPA groups also work with claimants and help them to get physical

and occupational therapy quickly. Sometimes the claimant's doctor can't see him for a long time. The TPA will gently suggest alternate routes, which helps the employee and you. What's that you are saying: "Why would I spend more money to manage claims when I already pay the insurance premium?" The answer is: you will save in the long run, guaranteed. TPAs work; speak with your insurance broker for direction.

11. Set-up a fraud tip-line in your company, maybe a special phone number, a private, locked mail box outside your office or a special email address. Make sure your entire company knows you fully prosecute fraud and that you pay a percentage of the savings as a reward to anyone who reports fraudulent activity. This is not limited to just workers' comp, but will certainly help with comp.

12. Pre-employment physicals are great for helping you hire physically capable employees; they also give you a leg-up in fraud prevention. (*See Chapter 66.*) If Al has a weak back before you hire him and later makes a claim, the starting point is not that he has a weak back, but how much different it is from his starting point. If you don't have a baseline, any weakness is on your comp insurance.

13. Hearing loss is a common fraudulent claim, especially for workers in factories or auto body shops like Larry's. Many people have hearing loss due to loud music played directly into their ears. If, after working at your company for a year, Al claims hearing loss, and his hearing is only 80 percent, you will pay a claim. If Al had this loss before you hired him, and you don't have a baseline, you will pay. Give a hearing test at the start of employment and then annually. If you work in a loud environment, this will save you much more than it costs.

14. Here is another question from Larry: "I have yelled at Al to wear his earplugs, but he often forgets. Isn't it his fault that he has hearing loss?" Nope. It is your responsibility to monitor the use of personal protective equipment in your employees. If Al gets a small

piece of metal in his eye while he was not wearing his safety glasses, you pay, no questions asked. You can fire Al for not following safety procedures, but you will still be responsible for the comp claim!

15. Be extra-cautious on Monday morning accidents, especially soft-tissue claims, like back or shoulder pain. Many come from weekend work around the house and by not going to the doctor or emergency room on Saturday; Al turns this into a fraudulent claim. Meet your workforce every Monday morning, maybe for a five-minute safety meeting, or to discuss a new product or procedure. See who is grimacing, who is walking slowly or who looks glassy-eyed from taking pain meds. Send an employee home before he starts physically working and you may save a claim. Once the employee makes the claim, your boat is taking on water. Listen to what your other employees are saying about Bill. Oftentimes another employee will have helped Bill put up sheetrock or cut down a tree. This is where the fraud tip-line and reward have value.

16. You should know who has a part-time job and what each employee is doing. The job may be off the books, offering no insurance. This makes the Monday morning look-see even that much more important. Train your supervisors to look for any employee coming to work in pain. This will prevent claims for you.

17. You can set-up a special bonus for your employees if your workers' comp insurance goes down. Place 50 percent of the year-over-year savings in the employee pool and make a big deal of giving out these bonus checks. When an employee knows he won't get a check because Bill is committing fraud, he may be more likely to speak up.

18. What about Al and Bill? What else can you do? Have the private investigator get their banking records when possible. Look for regular deposits, which may mean another job. Ask your competitors if Al or Bill has come in looking for work. If so, report

this to the fraud team at the insurance carrier. See if they attend their therapy appointments and work hard there. If they don't go to the therapy because they don't need it, maybe the accident is fake?

19. Should you do an alcohol or a drug test after an accident? If your state allows it, do it for each claimant as soon as you can. Check with your attorney on this and if you are allowed to claim contributing negligence on the employee's part. Sometimes a claim doesn't come in for a while after an accident occurs. If you can't do the test within 12 to 24 hours of the claim, don't bother.

Chapter 9

The Five-Minute Solution to the Whistle-Blower

Problem

On Wednesday, the local business reporter, Jerry Journalist, calls and asks for a comment on a story he is writing. Jerry says he is naming your company, The Acme Astounding Supply company, as one of several not paying income taxes because of accepting cash sales off the books. Jerry is fair and wants to hear your side of the story.

Possible Outcomes

- Jerry writes a fair article stating that this is an alleged situation. He quotes you as saying this is certainly not Acme's policy. Jerry has permission and tells you who his source is and you explain that you let him go a couple of weeks ago for being drunk at work. Jerry mentions this in the article.

- Jerry asks if he can meet you for an on-the-record interview. Jerry asks tough questions, but you answer them honestly and help diffuse the situation.

- Jerry has two sources and, while asking for your comment, he decides not to print your answer when you call him a liar and troublemaker.

- The article is on the front page with the headline "Fraud at Local Businesses" with a picture of your building.

- There is an old political saying predating Twitter and YouTube, "Never argue with a man who buys ink by the barrel and paper by the ton." Jerry writes an unflattering article and in six months you are totally exonerated by state auditors; you won't see that in the paper. You had six months of innuendo and gossip. Acme Astounding's goodwill is gone, along with its key customers.

- You think about your boat, which you bought for cash four years ago. Tonight, you plan on cutting a hole in the bottom of the boat.

What to Do When Jerry Calls

1. Talk with Jerry yourself; don't have someone down the line respond. When you talk with Jerry, have someone else in the room writing down what you say. This may prevent a misquote, and Jerry will realize you take this seriously. If this indeed is revenge by a fired employee, make this clear.

2. Talk honestly with Jerry, but don't admit any wrongdoing. Tell him you run an honest business. It's okay to say you are investigating this and will give Jerry an answer within a couple of days. Ask him

to read your written response before publishing his article. You don't want to start an argument with Jerry. You can't win. Ever. Get advice by searching for "countering negative publicity" at Bing or Google.

3. Responding with "no comment" is viewed by most people as hiding something. Use this chance to tell Jerry good things about your company and your people. Some of these thoughts will get into the article. Ask Jerry to let you see and review any of your direct quotes that he plans to use in the article.

4. If Jerry is a crusader and doesn't want your opinion, or tells you he will write the story anyway he sees fit, cut the interview short—you will be misquoted.

5. Call the paper's editor for a discussion. The editor will stand by Jerry, but perhaps will question Jerry enough that he will soften the article.

6. Tell your employees that an article will be in the paper, explaining that you disagree with the article. Call key customers as well, telling them your side before it comes out.

7. Contact Ann the Attorney and be totally honest with her. Tell her everything so you can come up with a realistic plan. It is very tough to sue a newspaper for libel or defamation when it reports a story that has some basis of fact. Threatening a suit will only make Jerry dig deeper. You don't want this. Whether you win or lose a potential suit, you will spend tons of money, and the publicity during the trial will always be about the allegations against you and will continue to hurt your business.

8. Contact your accountant to come in to do an audit right away to find potential problems that can be fixed as soon as possible.

9. If, perchance, you did the deed that Jerry is writing about, you can say how sorry you are that this situation occurred, and you and your loyal employees are working hard to do everything to keep improving Acme. You are not admitting guilt, but you can turn

this positive with the right attitude.

10. Call a local ad agency or public relations firm to work with you to craft a campaign that places you in a better light. Even if you get a retraction from the paper, the original article will be copied by your competitors and available on the web forever.

11. Get ready for the government audit. It will come.

Let's Try to Prevent This at Your Business

1. There are some businesspeople who have been tempted to be creative with a cash sale. A customer doesn't get a warranty repair in a timely fashion, or your customer is audited, and you are thrown under the bus. Don't fool yourself into thinking no one knows. Your bookkeeper will notice an inventory discrepancy. Your customer will tell his brother about the great deal you gave him for cash, and then he tells someone, and he tells someone who works for the Department of Taxation. You just don't know.

2. So, don't do it. Don't be tempted. Don't make excuses to yourself, and don't think you are owed because you pay so much in taxes already.

3. An employee comes to you wanting to work off the books; you know how much you will save and the employee is glad to do it too. Don't do it. What happens when the employee gets hurt and the workers' compensation investigator asks for time cards? If you utilize a state-run workers' comp fund, the information will be sent to the wage and hour department. Tell employees who ask for off-the-books hours that they will earn more in Social Security in the long run if their wages are higher now. I know that most workers don't think this is important, but you have to hold your ground.

4. The most important reason to stick to an ethical policy is: your employees, for the most part, will do the same. They will respect you. An employee who sees you cheat will not feel bad about

doing a side job or taking a small inventory item. Don't let anyone feel that this is okay! There will still be a small percentage of employees who feel it is their right to become your silent partner.

5. Begin sending press releases out about your company now, before problems exist. You can do this yourself, or hire a professional. You don't need a full agency; there are plenty of professionals looking for occasional work. You can find them by simply searching Google for "press release writers." Get lots of good PR, do an occasional charity job, and take pictures. Send these to the papers. You will be noticed.

6. The impact of newspapers is slowly waning. You now have to watch out for bad comments on YouTube, Twitter, business referral sites and Facebook. Every journalist I have ever worked with has strong personal ethics and will not spread malicious gossip. But on the Internet, you have little opportunity to respond effectively. Most companies larger than a dozen folks have a web or information technology person. Make sure part of that person's job description is to monitor your firm on the Internet. At the same time, monitor your competitors and copy what they do well. If you don't have a computer person, be sure to Google your company's name once a week.

7. If you belong to a trade association, its management may have experience in this area. Contact the association for advice on publicity; it may have PR releases into which you can just plug your company's name. Don't work with people mentioned in an unflattering article. They may be guilty and you will be, too, by association. Speak for Acme only after rehearsing your thoughts.

8. In the event that you get a sales tax or wage and hour audit, do what your accountant or chief financial officer tells you. Don't try to do this on your own.

Chapter 10

The Five-Minute Solution to the Great Production Mistake

Problem

Your company, Paul's Baseballs, manufactures sports equipment, including baseballs for youth baseball leagues. You manufacture about 500,000 each winter. You start shipping mid-February when baseball season begins. In early March, a coach named Kevin calls you and says that some of the balls he received were slightly larger than normal. You go back to your quality control logs and see that indeed 9 percent of this year's balls are a smidge larger than they should be. You investigate and find out it's due to a faulty measuring machine.

Possible Outcomes

- It's only one call from Coach Kevin. You decide to keep this under your hat as the ball size is so close. You get only two more calls throughout the season, and the problem disappears.

- You start getting frequent calls from coaches who notice that their pitchers are not holding the ball correctly due to the size. You begin to lose a little bit of sleep; you get through the season, but your advance orders for next season drop.

- You send out a letter/email/fax to all customers telling them about the error and offering to replace any balls the customers send back. This may cost you up to $150,000.

- An influential baseball website stops selling your balls. Coaches all over the country want replacement balls as soon as possible. A couple of bloggers question your products in their postings.

- You get a phone call from a national baseball organization questioning your baseballs. They are considering not renewing your marketing arrangement because of poor quality. You visit with them and stress that this is a small overall problem and invite them to tour your plant and see the steps you have taken to guarantee perfection in the future.

- ESPN sends a reporter to your plant to discuss your baseballs and all of the other equipment your make. You begin thinking about moving to Brazil.

What to Do When Coach Kevin Calls

1. You check your quality control logs and discover the error in the measuring machine. You have 45,000 oversized balls out there. You think about options, from doing nothing to replacing the balls. You send a gross of new balls to Kevin and thank him for alerting you.

2. After a couple of days, you get a few more phone calls and send each coach free replacements since you have a limited warranty that says your balls will be correctly sized.

3. If no more calls come in, you are okay, but you just can't predict that one major user will complain, and do so publicly. Are you willing to gamble?

4. Within a week, you have received a dozen calls asking about the ball size. You have to do something. The question is:

    a. Do you put up a stone wall and say the problem is nothing?

    b. Do you respond only to the coaches who call you, hoping no influential teams or bloggers get the news?

    c. Do you issue a letter telling the world about your problem, and hopefully turn your lemons into game-day lemonade?

5. Check with your insurance broker; you may have coverage for defective products!

Preventing This Problem and Reducing Its Impact on Paul's

1. So, what do you do when Coach Kevin calls? After tearing your hair out, send a note to your customers explaining you found a small problem and you are standing behind your products unhesitatingly. If someone wants to return a shipment, you will replace it and pay the freight both ways. Don't waiver on this promise, but do place a date on it, for instance, up to six months from now.

2. You can be big or small, but turning out a quality product for your pricing level is a key to success.

3. If you sell products, whether or not you make them, it is not a question of if you will be involved in a product recall; it is when.

4. Products are controlled primarily by several federal government agencies, including:

    a. Food and Drug Administration (www.fda.gov);

    b. Consumer Product Safety Commission (cpsc.gov);

    c. Department of Transportation (dot.gov); and

    d. U.S. Department of Agriculture (usda.gov).

If your product falls under one of these agencies, you have to be very careful with your quality control and recall situations. There are very specific guidelines and steps in the notification process that must be followed.

5. Check your quality control (QC) instrumentation daily, no matter what business you are in. Have control samples made which are known to be perfect; run them down your line and see if your instruments agree. Set tolerance levels and stick to them religiously. If you see a trend—let's say one percent too big today and two percent tomorrow—don't wait until the preset target is hit. You have a problem coming. Fix it now.

6. Some companies don't have a QC department. They have controls and checks at every step of a process. In this way, everyone is responsible for quality. Others believe that a professional QC department is the better way to go, doing product checks, training and teaching whenever a problem occurs. Whichever is your choice, do it and don't relegate QC to the backburner. Don't override your own standards when a problem is uncovered.

7. If you sell through distributors, you must also notify them. Either get their customer lists for notification, or pay them to do the notifications. Remember, you want to control the message by writing the letters for your distributors. Have your sales teams meet with the distributors' representatives to go over everything, and emphasize how good your company is and that this recall is an isolated incident, now under control.

8. If your recall needs 24/7 response or results in a heavy call volume to your office, Google "call centers" for lists of companies that might be able to help.

9. You should call in the local business media before they call you. Tell them about the little machine in QC that took a month off, and how you are solving the problem for thousands of baseball coaches around the country. Get your story out there before

your competition does (and they will).

10. Now, let's make some lemonade. When a coach returns balls and wants new ones, give a special deal on other equipment you sell, since you are paying the freight anyway. Many customers will reward your honesty with additional orders.

11. Donate the returned, oversized balls to any organization that wants them, and get good press over your donation. Get pictures when you deliver.

12. If you make precise machined parts that can't be used again, then make a big deal about recycling your mistakes.

13. Make the discarded balls, or whatever you make, into an eBay phenomenon. Sell your off-spec products as paperweights. Do something that will let your customers know you have solved the problem and stand behind your goods.

14. Teach your employees to always be on the lookout for products that don't feel right. If you have a QC person, don't let your employees feel that QC is not their responsibility. A product recall is a marketing and branding nightmare, but it is caused by a manufacturing defect. The cost of a recall is hundreds of times the savings from taking a shortcut. Inspect all incoming materials to the standards you have specified. Inspect five percent of your outgoing product, and verify that your standards are being kept.

The Five-Minute Solution to the Upset Customer

Five minute consultant™

Problem

You own Megan's Ultimate Unfinished Furniture, a retail business selling unfinished furniture where you average 30 customers a day. Today you received a complaint from Mrs. Olivia Day. She was in your shop yesterday to buy a bureau and said she was treated rudely by your clerk, Sandy. Sandy has worked for you for three years and you think she is terrific. Mrs. Day wants a written apology from you and Sandy or she will file a complaint with the Better Business Bureau and your local chamber of commerce.

Possible Outcomes

- You listen to Mrs. Day, thank her for bringing this to your attention, and then send a written note of apology. You chalk it off to one person having a bad day, but you are not sure which one.

- You offer an apology, but Mrs. Day is still not happy. She writes to the Better Business Bureau, which, in turn, sends you a copy of her complaint and asks for your comments on the incident. You speak with Sandy and are sure she handled Mrs. Day appropriately. The BBB puts you and Mrs. Day together for a conversation and another apology satisfies Mrs. Day.

- Mrs. Day turns out to be extremely insulted and writes a letter to the business editor of the local paper. The editor asks for your comments and doesn't write a story.

- It turns out Mrs. Day enjoys berating people. The business editor told you he gets a letter every week from Mrs. Day about something. He ignores her.

- Can it get worse? Mrs. Day did not buy anything from Sandy, and you are better off. Had she bought a coffee table, she would have returned it anyway. It was her ego that was bruised; you won't see her again.

What to Do When Mrs. Day's
Phone Call Comes In

1. One of the greatest retailers in the country, Stew Leonard's in Norwalk, Conn., has a huge rock outside its front door with the following credo carved into it:

    a. *The customer is always right.*

    b. *In the event that the customer is wrong, see #1 above.*

2. In your heart, you know Sandy would never be rude; nonetheless, you do apologize to Mrs. Day and listen to her complete story. Provide feedback by repeating parts of what she has said back to her.

Don't pick up a condescending tone of voice. Mrs. Day won't give a darn if you defend Sandy; she wants her ego massaged, and nothing less will do.

3. Speak with Sandy and listen to her side of the story. Mrs. Day was upset because Sandy would not honor a 10 percent discount coupon that expired six months ago. Sandy offered her a current 5 percent coupon, but Mrs. Day wasn't happy.

4. Your most important goal is not to get Mrs. Day back as a customer, but to prevent her from spreading malicious gossip about your store. Call Mrs. Day and explain that you have spoken with the salesperson involved and you are sure this will never happen again. Thank her for bringing this to your attention and for helping your business.

5. You probably won't get her back as a customer no matter what you do and that is okay. Take her off your mailing or email list. The next visit will be just as bad! Remember that her comments can end up on Angie's List, the Better Business Bureau, and throughout her circle of friends. One survey I read says that an average consumer will tell six people about a good experience, but will tell sixteen people about a bad experience.

6. By now, you realize Mrs. Day is a classic pain-in-the-back. You still have to be nice, as Mrs. Day can do a lot more to hurt your business than you can do to change her ornery personality.

7. Ask Mrs. Day for her address so you may handwrite a personal note. You know Sandy wasn't wrong; you don't have to say that, but you can acknowledge Mrs. Day's concerns.

Preventing the Problem

1. All employees should be greeted at the start of each shift by their team leader or manager. If an employee is grumpy or non-responsive, take him aside for a few seconds and ask what the problem is. Let him vent for a minute to get the problem off his chest. Your

goal is for employees to have a positive attitude toward co-workers and customers.

2. Many companies start shifts with a five-minute meeting, during which they discuss safety, customer relations, products and company business. Be sure to leave time for your crew to ask questions. This will make for better employees, which translates directly to better customer service.

3. Specifically for customer service people, like Sandy in the furniture store, make sure she has a sincere smile on her face. If Sandy is grumpy because of a real or perceived problem, customers will pick up on this, and will not purchase from someone with a frown on her face.

4. Have Sarah, Sandy's supervisor, spend at least five minutes twice during each shift with every customer-contact person. This includes receptionists, phone support staff, cashiers, delivery drivers, and each person who speaks with a current or potential customer. Sarah becomes part cheerleader, part friend, and all teacher and leader. Problems detected early can be resolved.

5. Whenever an employee has a tough time with a customer, right or wrong, the supervisor should be told. This way Sarah knows what is going on when Mrs. Day calls. Don't set this up as a 'blame' report—keep it informational; if one salesperson keeps popping up, though, you know where to focus training.

6. Have a monthly sales meeting where you role-play different customer scenarios. Don't throw softballs, either; make the situations honest and tough. This is the best teaching tool there is. Take videos of each session for further training.

7. Create training for your supervisors, including customer complaint resolution. Unlike Mrs. Day, you want customers to come back, and customers with properly resolved problems will come back, as they feel comfortable knowing you will resolve anything else in the future.

8. Try to have the supervisor resolve the complaint on the first call. Give every supervisor the ability to offer discounts, coupons, reduced or free service calls, or just about anything to keep customers happy. You do have to set some limits, and not every problem will be resolved, but the more you resolve on the first call, the better off you are.

9. With Internet and catalog shopping, you get fewer chances to see a customer face-to-face in a selling situation. Make the best of it by doing everything possible to keep customers happy.

10. Understand how the Better Business Bureau (BBB) works. This is a premier organization that helps consumers and businesses solve problems. In 2010, the BBB received roughly 67,000,000 inquiries, 844,054 of which were complaints, and successfully settled more than 75 percent of them. In the business of unfinished furniture, there were 4,467 inquiries and 27 complaints filed. By far, most requests are for information about a company in a respective region. Visit www.bbb.org for more information.

11. The new kid on the street is Angie's List (angieslist.com). This is a subscription model, where consumers pay to see business ratings. They don't have the breadth of the BBB, but do have a large user base among younger and more computer-literate consumers. If you are in a retail or service business, you should know this company.

12. I was always grateful when a customer called with a complaint. It meant they wanted to improve a situation so they could continue buying. If they were truly upset, they would have started buying from a competitor.

13. Yes, customers can be wrong and sometimes a pain in the neck. Remember this as you ring up the sale.

Chapter 12

The Five-Minute Solution to a Competitor Who Steals Your Employees

 ## Problem

You run a medium-sized company, Bud's Home Maintenance, with 35 employees working in plumbing, electrical work and HVAC. You have been in business successfully for 19 years. You make a good living and have considerable equity in your company. On a Friday afternoon at 3 p.m., eight people give their two-week notice; this is half of your licensed plumbers and electricians. You soon realize they are all going to work for Gary's Maintenance, a competitor across town.

Possible Outcomes

- You speak with each person; they all realize their mistake, and they all stay. If this happens, buy a lottery ticket; you are having a good day.

- They all work out their notice and go to work for Gary. Gary's business begins to grow and yours takes a stumble.

- As you realize your employees are going to be taking certain customers with them, you explode. You call them all traitors, kick them out, and do not pay for the two weeks they offered as notice. Your hair turns grey overnight.

- You call Larry the Lawyer and ask him about suing Gary. He reviews your employee manual and says you don't stand a chance.

- After talking, Larry says he might be able to get an injunction against Gary, but it is a long shot. Your legal fees will be at least $50K, with all the depositions and court appearances for so many people. Larry says you have a one-in-ten chance of getting the injunction.

- You realize your time is better spent working with your current employees and customers, keeping them loyal to Bud's.

What to Do When the Employees Start Walking into Your office

1. It is alright to be upset, but don't take it out on your workers. They are looking out for themselves, not you, much to your disappointment. After a couple of weeks, some will want to come back, and you will probably want them. Don't burn your bridges.

2. Follow the procedures in your employee manual. If you don't mention asking for and/or paying for notice given, and as these folks are going to a direct competitor, it is okay to ask them to leave your company right away.

3. If you need these people to cover work you have already booked,

pair them up with each other. Don't let them work with someone who is staying. In other words, isolate the cancer within Bud's.

4. Call Gary and tell him in no uncertain words how you feel about him. Even though you probably won't go to court, scare him a little with talk about your lawyer getting involved.

5. Start your plan for hiring replacements ASAP. It is a fair guess that Gary has talked to most of your people, and the ones who are staying are loyal to you. Ask them to refer their friends or family who have the skills you need. I have run programs in which I would pay a bonus to current employees who recommended a new employee who stayed 90 days. We hired great people this way.

6. Let the rest of your employees know what's happening. You are going to have a strong competitor, but you are sure that Bud's will continue to be a great company.

7. It is a given that your customers will be solicited. You and your salespeople should immediately reach out to all customers saying you are here to service them and will continue to earn their respect and business.

Preventing This Problem and Keeping Bud's Business Busy

1. If you didn't see this coming, it surely is a wake-up call for you. You haven't been listening to employees, customers or your industry. Just about all employees signal their intent to leave before they do so. They may ask for raises, new assignments, or different lateral positions. They may ask what the future holds for them, if you will ever sell stock in Bud's, or open a branch where they may become leaders. They are asking these questions because someone is offering one or more of these options, and they would rather stay with you. Your job is to listen. Think of this as your "early warning system."

2. Oftentimes you have one key employee who has great influence over others. He may not be a supervisor, but has a strong person-

ality. You want to keep this natural leader happy and excited to work at Bud's. If he starts to look around, others will follow!

3. Do your homework on wages and benefits in your industry. You don't have to pay the highest salaries to hold people, but you do need to be above average.

4. When your customers start to question pricing, or mention you have to stay competitive, you listen and probably adjust your service level and pricing. Your job is to listen to your employees as well.

5. If you haven't caught the buzz by the day everyone resigns, you are spending too much time away from your day-to-day business. You have to focus on Bud's.

6. When the eight people come in, don't get angry with them. Odds are three or four will see that the grass isn't greener. You will want them back, provided they gave the proper notice and did not bad-mouth you once they left. It is not the employees' or Gary's fault that they left. It is yours. You didn't keep them. The reason most people leave jobs is not money. It is to have an opportunity to grow, to learn more and to be better cared for as a person. If you just threw money at these eight, maybe one or two would stay, but they would jump as soon as someone else sweetened the pot.

7. Since so many people have left, there is something wrong at Bud's. To find out, hire an outside personnel company or consultant to do exit interviews with the eight, and some of your key people who stayed. Learn what caused the eight to leave, and take action to prevent further losses. There will be one or two common themes that you must work to improve. You won't be happy with what you learn. Treat it as constructive criticism.

8. There is nothing wrong with seeking out Gary's employees to fill your openings. Don't do it just for revenge; do it to get the best people for the positions you now have open.

9. Start more conversations with all of your people in place. If you are not doing annual reviews, here is a reason to start. Have

lunch breaks with your people and listen. See more customers more often. Don't get caught up in the fable that you have too much paperwork to do. Hire an administrative aide and get out of the back office.

10. You may want to create a loyalty awards program for your customers just like airline miles. These programs work. Visit www.fiveminuteconsultant.com to see many options. These work for big hotels and small sandwich shops. They also work at the wholesale and retail level.

11. Now is the time to review your employee manual's section about giving notice. Make it your option whether to accept an employee's notice if he is going to a competitor.

12. Do you ever share a contract with a competitor? Don't show off your star players in this case. Better yet, hope that your competitor does.

13. Place a blind ad in the local paper or online with Monster.com or careerbuilder.com. See which of your employees respond. Don't be upset with them, but quietly work with them and improve their feelings for Bud's.

14. Are you an angry boss? Do you yell and scream? If so, you will have a higher turnover of people. Count on it.

15. Do you have employees who have been job-hoppers before they came to you? If so, concentrate on their retention; maybe give them a different assignment at Bud's every couple of years.

16. By the way, did I mention this? Listen to your employees and customers.

Chapter 13

The Five-Minute Solution to Employees Who Become Romantically Involved

Problem

You own Matt's Marvelous Mighty Baseball Bats, a manufacturer of wooden baseball bats. At work, you never listen to gossip. But one day, your ears perk up when you hear that Sammy Sales Manager is romantically linked to Cathy, a customer service specialist in the office. Both are married and not to each other. You are especially worried because Sammy is her boss.

Possible Outcomes

- A couple of days later you hear the story of their break-up. You just dodged a high fastball.

- The rumors are true; looking through expense reports, you see that Sammy had a few extra nights in hotels at the same time that Cathy was on the road. Your alarm bells are ringing.

- As you discuss the situation with your attorney, you realize this will be trouble. With Sammy being her boss, Cathy easily can claim she was promised job advancement in exchange for being in a relationship. Your defense is …well, you have no defense. If Cathy claims harassment, all you can do is open your checkbook.

- It's possible that both Sammy and Cathy will leave their spouses and get married. This relieves you of legal problems. The chances of this outcome are about as good as hitting a Bob Feller fastball with a toothpick.

- You confront Sammy and he denies the whole thing. You fire Sammy and he storms out of the office.

- You confront Sammy and he admits to the affair, but doesn't see the harm. You know that he understands the law on sexual harassment, but he believes that Cathy would never claim this. You fire Sammy anyway.

What to Do When You See the Smoking Gun Proving That Sammy Acted Improperly

1. Until now, it has just been a rumor. But today, you have firm proof of the relationship due to the expense reports.

2. Don't "do nothing" and hope the problem goes away. Other employees know what is going on. They will look to you for leadership.

3. Review your employee manual, and hopefully you will find that

you have strong language against sexual harassment. Besides the legal problems, you are disappointed in Sammy due to his poor ethics and judgment.

4. Meet with your attorney to make plans for Sammy's termination. Discuss a non-disclosure section in the termination agreement. This is probably your key bargaining chip to make Sammy leave peacefully. Discuss Cathy's status. Should she be let go as well? Sammy, as the supervisor, is clearly in violation of your policy. It appears Cathy's only mistake is poor judgment.

5. Meet with Sammy. Never go into this type of meeting alone; have a trusted person take notes. Ask Sammy if the relationship rumor is true. If he says no and becomes confrontational, or says that it is none of your business, fire him on the spot, offering no severance or benefits. Make no promises about job references or unemployment. Don't discuss what evidence you have; you may need to save this for a possible wrongful termination lawsuit. If Sammy admits the affair, you still fire him, but with more understanding. Discuss the options: (a) he can go quietly and say nothing; (b) he can protest, which means you will be forced to reveal your information in a legal proceeding; or (c) you come to terms on his leaving and pay a certain amount of benefits and agree to non-disclosure.

6. Tell the rest of the company that you and Sammy have had a disagreement and that he has left Matt's Mighty Marvelous Baseball Bats. Don't bring Cathy's name up in any way, as this can lead to defamation.

7. Go about your business. Everyone will ask, but only say that you and Sammy had a business disagreement, and that Sammy is no longer employed. Don't be tempted to discuss a few choice details. The only time you should respond is if Sammy doesn't keep to the non-disclosure, or if the whole deal goes to court.

8. No matter what you do now, you can't win. The best you can hope for is that Sammy and Cathy both voluntarily leave Matt's.

Preventing This Problem

1. Have a bold and underlined statement about sexual harassment in your employee manual. Visit http://eeoc.gov/laws/types/sexual_harassment.cfm for solid information from the Equal Employment Opportunity Commission. You and all of your supervisors should know and understand this site. Your next step is to read the info at: http://www.eeoc.gov/policy/docs/harassment-facts.pdf. Also visit www.fiveminuteconsultant.com to see various statements written in different styles and languages. Pick one that fits the style of your employee manual, or call your attorney to write one for you.

2. Once a year have a meeting with every supervisor and leader at Matt's, covering all forms of harassment, not just sexual. The EEOC recognizes these discriminatory areas:

    a. Age;

    b. Disability;

    c. Equal compensation;

    d. Genetic information;

    e. National origin;

    f. Pregnancy;

    g. Race/color;

    h. Religion;

    i. Retaliation;

    j. Sexual preference; and

    k. Sexual harassment.

3. Some companies have a policy that two employees who become romantically involved must sign "consensual relationship agreements" (sometimes called love contracts) stating that the relationship is voluntary. This will not work in situations where one party doesn't want a spouse to know. Creating this affidavit is going too

far for small and medium-sized companies.

4. As soon as you get the slightest hint that something is going on, you must ask one of the parties about it, especially if there is a supervisor-employee situation. Generally the boss is the last to know, so by the time you hear, everyone else will be gossiping. You have to act quickly to prevent a possible legal problem.

5. You can transfer one person to a position that doesn't result in a supervisor-employee position. It is most common to transfer the senior person in the relationship to a different location or department. If you can't make the transfer, then you need to make sure the relationship is voluntary, and that may include getting written acknowledgments from both people.

6. Surveys say that about 40 percent of office workers have a workplace relationship at some point, and about 10 percent of marriages start from the workplace. In the Matt's Bats situation, both Sammy and Cathy are married, so you know the train wreck will be coming. If you can't get the written statements, you have a tough decision.

7. Even in a consensual relationship, other employees may be offended by personal displays of affection, such as holding hands or a quick kiss. Others will infer that favoritism is taking place when they don't get raises or new job assignments. How much faith do you have that once the relationship ends (and most do) that there won't be bitterness festering in your workplace? Whether or not there is a sexual harassment case, the atmosphere of a company can be poisoned when two parties won't speak to each other. Your office will quickly turn into a sitcom!

8. Do you request a resignation? Do you terminate one of them? There is absolutely no right answer. You face an elusive target: balancing employees' rights versus protecting your business interests.

9. You can't ever totally eliminate Cupid's Arrow from your workplace. What you can do is constantly stress to your leadership team

that an affair with someone they supervise is against every rule you have. Keep repeating that when you find out, and you surely will, there will be instant termination of the supervisor in all circumstances. The costs and aggravation of a sexual harassment lawsuit are enormous. There is not a company anywhere that should find a way to work around a supervisor-employee relationship. Whether one or both parties are married is irrelevant.

10. You can purchase insurance to cover your legal costs and settlements. This is enormously expensive and usually carries a very high deductible. Even if you have this insurance, you must still take actions to prevent a supervisor-employee relationship.

Chapter 14

The Five-Minute Solution to the Employee with an Offensive Tattoo

Problem

Tim works in the production area of your company, Thomas' Tremendous Toys. The plant environment is warm due to manufacturing processes, so employees usually work in T-shirts. On Monday, Tim comes to work with a Ku Klux Klan (KKK) image tattooed on his forearm. After lunch, five employees come to you saying they are offended by the tattoo. They tell you that none of them wants to work in the same department as Tim, and that his bragging about his new tattoo is harassment.

Possible Outcomes

- You ask Tim to wear a long-sleeved shirt at all times. He agrees begrudgingly. But he still rolls up his sleeve, talks about his approval of the Klan, and tries to show off the tattoo. Other employees are upset.

- You tell Tim that he cannot show the tattoo in the workplace. You warn him that his actions can be construed as harassing to other employees. A week later he begins showing the tattoo again. You warn him in writing that his actions may cause further disciplinary actions. Twenty-five percent of your workforce signs a petition against Tim.

- You check your employee handbook; it is silent on the subject of tattoos. Your handbook does clearly state that harassing signs or demonstrations can be cause for disciplinary action, up to and including termination. You suspend Tim for two days when he next shows up in a short-sleeved shirt.

- A week later you see Tim flaunting his tattoo again. You fire him. He promises to sue you. In the meantime, the upset employees have contacted the labor department to see what their rights are.

- You don't understand how you managed to upset everybody.

What to Do When Tim Comes to Work with His New Tattoo

1. As soon as this is brought to your attention, bring Tim into your office and look at the tattoo. Don't bring up whether you support or decry the KKK. The issue is that he has offended other workers and they have a legitimate claim to take to the Equal Employment Opportunity Commission (EEOC). You visit www.eeoc.gov and find this: "A hostile work environment is created when the 'workplace is permeated with discriminatory intimidation, ridicule, and insult that is sufficiently severe or pervasive to alter the conditions of the victim's employment and create an abusive working environment.'"

to establish a case of religious harassment, an employee must show that the harassment was: (1) based on his religion; (2) unwelcome; (3) sufficiently severe or pervasive to alter the conditions of employment by creating an intimidating, hostile or offensive work environment; and (4) that there is a basis for employer liability." To read more about this, visit www.fiveminuteconsultant.com. If you are not sure if Tim's KKK affiliation is due to racist or religious views, it doesn't matter. It is still harassment.

2. Bring Tim into your office with an additional person as note-taker, and explain to Tim that his tattoo is offensive to others and he cannot show it at any time at work. Tim strongly objects and says he has the right of free speech. Tell Tim that his time at work contains responsibilities to all members of your company and, in no uncertain terms, explain that he must keep this tattoo covered at all times at work or face disciplinary action.

3. Talk with all employees and explain that Thomas' Tremendous Toys will not allow harassment or discrimination in the workplace. Without mentioning Tim by name, explain that you will take all the actions necessary to maintain a proper work environment.

4. You hope that tomorrow this will quiet down, but you know that if Tim continues to show or discuss his tattoo, you have to take strong and decisive action.

Preventing This Problem at Thomas Toys

1. In the next revision of your employee manual make sure harassment and discrimination are broadly defined and that your disciplinary procedures are clearly laid out. Be sure to include that offensive tattoos, shirts, hats and articles of clothing are not allowed anywhere at Thomas' Tremendous Toys.

2. Years ago, tattoos were used by bikers and gang members. Today, "body art" is acceptable in many situations. Thomas has to walk

the fine line between artwork and something offensive to others. More often than not, Thomas will make individual determinations on what he sees.

3. Have yearly "respect for others" conversations with all employees. Explain why harassment is bad for the company and for individuals. Teach what harassment is, giving examples. Don't be shy. Be clear and passionate about not allowing harassment at Thomas'. Teach how a hostile work environment causes problems for the entire company by distracting employees and causing unfounded concerns.

4. Have more frequent conversations and training with supervisors. They should be able to spot and defuse harassing or discriminating situations before a complaint arises.

5. Set up an easy-to-use communication channel for all employees to speak privately with you about discrimination and harassment. It may be a separate telephone extension, a locked mailbox outside your office door, or a phone call to a trusted advisor who will then tell you.

6. Be sure to follow up on each and every contact stating discrimination or harassment. You and your company are responsible for providing a safe, secure, and non-hostile work environment. If you know about a problem and do nothing to solve it, you and your defense attorney will become close friends.

7. Give clear and prompt answers to any complaint. You may find some complaints totally innocuous and without evidence of a hostile environment, or you may find you have a problem that needs immediate attention. Either way, react quickly. Don't just laugh it off as idle talk.

8. If you have a uniform policy for employees, enforce it. You can have a different policy for workers who meet the public than you have for production or office workers who don't. It's fine to have customer contact personnel dress to a higher standard. If you re-

quire a uniform, in just about every state you have to provide it or pay for it. Make sure that you get the best you can afford. A neatly dressed customer-contact person is one of the best advertisements you can create.

9. Do not, under any circumstances, allow political buttons, advertising messages (like beer shirts) or social commentary among customer-contact people. If a customer-contact employee has a tattoo, you may require him to wear something that will cover the tattoo. There are many types of cosmetics available that will cover tattoos as well. The important rule is to enforce this on an even-handed basis. Don't allow your politics to be shown while disallowing other's positions.

10. If you don't have a business dress policy, now is the time to create one. Ask three people from the plant and office to be on the committee with you. Use their input as the main ingredient in your dress code and teach them the rules about harassment and the importance of a good appearance for all face-to-face customer contacts. At first, be strict on the policy. It is easier to relax a policy three months down the line than to tighten it up.

11. Include body piercings in your dress code. Surveys have shown that customers often find piercings more off-putting than tattoos.

Chapter 15

The Five-Minute Solution to Your Cash Flow Turning Negative

5ive minute consultant™

Problem

You own Homer's Home Store, where you sell household appliances, kitchenware, closet supplies and other trendy items. Your sales have slowed down, dragging cash flow into negative territory. You have maxed out your line of credit at the local bank; you are paying your bills at 60 days and heading toward 75. A couple of key vendors have started asking for prepayments and COD shipments.

Possible Outcomes

- All of a sudden sales pick up; you pay all your bills and have no problems. You're better off buying a lottery ticket.
- Your long-lost Uncle Herman passes away leaving you enough money to pay your bills. Stop laughing–it can happen.
- You lay off two people, cut your advertising and other local expenses. This helps, but just not quite enough.
- Sales pick up due to revamped advertising and a new line of bedding you bring in. You are back to positive cash flow.
- You fall farther behind and most of your vendors cut you off. You realize the end is near and call your attorney to discuss your options.
- You have owned Homer's for 30 years and sink into a deep depression on the day you lock the door. You spend three months in your bedroom, curled up in a ball, watching reruns of Rocky and Bullwinkle.

Dear Homer, There Are a Lot of Paths for You to Take ... Let's Look

At this point, cash flow is more important than profit. Cut margins for a month and sell excess inventory. No successful business has high margin inventory and low sales. This sounds so basic, but many inventory-rich companies go south. Don't be so proud that you can't have a "sale."

There are two ways to solve this problem: increase revenues or cut expenses. You can do both, simultaneously. These ideas work for a retail company

1. In a retail business, expand open hours. You'll have to work longer hours yourself, but that is the definition of entrepreneur.

2. If you rent your space, meet with your landlord and be honest about your situation. Ask for a rent holiday for three months, of-

fering to begin paying back in the fourth month through the twelfth. Prepare for this conversation by doing homework on the real estate in your area. Threatening to move to a lower rent space would ring hollow if there is no space available. If you pay real estate taxes as part of your lease, pay them as a show of good faith. Also, ask for a lower base rent. In tough economic times, most landlords will prefer a lower rent than an empty space.

3. If you own the property, consider a sale and lease-back situation. This won't happen overnight. Talk with your attorney and a trusted real estate broker. This won't solve short-term problems. If the purchaser knows you are in trouble, you won't realize the full value of your property.

4. Cut all extraneous expenses. If you don't need whatever you are buying during the next 90 days, don't buy it. You used to buy a quantity of an item for a price break; now buy just what you need. Cut down on the little luxuries of life: company-paid coffee, high-end office supplies, air conditioning and heat at the coolest and warmest levels. Take the garbage out and vacuum the office yourself. Don't renew expiring service contracts right now, or work out a 90-day free period as a renewal bonus.

5. Don't take any bills that come in for granted. Sure, you have been paying the electric company for years ... call them and make sure you have the lowest commercial rates. If you heat with oil, let the tank go to its lowest level before filling up. Fix that leaking toilet to reduce your water bill. (Every company in America has one leaking toilet.)

6. Call your key vendors and ask for extended terms. It is better for you to call them than for their collection attorneys to call you. Ask them to place a hold on what you presently owe, and sell you new goods on COD, maybe with a 10 percent add-on towards the old balance. Let your current vendors know what you are doing. Communication is the key to keeping these relationships. Ask your key vendors for a bigger cash discount. Do the math; paying these ven-

dors more quickly may actually improve cash flow.

7. Look to new vendors who may be eager to sell to you. It is not particularly ethical to replace vendors who have been working with you—but these are tough times.

8. Look at your inventory, whatever type of business you are in. If you have owned inventory for more than 60 days, it is time to get rid of it. Create interesting advertising around your "specials," whether it be in media or just within your store or company website. Increase the payment terms on lay-away purchases. Sell out your slow movers and increase your inventory of bread-and-butter items. Give a small incentive to your sales staff to sell certain products. If you are in a service business with no inventory, train your people to ask, "What else can we do for you? Or, "Did you know that we do_____?"

9. Set your retail pricing with product combinations in mind…Sell three of the same item at a 10% discount; sell charcoal along with grills; sell larger sizes of current products or sell case quantities of items that are good sellers. These all increase current revenue. Work with vendors to get sample sizes of items that you can give away… if the products are good, count on a high percentage of customers to return and buy the product.

10. Do you have a gift card program? This is a great way to generate current cash for purchases in the future. Give a 5-10 percent discount on gift cards to generate immediate cash.

11. Stop all business travel. Have meetings by phone or email. Use your accumulated credit card points if you have to travel. No more overnight mail either; fax or email documents.

12. Use Skype for long-distance calling, especially international. Look at your phone bill … it may be cheaper to start unlimited calling plans rather than being billed for each call. Combine your fax lines, reducing to one company-wide number. You don't need the latest gadget-filled phone. If you switch cell phone carriers for a better

price, negotiate the new carrier paying the cancellation charges on your current plan. Ask for it, you will get it!

13. Is your building at a high point of geography? Call the local cell phone companies and see if they want to put up a cell site and pay you rent.

14. If you are not on the web, get there. A simple website is better than no website, but don't do it poorly. This doesn't have to be expensive. Call the computer teacher at your local high school and ask for a recommendation on a student who creates websites.

15. The best people to help are your employees. They know where revenue is not maximized, or expenses are running unchecked. Set up an employee group to help you and consider giving part of the savings to the group.

16. Set up employee benefits programs that don't cost you anything, such as a flexible spending account. In fact, you save money by not paying the employer's share of FICA here. Contact your benefits advisor or health insurance provider. (*See Chapter 48 for more on this topic.*)

17. Work to reduce turnover of your staff. One of the biggest costs you have is the hiring and training of people.

18. Stop paying for all alcoholic drinks at company lunches and/or events.

19. Look at your bills from professional providers, lawyers, accountants, etc. (but never consultants!). Get them to drop travel time, and look for more phone conferences than face-to-face meetings. Put off all non-necessary projects.

20. Check your property tax bill. Companies will work with you for free to reduce your bill and then take a percentage of the savings. The same concept works for utility auditors.

21. Check your bank and credit card fees. Combine all accounts with one bank to get lower fees. Pay your bills with electronic bill pay from your bank. This will always be cheaper than writing a check.

Look online to get the lowest credit and debit card fees. American Express charges the highest merchant fees. Consider the impact to your business if you don't take American Express cards.

22. Place all charitable contributions on hold for 90 days. It hurts to withdraw from favorite programs, but the health of your own business comes first.

23. Start approving every check yourself. Don't delegate. You will learn more with this exercise than any other. Review every invoice from every vendor. Make sure you are not paying sales taxes on materials for resale. Many states allow you not to pay sales tax on electricity used in manufacturing.

24. Don't even think about <u>not</u> paying your payroll taxes.

25. Question every expense, every day.

Chapter 16

The Five-Minute Solution to Trying to Collect Past-Due Money

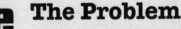

The Problem

You own Babe's Candy, where you are the Sultan of Sweets. You sell mainly wholesale to candy stores and gift shops. Last month your accounts receivable bookkeeper, Betty, won the lottery and moved to Las Vegas the next day. You tried to hire an experienced person but no one answered your help-wanted ad, so you hired your wife's cousin's niece, Nancy, a nice kid, with some office experience, but no collection experience.

Possible Outcomes

- Niece Nancy comes in, looks at your accounts receivable, organizes all of the paperwork, and is on the phone by noon calling people overdue by 60 days. She gets everyone to promise a check. Sure.

- Nancy looks at everything for a week, eats $185 worth of jelly beans, and decides the job is not for her.

- You place another ad in the paper, increasing your salary range. You still don't get any good candidates.

- You decide to do the job yourself; you know the business, but don't have a feel for collecting money. You feel like a babe in the woods.

What Can Babe's Do When Niece Nancy Starts Working?

1. Babe, you should have held out for an experienced person.

2. Since you didn't, and Nancy doesn't know what to do, give her a day with your accountant, going over business protocol and terminology.

3. Your accountant is at the ballgame, so ask your best business buddy to let Nancy shadow his accounts receivable person for a couple of days.

4. Hire a temp person from a service that specializes in financial temps, and have Terry the Temp mentor Niece Nancy for a week.

5. Surely you have cross-trained the other people in your office to do this, so you really won't have a problem, unless, perchance, you didn't quite get that into your staff training agenda.

6. You can thank Nancy for her effort and decide to do it yourself for a month, so that you can then train the next candidate.

How Can Babe's Begin to Collect 60-Day Past-Due Money?

1. Get an aged accounts receivable from your bookkeeper. If you have QuickBooks™, or any other computerized system, this should be very easy. If you are still writing on ledger cards, consider taking your head out of the sand. I understand why Betty bought lottery tickets.

2. You have your aging. Your terms are 1% 10/net 30. Starting out, look at the largest dollars rather than the oldest dollars. Your goal is to collect money first, and clean up problems as you go along.

3. There are different techniques based on the age of the receivable. In this chapter I'll discuss collections up to 60 days.

4. Rule Number One: You want to keep the customer buying and paying. It does no good to so upset a customer during collection that they go to another vendor. Nice works better than angry on a collection call. Never threaten unless you are willing to lose the customer.

5. Customers will say their cash flow is uneven and can't predict when they will pay you. In a hard goods business, inventory can sit on shelves. In the candy business, you know the inventory turnover is always less than 30 days. If you are not getting paid, customers are using your money for other needs. You will be more forceful knowing what your customers do with your products and their stock turns. Watch the calendar. A week before taxes are due, you won't receive much cash. In the candy business, you should expect payments immediately after big holidays.

6. When you send 30-day statements, write a short note to customers who are past due. Avoid the stickers and stamps that say "past due." A short personal note on the statement works wonders.

7. If a customer traditionally pays you in full in 60 days, your conversation starts with the owner, not the accounts payable person. Thank him for his past business, and ask what you can do to help him start paying in 45 days. Does he need invoices sooner? Can

you fax or email rather than using postal mail? Remind him that your one percent discount will be better for him than withholding your money for 60 days. Can he pay in 10 days if you offer a two percent discount?

8. Not too many people are going to improve their paying habits just because you say "please." You have to give them some reason: a discount or a better offer on products; or maybe an exclusive product or a quantity discount. You have to give something, so try to give something that will improve your sales at the same time. Many of you will ask, "Why do I have to give something? I gave him my candy to sell!" Because the only answer to that is withdrawing your candy from sale. Babe's is great candy, but there is competition.

9. Do you charge a finance charge? You should, and the common number is 1.5 percent per month. Call your attorney for your state's rules. You will need to detail the finance charges on your customer application and notify all customers when you start the program. Then, you have a negotiating tool. Explain you will drop the finance charges for a payment. This really does work, as simple as it sounds! Some customers will pay the charges as well. We were paid about fifteen percent of the finance charges we billed. Remember, at your fiscal year-end, write off the accrued finance charges from your profit-and-loss statement, but not from your accounts receivable. You don't want pay taxes now on money you probably won't collect.

10. Ask your customers to give a credit card number that you will automatically bill on the 29th day from shipping. They then pay the card in 30 days and get their 59 days, plus their airline miles. This will cost you a couple of points, but by guaranteeing your cash flow, it's worth it.

11. Call your customers when they are 35 days from invoice—every single one. The squeaky wheel gets paid first. Get a firm promise for a check date. You will get paid ahead of vendors who don't call. If a customer tells you he will pay in ten days, politely call on the

seventh day and remind him. Three days after the expected date, if the check is not in, follow up. Let the customer know you are serious about following his commitment. At 60 days, you are not near the "Call the collection attorney" stage, but constant, polite communication will get you paid.

12. You want to encourage prompt payments, so create a sale and send info to every customer. Boldly state that only customers who are current can take advantage of this special. When Sally's Sweets calls to order your big deal, politely explain that she is not eligible as she is past due. Offer to extend the sale to her for a couple of days so she can send a check. It will get around the industry that you offer great sales only to customers who pay their bills. Customers who do pay timely will take advantage of your deals.

13. You need to set a firm policy about cutting off shipments. Generally, 60 days works for just about everyone, but competitive and industry standards have an impact here. After three phone calls to the same person, change tactics. Ask for a supervisor or owner. If you have been speaking with the owner, and he has lied to you about sending a check, don't feel badly about cutting him off from your product. One alternative is to work out a plan for shipping COD, with a 15 to 20 percent add-on for the old money.

14. If the customer owes you a large amount, and won't or can't pay COD, ask him to send you a weekly check, just like payroll. I had customers do just that, putting us on the payroll for a small amount each week, and the bills got paid. A series of post-dated checks is okay; better yet is a group of checks all dated today from which you deposit one a week. A bounced post-dated check is just paper, but a currently dated check that doesn't clear is a felony.

15. It is easy to say, "Sally's Sweets always pays in 60, so she is okay." Don't fall into this trap, you can move them up to 45, and then slowly move them to 30. You are entitled to your payments within your terms. This is the implied contract of your sale.

Chapter 17

The Five-Minute Solution to Two People in a Row Quitting the Same Position

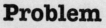 **Problem**

You have hired two people for the same position in just three weeks. Both have quit within a week. Why is this happening? It is costing you to advertise and hire and you have a high loss of productivity. The biggest problem is the negative impact on morale for your employees.

Possible Outcomes

- You keep on hiring until you find the "golden child." You accept the costs involved and chalk it up to overhead.

- You eliminate the position all together, figuring you can't get someone to fill it; you spread the duties to others, who all ask for raises with their new work.

- You call an employment agency and pay three month's salary to hire a low-level candidate.

- You rethink your entire hiring approach and hit a home run with your next hire.

What to Do When an Employee Quits Unexpectedly

1. Stay calm. It happens. I never try to talk someone out of quitting. If the person didn't come in and say he had a problem, and ask, "Can we work it out?" then he isn't worth saving. Ask him why he is leaving and what can you do better to ensure that his replacement will like the job.

2. Many companies do an exit interview, and, if the interview is done well, it can be very informative and helpful. Even an employee who has only been at your company for a week can offer insights. If you have a personnel manager, have her conduct the interview. If you do it yourself, don't argue with the employee over anything; don't rebut his comments. Just listen, take good notes, and try to understand what made this decision the right one for this person.

3. A short-term employee who quits should not be given severance pay, unless you have a contract of some sort. He should not continue working either; he is a source of discontent that can spread like a virus. Pay him for the remainder of the day he quits and move on. If the employee gives you two weeks' notice, decide whether it is worth keeping him, or paying him the two weeks and requesting that he leave anyway. In your employee manual you

may want to add a phrase, "Employees who resign during their first ninety days of employment are not eligible to be paid for their two-week notice."

4. You have to decide if this was a poor employee or a poor hire. Did you hire a great person for the wrong job, or did the employee not fulfill your expectations? My nephew recently received a job promotion at General Electric Co. He had to go through five interviews, even though the company already knew him. Getting hired at Google requires at least six interviews. Many small companies hire after just one interview and most hire after the second interview. Don't just hire the next one in line. Keep on interviewing until you are sure you have a winner.

5. When two people quit from the same department, you need to examine the department's supervisor. Ask other supervisors what is happening. Talk to other employees in the department. Is the supervisor providing the right training? Maybe dumping all the dirty work on the new person as an initiation? Is the supervisor afraid to have a good worker in the department? Ask the supervisor why he thinks the people quit and what he will do to prevent this in the future. The supervisor most often will say "Let me do the hiring." This is one of the best solutions!

6. Keep this treadmill going until you get the right employee, or read the next section on how to prevent this horrible waste of time and money.

Preventing This Problem

1. It starts with writing a good job description. Understand what the job entails, what the qualifications for the job are, and what the commitments are on the part of the employee. These might include the ability to work overtime, willingness to learn new products or procedures, travel, early or late hours, etc.

2. Before the initial interview, have the applicant fill out a job application at your office. You already have the information from

the person's resume, but the application can help you learn several other tidbits.

a. Does the person fill out the application completely? If he completes his name and address and then writes, "see resume," he goes on my back burner.

b. Is there care taken? Is the person's writing clear? If he scribbles the answers, he doesn't really care about the job and is not trying to impress you.

c. Does the applicant answer all questions correctly? If he can't follow the simple directions on the application, how well will he follow his job description?

d. Watch the person complete the application. Is he nervous? Does he fidget and look at his watch? Or does he look around the office, trying to get a feel for your company?

e. If you have a release for a background or credit check, or a pre-employment drug test or physical, is it properly signed? Ask the applicant a question about this during the interview. See if he retained what he read.

3. When you do the initial interview, provide a five-minute description of the job and see if the employee is excited about it. You don't want to hire someone who is just seeking a paycheck. If the person is truly interested in your company and the position, he will work to be successful. You should be listening more than talking; the applicant should speak about 70 percent of the time during the interview.

4. Ask intelligent questions. Avoid the theoretical questions such as, "What is your favorite color?" You should always ask open-ended questions, and let the candidate speak. You can throw a curveball question, but make it relevant to the job at hand. Avoid political or religious questions or statements, unless they relate to potential job duties.

5. Conduct at least two interviews. When you are serious about a

candidate, take him to lunch. See how he reacts to waiters and busboys. If he is polite to these working people, he will be polite to your customers! During the second interview, have the supervisor of the position join you. The supervisor's opinions about the applicants should be one of the most important aspects of your decision, giving the supervisor a stake in the success of the new hire.

6. Walk with the applicant through his possible job area. See if he is surprised by what you do, or if he understands it. This helps validate his previous work history. Try to climb stairs, if possible, so you can observe the applicant's physical ability. Later ask questions about what the applicant saw. Was he observant?

7. Ask the applicant when he would be available to start work. If he is working presently and says he can start right away, you should run away. If he doesn't plan on giving his current employer proper notice, he won't give it to you either.

8. Do a thorough job of checking references. Many people spend more time reading movie reviews than they do checking references. Yes, it slows down the hiring process, but it is one of the keys to success in hiring. Consider doing pre-employment drug testing. (*See Chapter 20 for more on this*).

9. The first day of employment is the most important day of an employee's future success (or lack of it). Greet him yourself. Give him a five-minute pep talk about the company's history, type of work done, and the values and culture of your company. Have the new employee's supervisor give him a thorough tour of the facility, introducing key people he will come into contact with. Show him where the lunchroom is, the bathrooms, parking, dress codes and all of the non-direct job-related things that go into helping people enjoy their work.

10. Assign a "job buddy" who will guide the new employee through the ins and outs of his specific job. Make the supervisor and job

buddy responsible for the success of the new person. When the new employee finishes a full week, give all three a $25 gift card for achieving this milestone.

11. At the end of the second day, you should meet with the new employee for just a minute or two and see how he is doing. Let him know you care about his success in your company.

12. Have the supervisor give you a two-minute update daily. This ensures the supervisor is involved with the success of the new hire.

Chapter 18

The Five-Minute Solution to the Liquid Luncher

5ive minute consultant **Problem**

A good employee comes back from lunch and you distinctly smell alcohol on his breath. Your employee manual specifically prohibits drinking on the job or being under the influence at work.

Possible Outcomes

- You do nothing. The employee, Steve, goes about his job, and at the end of the day you breathe a sigh of relief.
- You do nothing. Another employee comes up to you, says he smells alcohol on Steve, and asks not to work near him for safety reasons.
- You do nothing. Steve has an accident, hurting himself and another worker, and causing damage to a machine in your plant. Now it is expensive.
- You confront Steve; he says he had one beer with lunch. You say, "Okay, it's only one beer," tell him not to do it again, and hope for the best.
- You send Steve home for the day, and tell him to come back tomorrow for a disciplinary lecture.
- You ask another worker to drive Steve home, or call his wife to come pick him up, embarrassing Steve.
- You call your drug and alcohol testing lab and request a mobile breathalyzer reading.

What to Do When Steve Comes in with Alcohol on His Breath

1. Show Steve your disappointment and frustration. Be upset. There should be no middle ground in this situation. Steve has clearly violated a rule, and has placed himself and others in a possibly dangerous situation. If Steve happens to drive a company vehicle and is involved in an accident, you will be in serious trouble. If Steve injures another employee, that employee can sue you for contributing to the injury.

2. If your employee manual calls for zero tolerance on alcohol during the work day, follow your procedure—whether it is a warning, suspension or termination. If you have an alcohol policy, make

sure you retain a testing lab that does breathalyzer work. Also, there are mobile labs that will come to you. It is very important that you have these options clearly established when you publish your manual. If Steve refuses to submit to testing, your employee manual should state that this is the same as flunking the test and appropriate disciplinary action will take place.

3. It is virtually impossible to know how much alcohol a person has consumed by smelling his breath. A heavy drinker can consume multiple beers and act fairly normal, but he may still be over the legal limit for driving or over your company limit.

4. Never let Steve drive to the lab himself or drive home for the rest of the day. Think about it. You suspect that Steve has consumed an unknown quantity of alcohol, and then you say it is okay to drive. His accident is now your lawsuit, and you will lose. Insist that Steve not drive; if you must, block his car or take away his keys. Tell Steve that if he does drive away, you will call the police to report there is a drunk on the road. This sounds cold and heartless. It is not. You are doing him a favor in the long run, and possibly are preventing him from involvement in an accident. You are also protecting yourself and your company from legal troubles.

5. The following day, hold a disciplinary meeting with Steve and one other person. Never do this alone; have the other person take notes. Follow the guidelines in your employee handbook or, if you have no employee guidelines or handbook, decide if this incident is a one-timer or if you have a long-term problem on your hands. Without a prepared guideline, you probably will do the wrong thing.

Preventing This Problem

1. Changing the company culture is key. You should have a zero-tolerance policy during the workday. Whether you are in heavy manufacturing or are an office-based business, zero tolerance works. Today, there is total acceptance of going to lunch with a

client and ordering ginger ale. Business dinners are slightly different, as you are not going back to the workplace. Have one drink, sip it slowly and enjoy the evening, setting the tone for others. If your client continues to drink, you will have the clearer head and will be one step ahead in business conversations. If the evening is strictly social, then go ahead and enjoy yourself, but always appoint a designated driver.

2. Let's set some employee guidelines for your employee manual:

   a. **Zero tolerance.** If you have a company where machinery is used, forklifts being used, or physical labor, this is the program for you. Safety has to be your prime concern here; even one beer during lunch will reduce reaction time in trying to avoid a dangerous situation.

   b. **A Specific tolerance.** A .08 blood alcohol content (BAC) is legally drunk in all 50 states. You certainly don't want to set the level this high in your company. What level do you want in your company? Do you want to allow one beer during lunch? Two?

3. Whatever you decide, explain the policy clearly to all employees and new hires. Remember, you are not trying to manage their personal lives, but are managing your company for safety and for doing the best job possible for your customers.

4. You have to set the example—no drinking by you during the day.

5. Now set up the disciplinary program. It has to work at various levels. Employees who test at .08 should be immediately suspended, without pay for at least 30 days, and be required to attend and graduate from an alcohol recovery program. No exceptions. They also have to agree to be randomly tested a minimum of six times in the next year, at their expense. A second positive test should result in termination.

6. Whatever tolerance limit you set, those exceeding the limit but below .08 should be suspended for at least two weeks, and at a

minimum be subject to random testing four times in the next year, at their expense.

7. Check with your group health insurance company. Many will pay for either inpatient or outpatient alcohol abuse programs. Use this to encourage employees to get help.

8. When someone is suspended or terminated for violating a policy, don't be the one to spread it around the company as an example of what you have done. Word will get around on its own.

9. Consider offering an Employee Assistance Plan (EAP) to your employees. This is usually a phone-in assistance program that helps employees with many different types of issues. Substance abuse is always high on the list. These generally run between $3 and $9 per month, per employee. Talk with your benefits provider for details.

10. Be observant. Realizing that an employee came back from lunch a little tipsy may be just one indicator of a drinking problem. Here are some others:

    a. Frequent tardiness;

    b. Abuse of sick leave policies;

    c. Many absences on Mondays and Fridays;

    d. Careless and sloppy work output;

    e. Arguments and disagreements with coworkers;

    f. Obvious financial problems, borrowing from coworkers;

    g. Bloodshot eyes;

    h. Constant use of mouthwash and breath mints;

    i. Avoiding supervisors, especially after lunch;

    j. Tremors or unexplained body aches; and

    k. Catnaps at work, most often after lunch

    Just one of these signs may not be cause for alarm. After all, we all have rough days. But when two or three of these alarm bells start ringing, it is time to ask serious questions.

11. Your employee manual should state that all employees involved in any type of accident while at work will be tested for drugs and alcohol. Speak with your lawyer about drawing up a short acknowledgment to be signed by new hires.

12. Few alcoholics can stop on their own, even though many say they can. Make attending a supervised program mandatory before returning to work; this often is covered by insurance.

13. Most alcoholics know they have a problem, but don't have the inner strength to resolve the problem. If you take the time and effort to help a good employee stop drinking or taking drugs, and the program works, he will, just about every time, be so grateful that he will become one of your best employees. You get an emotional return for helping someone, and your business will regain a great employee.

14. Never have an open bar at company events, dinners or picnics. Give employees one or two drink tickets and ask them not to share their tickets.

15. Is your company environment stressful? The more stress in a job, the more likely it is that employees will turn to alcohol to relieve their stress. While you may get more productivity from employees by constantly getting on their backs, you may cause long-term problems that will affect your company greatly.

Chapter 19

The Five-Minute Solution to Giving an Employee a Loan

Problem

Your company, Larry's Leisure, has 31 employees. Doug, from the swimming pool division asks to meet you. He says he needs $2,000 for an emergency repair to his car. Without fixing it, he can't come to work and would have to quit. Doug has been with you for three years and is a good employee. You've never given an employee loan and are afraid if you do every employee will ask for one. You want to help Doug, but don't know what to do. You ask him to come back in an hour.

Possible Outcomes

- You decide to stick with what you have done in the past, telling Doug you can't give him a loan. Regretfully, he tells you he can't get to work and resigns.

- Three weeks after you give the loan to Doug, he pays you back, gives you a plant for your office and says you are the greatest boss he has ever had.

- You give Doug the loan and ask him to pay it back in four weeks. In four weeks, Doug walks in with just $1,000 and tells you he can have the balance in another four weeks. You are upset and yell at him.

- Even though you and Doug agreed that no one would be told of the loan, word gets out from your bookkeeper who wrote the check. Five more people come to you for loans. You turn them down and have five people who just don't understand. You start looking for a new bookkeeper.

- You get the idea … the outcome can be anything from successful to a disaster. You need a better plan.

What to Do When Doug Comes into Your office

1. Since you don't have an established policy, you did the right thing by asking Doug to come back in an hour. You need a little time to think this through.

2. A quick call to Anne, your attorney, tells you that you cannot garnish Doug's wages without his permission. Doug can sign a note giving you permission to take a fixed amount each payday, and, if necessary, to withhold a final check in the event he leaves the company. Anne faxes you a basic form.

3. You recall that other people have asked for a loan, and you said no, mainly because you never had any extra money. Larry's has

grown and you do have the funds available. Is it time to change your point of view?

4. You made it through life without asking for help, so why can't Doug? But you know that you are not most people.

5. You decide to help Doug, but with no mention of employee loans or advances in your employee manual, you don't know how to structure it.

6. Doug comes back to your office saying he can repay you in four weeks, giving you the answer. You call Beatrice the Bookkeeper and ask her to write a check for $2,000 to Doug. When she asks how to record this in the books, you are not sure, but finally decided to call it just what it is, an employee loan. Doug tells you he is proud to work at Larry's.

Let's Try to Make This Better for Doug

1. Employees will ask for loans. Even if you have a firm "no loans" policy, people will still ask. There is no right answer on whether you should give loans. The bigger the company, the harder it is to administer a once-in-a-while loan and payback program. You may have a strong reason for saying no; possibly a previous employee stiffed you and left you with bad feelings.

2. On the other hand ... giving loans gives you an opportunity to help your employees, who almost always repay with enthusiasm for you and the company. Employees who have money problems think about it at work, move their focus from your products, and cause an impact on productivity, safety and customer service.

3. Whatever you feel, place your policy in clear language in your employee manual. Don't vary ... a discrimination complaint can follow if you pick and choose who receives loans without a guideline. In your employee manual be sure to state that the program can be modified or canceled at your discretion.

4. Let's look at some program basics if you want to offer employee loans:

a. Set a minimum time employed before you will offer a loan. One year worked for me.

b. Require that payments be deducted from each paycheck, no exceptions. Payments should not extend beyond a certain time span. 26 weeks was my maximum length.

c. The employee must sign a form giving you the right to take funds from his paycheck and to withhold all monies due from a final paycheck if the employee leaves.

d. Employees can have only one or two loans a year, whichever you are comfortable with. You may even want to say one loan every other year.

e. In your program, there should be a loan maximum amount, maybe one thousand or two at most. There should also be a minimum; you don't want to go through the paperwork for $50. If someone needed a small amount of money, I found it easier to give it to him from my pocket, which was a mistake, but I did it anyway.

f. The employee has to tell you the purpose of the loan. In your program, you can state that it must be for medical needs only or to cover housing emergencies. You can leave this vague, but be careful to follow the precedents you have created. If Maria is given a loan to cover a blown heating system at home, and then you deny Donald a loan for the same reason, you may be open to a discrimination investigation.

g. If you have alternate sources for loans available to employees—a company-affiliated credit union, or a labor union welfare plan—the employee has to show you a denial letter from this source. Company loans should be the last source, not the first.

h. All paperwork and details relating to employee loans has to be done when the employee is off-the-clock.

5. Think about interest. We did not charge interest. You may want to. If you don't charge interest, the imputed interest can be a taxable

income to the employee and must be reported at year end. The broad exception that covers just about everything is: if the loan is under $10,000, and the intent is not to avoid federal income taxes, you don't need to record the imputed interest. The other exception is for a bridge loan to an employee buying a new house. If the loan is paid back within fifteen days of closing, no matter the amount, you do not need to record the value of the unpaid interest.

6. Many companies do not put employee loan information in their employee manuals as it advertises this unnecessarily and just about guarantees everyone will ask for a loan. Some mention that a program is available and to see management for details.

7. Payday loan companies are springing up all over the nation. It is very tempting to tell your employees to go to one of these storefronts. This relieves you of all responsibility. But these companies consistently charge obscene amounts of fees and interest. One average I have seen is that for a five-day loan of $500, the fees are $75, which is equal to an annual interest of 1080 percent. Often times, an employee gets into deeper trouble with payday loans and you get an employee who may have to skip out, or take a second or third job, reducing productivity for you.

8. Don't give an employee loan to someone who is on probation, is on a leave of absence or vacation.

9. There is a large difference between a loan from your company, and an advance on a paycheck. A loan is paid back over time, while an advance is: Can you give me Friday's paycheck on Tuesday? This can be a bookkeeping problem, but not an insurmountable one.

10. My company had a couple of hundred people. At any given time we may have had ten open employee loans, adding up to hundreds of loans over 22 years. I remember only one that went bad and we lost our money. But the goodwill created among our employees was huge. The smiles and thanks I received are among my fondest memories. This helped employee retention and company productivity.

Chapter 20

The Five-Minute Solution to Deciding to Start Drug Testing

 Problem

You own Bernie's Bumpers, an auto body shop with 24 employees. Most have been with you for years, although lately your old-timers are starting to retire. Bobby, who has been with you for four months, had an accident in the shop today and received a severe gash on his forearm. You went to the emergency room with Bobby, and overheard him yelling at the doctor, saying his blood tests were clean and the doctor was wrong. You have been putting off thinking about drug testing for new employees. Is now the time?

Drug Testing   **105**

Possible Outcomes

- Bobby heals quickly, returns to work in three weeks, and all is fine. Your workers' comp rate goes up a little.

- Bobby heals slowly, especially after he sees multiple commercials about suing the boss. Four months later, Bobby is still collecting comp and you can't do a thing about it. Your comp rates go up a lot.

- Bobby finally comes back to work after six months, but gets a 10 percent lifetime disability from the workers' comp board for numbness in his arm. Your workers' comp rates go through the roof.

- You begin to wonder if Bobby was a good hire with a little bad luck, or if something else contributed to the accident. You'll never know the answer but vow not to let it happen again!

What to Do When Bobby Gets the Gash in His Arm

1. You did okay on the first day when you went to the hospital with him and let him know you cared.

2. Follow up with Bobby every other day for a week or so. Tell him to come back to work as soon as he can, where he can work light duty, at full pay, maybe running errands or picking up parts. The key is to get him back to your workplace as soon as possible. The longer he stays home, the more it costs you. It is cheaper to have him at work earning full pay for less than full work than to pay the comp insurance premium raises for the next three years.

3. Since you don't have a drug testing policy in place, you can't ask for the blood test results. You have decisions to make now–drug testing–and to what extent?

4. You are not sure that drugs played a part in this accident, and you trust your employees. If you start testing, will they be upset? Will they think you don't trust them? Will the costs and paperwork in-

volved be a pain in the neck?

Let's Get Serious About Pre-Employment Drug Testing

1. Remember your visit to the home center the other day? As you walked by the customer service desk you saw the sign, "We drug test all people applying for work." Roughly half of all new employees in the United States are drug-tested, including all government and military personnel. That means that all those people who know they won't pass a drug test come to businesses like Bernie's.

2. At my company, where we did pre-employment testing, about a third of applicants failed the drug screen. Think about it. This was after we agreed to hire the person, and all they had to do was pass this test. If we didn't test, they would be on the production floor the next day.

3. The same is happening at Bernie's Bumpers. If you are hiring six people a year, odds are two of them will test positive. Here's your dilemma: What is it to you if Andy Applicant does a recreational drug on Saturday evening, and comes to work on Monday morning? You have never taken an illegal drug yourself; can you impose your morals on Bernie's Bumpers? The answer: of course you can. You own Bernie's and set the policies. You pay your people to work safely and to be 100 percent alert while handling power tools and heavy machinery.

4. We are talking pre-employment here. You don't yet have a relationship with Andy Applicant. You don't owe him anything at this point. You told him you do pre-employment testing, he says he is clean and then comes up dirty. Andy lied to you; he has the arrogance to think he can pull one over on you. Do you want Andy on your payroll? I think not.

5. How often have your employees complained about a new hire, that he wasn't pulling his weight or worked sloppily? You have

fired a few new hires, wasting all the time and effort placed into hiring and training and impacting your unemployment insurance rate. Does it seem that your shop has more accidents with your new hires than your veterans? In fact new people do have more accidents in all sorts of industries, including yours. Is this because of drug use? Poor training? Youth? No one knows for sure, but you can eliminate one of the possible reasons.

6. Your current employees will thank you ... I promise that this will happen if you do pre-employment testing. You will hire better people, and this will improve Bernie's safety and productivity. Remember, it is your responsibility to provide a safe workplace.

7. You have heard stories about the legal hassles of testing, and you hate paperwork. Yep, there is some paperwork. But you don't have to do any of it. Outside labs will take care of everything. It is not expensive, probably about $50 a person. This is very cheap insurance when you are planning to spend thousands to train and pay a new hire. Ask your attorney or insurance agent to recommend a local drug testing agency, or visit www.fiveminuteconsultant.com and you will find many companies that handle everything for you—all the forms, everything. There is a great website, www.dol.gov/elaws/drugfree.htm, that answers every question related to this. Each state's regulations are different; run the papers from the testing service by your attorney.

8. There are five broad categories of drug testing: Pre-employment, random, reasonable cause, post-accident and DOT (Department of Transportation). Start for a year with pre-employment. If you feel there is still a drug problem, go to the next levels. For the other plans, you will have to set up a written plan, disseminate to your employees and follow it to a "T"—no exceptions. You will also need to decide what will happen when a current employee tests positive—automatic termination or a chance at rehab.

9. What about alcohol for pre-employment testing? The tested drugs usually stay in the blood stream for up to a month, alcohol only a

couple of days. I have not found alcohol testing relevant in pre-employment, but it is useful at the other levels.

10. You can find many sites that will sell you drug testing kits cheaply online. Don't go anywhere near these. Only use a licensed and professional collection site.

11. Drug testing is an intrusion into someone's personal life; nonetheless I instituted it at my company. Responsible business owners know they have to do this. If you hire someone who may hurt another employee, who may run up your insurance rates, or may have an accident that involves a customer, it should be a no-brainer to have pre-employment drug testing.

12. Once you decide to hire someone, offer him a "conditional offer of employment." It is at this point that you send him for the test; if he passes, he is hired. You are not going to test all applicants, just the ones you plan to hire. We hired about a hundred people a year, and all were tested. And every one who flunked said our testing was bad and they were going to sue us. No one ever did. Don't be afraid of this if you use a reliable testing company.

13. One thing to think about: Which new employees do you want to test? If someone is a part-timer, only-for-the-summer file clerk, do you want to test? Probably not. You do want to test anyone who works around power equipment, even if part-time. Though it is at odds with consistency, it is a wise idea not to test members of your family if and when they come to work for you. There are some things better left alone.

Chapter 21

The Five-Minute Solution to the Resignation of a Key Employee

Problem

Katie, your chief financial officer and business confidante, tells you she is leaving your company, Phil's Faucets. Katie has been with you for 11 years; she handles financial work, bank lines, billing and payments, computer operations and personnel. You are speechless, as you never expected Katie would leave. She makes a good salary and you tell her every year how valuable she is. Last year she asked for an equity option, but your accountant and lawyer both said, "No, keep it in the family."

Possible Outcomes

- You convince Katie to stay with you, giving her more money and an extra week of vacation. I'm betting the same thing will happen next year.

- It may be that Katie is crying out for help and this is the way she gets your attention; well, it worked.

- You ask Katie to stay for three months while you sort things out. She can only stay one month because of her commitment to a new company.

- You offer Katie a consulting role. She agrees only to be nice; her heart is not in it. She wants to devote her energies to the new company.

- You scream at her, asking how she could do this to you. The conversation escalates; Katie walks out, never to return.

- You go home late that night and cuddle up with a bottle of Southern Comfort®.

What to Do When Katie, the Key Employee, Walks into Your office

1. Don't explode and make the situation worse. Count to ten, calming yourself down.

2. Take time to understand what Katie is telling you. Otherwise, you will be so upset that you will miss key thoughts. Is Katie calling out for help, or is this truly her giving notice? If she gives you the start date of her new position or where she is moving in another city, consider her career with you over. If she has not made any plans and wants to take time off before starting her job search, then you may be able to reach out and resolve the issues that are on Katie's mind.

3. If Katie is going to a competitive firm, skip to number 7.

4. Don't let the bridges burn. You have trusted Katie for 11 years.

Don't stop now. You will want to call her for advice and to help train her replacement. Don't let your hurt feelings get in the way of a good business decision. At this point, don't negotiate her pay as a consultant or advisor. Do that at another meeting a week from now.

5. Discuss with Katie how to make this announcement to employees, customers and vendors. You want this to be a positive plan, giving Katie good blessings in her new career and assuring all concerned that Phil's Faucets is strong and ongoing. Get this announcement out today or tomorrow. The gossip drums will pick this up long before you think they could.

6. Ask Katie who she recommends to replace her. Listen, but don't make a decision today. This may be an opportunity for you to re-cast the position, elevating two or three people to managerial level without declaring one to be the leader of all the departments.

7. What if she is going to an across-town competitor? Everything changes. In this case, it is okay to be upset. Politely thank Katie for her notice and then escort her out the door. Change her computer passwords; call the bank to withdraw verbal password authorities and do a walkthrough of her work area and look for anything missing. Tell your staff that Katie is no longer an employee, is not allowed on the premises, and that Katie has gone to work for a competitor.

8. Katie obviously knows many trade secrets about your organization. Normally, she can use what she knows in her head, absent a contract. If she took documents or customer or vendor lists, though, you may have a legal case.

9. No matter why Katie is leaving, you should personally speak with all of your managers and supervisors and assure them that everything is all right. Have them carry this message to the troops.

10. Talk with your accountant about the position and get input. Can she send someone to fill in two days a week until you get the departments organized?

Let's Not Lose a Key Person and What to Do When It Does Happen

1. First thing … this happens. It happens at Phil's Faucets and every other company that exists. It will happen at the worst possible time and will upset you. So get over it quickly and go forward.

2. Work hard to retain key people. They are more important to you than any other resource or asset you have. One survey says that replacing a middle or upper management person costs roughly one year of that person's salary! Think of the training time, lost knowledge, time spent with insecure coworkers, candidate search, and relocation expenses.

3. Key people are just that. They use their talents for the benefit of the company. Help them exercise their minds, and give them opportunities to attend training seminars to advance their skills. They will appreciate this!

4. Every manager at Phil's should present you with plans, at least annually, about who is promotable in their departments. Also, at your annual managers' meeting, ask each manager who would replace him if he won the lottery and retired. Make a point to know who these replacements are and evaluate them yourself. Understand what drives their needs.

5. Get to know your key players in every way you can—what their spouses do, how old their children are, if they have elderly parents to take care of, and what their goals are for their lives. If someone's last kid is graduating high school or college, watch for changes. If one of your employees' parents live far away and has a medical condition, allow plenty of creative time use or you may lose a key person. By the way, if you have more than eight key people reporting to you, you are inefficient.

6. Have a cross-training program in place, where every key person's job is completed by another person for a one week a year, usually during vacation periods.

7. Give yourself an exercise every six months: plan your moves if any employee decides to leave. This will show you your company's weaknesses and help identify lower-level people you want to start training and grooming.

8. Learn what your competition is offering its key employees. When the opportunity knocks, interview a key worker from a competitor. Also check out other companies in your geographic area who are your size. There is plenty of knowledge to be gained at your local Chamber of Commerce.

9. Employment contracts have some advantages, but if someone wants to leave your company, he will, even if it means breaking the contract and forfeiting deferred money.

10. In general, though, deferred income is an excellent retention tool for medium- and large-sized companies. It allows you to give employees a tax-advantaged amount of money that is payable two or three years down the road. Speak with your benefits provider and your accountant. You can have unique programs for different people. One may want more salary while another needs child-care options. Be creative; it will help you retain your stars. Building a custom set of "Golden Handcuffs" for key people will help every company.

11. Consider opening up shares of ownership to key people. Nothing retains good people like knowing they are a part of the company. Do the research with your financial advisors and your attorney. Don't do this on a whim; think it through carefully. If it is done right, you, your company and your key employees all come out ahead. One statistic I read said that in companies with key employee ownership plans, key person turnover was reduced by 200 percent.

Chapter 22

The Five-Minute Solution to Being Involved in a Lawsuit

Problem

You own Jessica's Decorating and Home Improvements and employ 53 people in retail and field work. Your husband, Bobby, handles the construction side of the business and you do the decorating. Three months ago, Mrs. Hastings called Bobby to rework a construction job that had been started by Acme Construction. You did $30,000 worth of work, got paid in full and have a happy customer. Now, Mrs. Hastings' lawyer has called. She is suing Acme for shoddy and incomplete work and wants Bobby to testify.

Possible Outcomes

- Bobby testifies as an expert witness and earns big bucks, and Mrs. Hastings wins the case. The owner of Acme is no longer your friend.
- Bobby doesn't want to testify against his friend at Acme, gets subpoenaed as a hostile witness, and spends two days in depositions and two days in court, earning nothing. Mrs. Hastings wins the case but bad-mouths you for not cooperating.
- Bobby testifies that Acme did a good job and that he found no problems when he came to the job. Mrs. Hastings loses the suit, and then sues you for overcharging on the job. Your lawyer goes on the payroll.

What Should Jessica and Bobby Do When Mrs. Hastings Calls?

1. Absolutely, whenever you are called in to finish someone else's work in any industry, whether designing computer programs, or fixing construction, be wary. People are upset and you may innocently end up in the middle. Hear all the info on why the customer wants to change vendors.

2. Contact the previous supplier, get the other side, and remember: there are three sides to every story.

3. Find out if Acme or Mrs. Hastings have already sued each other. Your lawyer can do this research fairly easily. If so, don't take the job.

4. Your lawyer can find out if Mrs. Hastings has been involved in other lawsuits. For many people, filing lawsuits is a form of entertainment. If Mrs. Hastings has a history, run away. (Remember the guy who sued his dry cleaner for a couple of million for losing his pants?)

5. Make sure your work order/contract gives you the right to stop work when payment is late. This should be in bold type in your contract, and it is even better if Mrs. Hastings initials this statement.

6. If Acme has given you referrals in the past, expect those to stop. Is it worth it?

7. Mrs. Hastings may be a sweet old lady and Acme an honest business, but something went wrong. Maybe there were building permit issues, or Mrs. Hastings' son doesn't want his mom to spend his inheritance. Some things you just can't control.

How Can Jessica and Bobby Take This Job and Steer Clear of Trouble?

1. Don't take this job without doing a lot of research. Your instinct is to take any work you can in a tough economy. Don't be tempted.

2. Since you know Mrs. Hastings is litigious get a substantial deposit and a schedule of progress payments. You should never be out-of-pocket on this job. With each weekly check, get Mrs. Hastings to sign saying she is satisfied with your work.

3. If you are using a preprinted order form, it is time to have your lawyer advise you on a custom one for your industry and your business.

4. When you step into the middle of an ongoing job in any industry, do extra diligence in studying the work done to date. You may learn a new technique from the work already done. You may also clearly see the problem that caused the work interruption and how you can easily solve what another vendor couldn't. This is where you can earn money based on your knowledge, not just on physical work.

5. When you testify for Mrs. Hastings, there will be an expert witness hired by Acme who will refute your every word. Every little mistake you ever made will be brought up in an attempt to discredit you. It is not personal, and don't take it that way. Be prepared for this by practicing with Mrs. Hastings' attorney. Tell her about all of your previous work and where a landmine might be buried. If your attorney is prepared, she can defuse it easily before a jury. She will keep it in confidence and will never have to disclose what you say.

6. Written reports by you to Mrs. Hastings or to her attorney may be made available to Acme's attorney. When you put anything in writing concerning this job, remember others may read it.

7. Is it ethical to testify against a competitor? Yes. Keep in mind you are not attacking the owner of Acme, but the work of the company. Don't make it personal.

8. Have you ever appeared in court? Or been deposed? It is not like the movies where Perry Mason asks three questions and the case is over. You will be asked questions by a person who has been trained for years to ask questions that will elicit the answer they want. Just about every attorney I have ever met is sharp. Attorneys know what they are doing, and they are staunch advocates for their clients.

9. There may be times when an attorney asks you to be an expert witness. He will ask you to review someone else's work and then testify if the work was in line with the generally accepted practices of your industry. No matter which side you are working for, the other side will attempt to discredit you, with every tool in its kit. They may attack your credibility, your own work history, your educational background and your expertise in your field. It is disconcerting to think that someone doesn't trust you. Also, check your insurance … do you have coverage for any mistake you might make as a witness? Your standard liability policy should be reviewed before you agree to be a witness.

10. Just in case you don't get the hint—research the job completely before you accept a deposit check, whether as a working contractor or as an expert witness.

Chapter 23

The Five-Minute Solution to Setting Up an Emergency Book

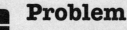

Problem

You own Elegant Ella's Music, which started out selling sheet music in the 1940s, and now manufactures string instruments, and publishes and sells music and CDs on the Internet. You get a call at 3:00 in the morning saying that an earthquake has rattled your building, causing a wall to fall.

Possible Outcomes

- It turns out to be just a small warehouse wall; no one is hurt, and the impact to your business is minimal. You dodged the bullet on this one.

- The bullet grazed your shoulder. The main manufacturing building for violins has a gaping hole. Almost all of your finished goods are ruined as a sprinkler pipe burst and no one on your night shipping crew knew how to turn it off.

- You caught one right in the shoulder. Two people were slightly injured and taken to the hospital for a precautionary checkup. Your computer center is totally destroyed by water from the fire department putting out small electrical fires. It will take a couple of weeks to rebuild the infrastructure and you are in the middle of the Christmas selling season.

- You are going to survive, but the bullet did damage. You lost inventory and your computer center from water damage. The building inspector won't let you into the building until structural repairs are finished.

What Should You Do When the Phone Rings at 3 a.m.?

1. Your first question should be: is everyone alright? The good news is yes, they are. But there is water everywhere and right now, the fire department is not letting anyone into the building.

2. Call your leaders and ask them to come in ASAP. What? You don't have their phone numbers by your bed, or in your smartphone? You waste valuable time looking up key numbers.

3. By the time you get to the plant the fire is out; the water is draining. You begin to understand the depth of your problem. You need help, ASAP. Start delegating specific tasks to managers. Call your insurance agent. A good insurance agency will have links to disaster recovery companies. Call a structural engineer. Contact your

computer support company (even though they don't answer the phone until 8 a.m. West Coast time). Get workers in for a clean-up … oops, you can't do that until the engineer says they can go into the building.

4. Your head is swimming. You stop for a cup of coffee, calm down and start to formulate a plan for rebuilding Elegant Ella's.

5. You get the drift. It is better to spend a week planning for emergencies than to struggle for a month trying to rebuild without a blue print to guide you.

Let's Set Up a Proper Emergency Book

1. An emergency book is a loose-leaf binder with multiple sections. The first section is employees, their addresses, phone and cell numbers, and email addresses. Your personnel department should update this section at least twice a year.

2. The second section is key companies to call for the basic operation of your company. This would include:

a. Local Police;

b. State Police;

c. Local Fire Department;

d. Local Ambulance;

e. Plumber/Sprinkler Repair;

f. Electric Utility;

g. Electrician;

h. Natural Gas Utility;

i. Gas Fitter/Plumber;

j. Computer Back-Up;

k. Computer Repair;

l. Phone Company;

m. Insurance Agent;

n. Lawyer(s);

o. Alarm Central Station;

p. Payroll Service;

q. Bank/Banker;

r. Accountant;

s. Taxi/Car Service;

t. FedEx/UPS & Account Number;

u. Truck Maintenance/Repair;

v. Tow Truck;

w. Trash Hauler;

x. Landlord; and

y. Neighboring businesses

3. The third section is for disasters, both natural and man-made. We are all subject to different types of problems: hurricanes, snow, earthquakes and tornadoes. Man-made disasters include fire, water damage, mud-slides, chemical spills, medical emergencies and power-outages. Collect info for:

    a. Fire/flood remediation firms;

    b. Office/building cleaners;

    c. Generator rental/service;

    d. Hazardous material clean-up;

    e. Poison control center;

    f. Counseling professionals to help employees;

    g. Disgruntled employee situations (*See Chapter 34.*);

    h. Companies that provide day-workers;

    i. Construction contractors;

    j. Demolition contractor;

    k. Water pump rentals;

    l. Oil spills/cleanup;

    m. Asbestos cleanup;

    n. Sprinkler system repair; and

    o. Forklift/crane rental.

4. One of the most important needs is temporary space. Once a year, talk with a local real estate pro to keep a handle on short-term rentable locations.

5. The fourth section is each of your key material vendors' information, including contact info for:

    a. Local reps;

    b. Regional sales manager;

    c. National sales manager;

    d. Plant manager;

e. Executive officer;

f. Key customer service rep;

g. Warehouse/loading manager; and

h. Truckers often used.

Why are your vendors so important at this point? They need to understand you may not be able to pay bills for a while; that you may need a lot of inventory, quickly, and to squash industry rumors that you are out of business.

6. You have now completed the easy part. It is time to sit down with each manager and foreman in your firm and discuss what would they do in the event of different emergencies. Take very good notes and then write the procedures down for each department because you know the experienced manager will be on vacation when an emergency hits. This may take months to complete. It should not be more important than running your business! Don't become the most well prepared, going-out-of-business, business. A little bit of this weekly will get the job done.

7. Assign one person to be your spokesperson during a time of emergency. He should reach out to all local and industry media telling the story and your plans to continue the business. This person and his pinch-hitter should have a special page in his book listing the phone, fax and email of the news offices and reporters that will cover the story. He should be very Internet-savvy, working Facebook, Twitter and blog sites.

8. Next, set up a series of Saturdays where you can practice different emergencies. Have everyone familiarize themselves with the water turn-off valve for the sprinklers. Give everyone confidence that they can take care of an emergency. On one Saturday teach first aid and CPR. Everyone should be able to locate every first-aid kit in your place, and if you have a defibrillator, where it is and how to use it. Teach the rules on handling blood, bloody injuries and moving of people with injuries. Every person should

be familiar with fire extinguisher locations and how to use them. This may take a couple of Saturdays; pay your crew extra for this, even if they are salaried.

9. Now prepare a plan on what to do when your computer center is down. You should have a remote site where you can download to and set-up work. In most companies, a down computer system is more unsettling to the business than a physical disaster.

10. Two copies of the emergency book should be given to every manager—one for their home and the other for the office.

11. Do you have a warehouse where you could temporarily stock merchandise? If there is no place to work, what will your employees do? Will you pay them if you have no work, but it is not their fault? What does your employee manual say on this subject?

12. Speak with your insurance agent about business interruption insurance. This can be a life-saver for your business.

13. When you bring in a new product line or vendor, update the page in the emergency book.

14. If you have multiple locations, even within the same city, create a section for each one with detailed maps of sprinkler systems, electrical panels, gas lines and egress procedures.

15. Speak with your local fire department and sprinkler company about putting chemical fire suppressors in your computer area, rather than water lines. This is more expensive upfront, but will save you a fortune after an emergency.

16. Make sure no exit door is blocked, every electrical panel is accessible and that aisle ways are free. If the siren sounds to evacuate to a shelter, you don't want people tripping over stuff.

17. It is very important to have an exit plan. Set a place where people meet once outside of the building. You need to account for every person so firefighters know what to do when they arrive.

Chapter 24

The Five-Minute Solution to Working with Your Key Vendor

Problem

You own Amy's Heavenly Hair Salons and Products. You have three salons and do a large business selling hair care products over the Internet. Your products are privately labeled by Sampson and Delilah Chemicals, owned by Samuel Sampson. Recently, you have been receiving poor service from Sampson and Delilah, which in turn has reduced your sales.

Possible Solutions

- You meet with Sam and explain your problems; he makes everything right and you are pleased.
- Sam tells you everything will be all right, but his company is very busy with a new customer who is taking a lot of attention right now.
- Sam shrugs his shoulders and suggests that your account is not important to him anymore as he landed a national chain as a customer.
- You realize that you have to find another vendor for your products; this seems like an insurmountable task.

What Amy Should Do at Her Visit with Sam Sampson

1. Come prepared with last year's purchase volume and your estimates for the coming year. Know Sampson and Delilah's sales, which you can usually learn online or by using a service like Dunn & Bradstreet. If your volume is more than one percent of the company's total, you have an impact.

2. Go into Sam's office positively, without complaining. Ask what you can do to help improve the service. Maybe less frequent but larger orders? Can Sampsons' marketing team help train your people to sell more products? What other products does Sampson make that can be worked on together?

3. Keep your ear tuned to the industry. You should have known that Sampson's landed that big new account.

4. Sam tells you that your lead times will now be twelve weeks, rather than the four weeks you had. You will have to predict your usage accurately and store more inventories, costing you a bundle. What will Sam give you in return? If nothing, he just wants to get rid of you. Take the hint.

5. Sam offers you better service, but it means giving up your private label program. You have worked hard to establish your brand and don't want to do this.

6. You leave Sam's office totally dejected, vowing to never let someone else have this much control of your business.

How Could Amy Keep Control of Her Inventory and Vendor?

1. Amy should have one secondary vendor packaging her products. Even though there is more paperwork, inventory stocking questions and overall more costs, give no more than 80 percent of your purchases to one source. Twenty percent to a secondary vendor will keep it hungry and wanting to earn more of your business.

2. Economic interruptions often are a result of bad weather. Your secondary source should be located far from your primary one.

3. Have an annual meeting with your primary source and discuss the upcoming year. Let this vendor know that you are counting on it and the company is your number-one vendor by:

   a. Asking the company to help train your staff to sell more products;

   b. Having the company's reps in your stores for one-day sales and demonstrations;

   c. Letting the company make a profit along with you. If you negotiate such low pricing that you are marginal for them, the company will drop you when it can;

   d. Developing a personal relationship with key players at the vendor. Take them out to lunch, dinner, or, better yet, a ball game. Most importantly, develop a relationship with the shipping manager;

   e. Don't ask for favors too often. You will get help, but if it becomes burdensome for your vendor, its management won't be upset to lose you;

f. Discuss a three-year plan. This shows your seriousness in keeping a relationship. If the company hesitates, your alarm bells should ring; and

g. Work together on the hidden cost of freight and inventory control. Maybe the vendor can piggyback your shipments on another customer's truck and save money. Ask to get inventory on consignment or get extended payment terms so you can order more goods less frequently.

4. If you have a contract with your vendor, look for parity in the termination clause and the remedies clause for breach of contract. If your vendors ship for you, have a strong clause covering their returning and/or non-use of your confidential customer data. Your vendor should add your company to its liability insurance for the products it packs for you.

5. Follow the same steps with your secondary vendor. If the company is more helpful and eager to work with you, it may be the time to reverse the roles! If you decide to switch, plan carefully so you always have inventory. Use this time to introduce new items or hold a sale. Send a press release to your local papers announcing your new and/or different products. It is a great time for an Internet sale!

6. Study your industry; attend trade shows; talk with your friendly competitors ... all to learn about other sources for your products. I strongly believe in buying local, first in your city, then state, then country. You may consider going overseas if no domestic source fills your needs. Alibabba.com lists just about every manufacturer in China. Globalsources.com is also a good site to visit. Importing should really be your last option. It is complicated and contains many hidden costs, such as broker fees, insurance and duties.

7. It may take six months or more to set up a second vendor. Don't rush. You don't want to do this again in three years. Get customer

references from potential vendors. Make a thorough visit of potential new vendors. Invest more time on a vendor's plant floor than in its offices, checking if it is clean, organized and if the workforce looks happy. Speak with the company's shipping foreman. Ask how the company resolves late shipments and how it prevents breakage. If the company is a union shop, ask to speak with the shop steward for his point of view for the future.

8. Find out if the company will take back your shipping pallets and cardboard for recycling. At what purchase level will it absorb all the freight costs?

9. Your new vendor should give you product for sampling to gain new wholesale customers. At the start of this relationship, the company will be most eager to help you.

10. Maybe you should think about the next big leap ... packaging yourself and selling on a broad scale. You may be surprised how easy it is. Go to EDA.gov (the U.S. Economic Development Administration, part of the Department of Commerce), or to SBA.gov (the Small Business Administration) for tons of free and very practical advice. Becoming your own packager is not an easy decision, but it may be right for your future.

11. If you are going to grow your business, consider carrying multiple lines of hair care products and give your customers more choices. You will be competing with yourself, which is the best position to be in. Keep your namesake brand in front, and follow with a lower and a higher price brand.

12. Part of this decision comes down to your philosophy of business. Do you want to be a key customer of a small vendor, or do you want a large vendor, who may have more services, but where you are not so important?

Chapter 25

The Five-Minute Solution to Working with Smokers in Your Company

5ive minute consultant™

Problem

You have finally decided to ban smoking at your company, Dick's Hardwood Furniture Company. You currently have "no smoking" rules in areas where there is sawdust in the air, but not in the general plant or office. You employee 85 people and your best guess is that 30 percent of them smoke.

Possible Outcomes

- Everyone understands the problem of second-hand smoke, and you get no pushback setting up rules and a couple of smoking zones outside the building. Your insurance broker reduces your plant insurance rates for implementing a no smoking policy, and predicts your comp and health insurance rates will go down in future years.

- You offer to pay for smoking cessation programs for all employees. Seven take you up on it and really appreciate the help you give them.

- The non-smokers love it, but the smokers are upset. Many complain about having to go outside, especially in bad weather. Five people quit.

- The non-smokers complain that the smokers get to take an extra 10-minute break to smoke. They want the same time off. Your productivity decreases.

Let's Implement a Successful Smoking Program for Dick's

1. Undertaking a program for employees to stop smoking will improve the health of the smokers and the non-smokers. There are a great many financial incentives as well, but the number-one goal is health. Remember this.

2. Planning a program is key. There are choices Dick has to make before the program starts ... let's review them.

   a. Should you allow smokers to take time away from work to go to the smoking areas? Yes, for three months at the start of the program. This allows smokers to begin changing their habits. After three months, limit the smoking times to coffee breaks and lunch.

   b. If you are going to erect a shelter for the smokers outside the building, it should be at company expense. You should make it very clear, though, that the cleaning and maintenance of the shelter is the responsibility of the employees using it. If there are cigarette butts on the ground, you have the option of closing the shelter. Also, enforce no smoking in the restrooms!

c. Should you offer smoking cessation help? Absolutely, yes. Don't look at this as giving one set of employees something that another doesn't have. You are helping your employees get healthy. If your insurance doesn't cover smoking cessation, it is a good practice for Dick to pay for the doctor's visits and the patches.

d. Quitting smoking requires both physical and mental help. Pills or patches alone won't do the job. Most people will need emotional help. Every single state offers this type of program for free. Visit www.fiveminuteconsultant.com for more information.

e. Get all employees, not just the smokers, involved in setting up the program. Form an employee committee to make all the decisions. Give the committee three to four months to establish the program, giving everyone a long time period to get ready for the start date. Make sure that everyone understands the smokers will be irritable for a couple of months.

f. Should smoke-free (chewing) tobacco be included? From a health standpoint, this is just as dangerous as smoked tobacco, but there is no second-hand smoke issue. Since health is your main concern, this should be included in the cessation programs.

g. Do you allow smoking in company-owned cars or trucks, even if the only person in the car is the smoker? If there are two people in the car and one is a non-smoker, there is no choice—no smoking is the rule. But what do you do when the smoker is alone? Let the employee group decide this one, but push for no smoking.

h. Do you take it one step further and go for a weight loss program as well? (Take away my peanut butter cups and I will revolt!) Not now. Do one program at a time. In a year, start your next healthy program after the success of this one.

i. Do you want to ban smoking completely for your employees? This is a tough call, trying to ban an activity that employees do at home. Many employers only hire non-smokers, and do nicotine tests, similar to a drug test, to enforce the policy. I feel this is just too much to tackle for the start of a program. Tell job applicants about your smoking policy at work, and you will find that the heaviest of smokers will go work someplace else. In a couple of years, when the smoking cessation is working at Dick's, consider a total ban, but check with your attorney for laws in your state.

j. Some states do not allow you to ban an activity done in the home of an employee. Go to http://www.cdc.gov/tobacco/data_statistics/state_data/state_highlights/2010/map/index.htm, for an interactive map of the 50 states and their policies published by the Center for Disease Control (CDC).

3. Some other thoughts to consider are as follows. Cigarette smokers are less productive than non-smokers. There are many numbers out there, but the logical conclusion is that smokers take time away from work to light up. In an office environment, furniture, carpeting and ceilings need to be replaced or cleaned more often in a smoking situation. This costs you extra money.

4. Aon Hewitt, a leading human resources company, has an excellent report on smoking and other health issues in the workplace. This report estimates that a smoker costs a company about $3,000 per year in increased absenteeism, lost productivity and increased insurance costs.

5. PepsiCo now charges smoking employees an insurance surcharge of $600 per year. Macy's charges $420 per year. This may not be the path for small- and medium-sized businesses just yet, but it is a growing trend. Concentrate on the cessation side and give rewards for stopping rather than penalties for smoking and you will have greater success. At the end of the first day, at the end of three days, at the end of a week, give a reward for each milestone—maybe a pat on the back, or a smile. Acknowledge each small anniversary.

6. Consider this, the U.S. Surgeon General's office estimates that smoking men live 13.2 fewer years than non-smokers, and women smokers live 14.5 years fewer. Aside from this as a gruesome statistic, think what this impact will be to your trained workforce.

7. It takes time to implement this type of program. Don't expect results overnight. The average smoker will go through two or three attempts to quit smoking before being successful. When you pay for cessation programs, keep this in mind. Even if you pay a thousand dollars, two or three times, in the long run you and the employee come out way ahead.

8. Great information comes from the American Cancer Society: http://www.cancer.org/Healthy/StayAwayfromtobacco/Guideto-QuittingSmoking/index and from the U.S. government: http://smokefree.gov/

9. What if you smoke? Can you ask your employees to stop what you can't? Yes, you can. But you do have to control your smoking at work. No special privileges. If you smoke, go outside to the shelter. No smoking in your private bathroom, not in your company car.

Chapter 26

The Five-Minute Solution to Balancing Your Customer List

Problem

You own Miss Molly Mutt's, a manufacturer and distributor of pet foods and supplies. You have been in business for 23 years, have 75 employees and are financially stable with about 2,000 customer accounts. You begin to notice a trend of large orders to chain stores and a reduction of small- and medium-sized orders to individual pet stores.

Possible Outcomes

- You start to service the big box stores exclusively. Molly Mutt's grows, along with the economy, and you have many less headaches.

- You implement minimum orders, forcing your small customers to buy from regional distributors. Too late, though—you realize the distributors also sell lines that compete with yours at lower prices. Your overall volume drops by 7 percent this year.

- Your biggest customer calls and asks you for a five percent rebate on all products. While the customer did "ask," you understand you have no choice. Your profit on this account goes into the cat litter box.

- Your biggest customer now makes up 20 percent of your volume. Without warning, this customer tells you it is going to source the products you make from overseas, devastating your business.

- You go back to your roots, working with smaller customers who are loyal to you, and your business prospers.

What Can Molly Do When Big Customers Implement Their Version of Price Controls?

1. Not much. Molly has been put on a leash by the big customers. She can try to reinvigorate her small and medium customers, but this will take years.

2. She can attempt to negotiate with the big customers. If her products really are unique, she stands a chance.

3. Molly offers to meet her biggest customer half-way, and asks the company's cost control department to come into her business and help to reduce costs, which then would be passed back to the customer. This works and Molly is saved.

4. The cost controls work, but the customer knows this, and asks for another round of discounts. Molly now understands a radical

change in her business came about without her making the decision to do so. She has to decide which business model to follow—a few big customers or many small customers.

Let's Help Miss Molly Make Some Decisions

1. All surviving businesses change. The question is, are you going to control the changes or will they control you? Every business owner should take a day or two each year to disappear from the business with trusted advisors and key managers, to plan the upcoming year and the future 2- to 4-year period. Yes, it is hard to keep plans, especially in unpredictable economic times, but without a plan, you will only be reacting to situations.

2. There is nothing like getting your first order from Wal-Mart. You have hit the big time. But you have to understand the pluses and minuses that go with it, which are both emotional and financial.

    a. Your sales numbers (and hopefully profits) will go through the roof, like riding a rocket. It can be great, until it isn't, and you can't control when that changes.

    b. You need a giant inventory and a logistics infrastructure to meet strict shipping directives to service a big customer. You also must acquire the technology to bill electronically, enable electronic shipment tracing and handle returns and allowances.

    c. You will have to expand faster than you have ever imagined. You will hire a new breed of people, possibly very different than you worked with before. Beware of the culture clash coming with your current workforce.

    d. Your current customers will be upset. There is no way around this. The products they sold will now be down the street at a cheaper price. You will give them slower service. Customers will complain to you, upsetting relationships that took years to cultivate.

3. When a customer becomes larger than two or three percent of your sales, it is in a position to be your best friend or a pain-in-the-neck. But, when a customer starts buying, are you going to say, "STOP?" Of course not. Set up a different customer service group for your very large customers. The people in your office may not be used to dealing with professional purchasing agents, who will do the job of protecting their company, not yours.

4. Set up a different branding program for your larger customers and your smaller ones. Give each one different packaging and marketing themes. The products will be the same, but the customer experience will set them apart. You may take the step of separating the divisions of your company or spinning off the large or small customer side.

5. Bigger sales mean more risk. Control this risk through correctly drawn supply contracts with your customers and your vendors. You will need greater liability insurance. Most big box stores will want you to indemnify them for anything related to your products. Check with your lawyer before signing anything. The big customers will also want a very detailed walk-through of your plant, checking on working conditions, labor law violations and the main thing, your capability to deliver products.

6. How do you tell if you may be in trouble? It's easy. Go to your accounts receivable spreadsheet. If your largest customer filed for Chapter 11 tomorrow, and you got nothing as an unsecured creditor, would that destroy your business? This will happen to any business that has a high exposure in one or two customers. The wider you spread your customer base, the stronger you will be.

7. You can still go through your customer list and state that if a customer doesn't buy a certain amount, say $500 a year; it is not a wholesale customer. Write, call and visit, asking the customer to buy just a little bit more to keep its line of communication open with you. Work with your accountant or CFO to decide the

level at which you break even for carrying an account. Use this as your basis to set the minimum sales number.

8. Be flexible. There will be large potential accounts that may not have bought from you. Find out why and solve the problem. Make each customer decision with your sales or customer service manager.

9. There is an unwritten rule of business: 20 percent of your customers will give you 80 percent of your business, and the corollary, 10 percent of your customers will give you 90 percent of your grief. If you see your company slipping below (i.e., less than 20 percent of your customers give you 80 percent or more of your business), look at rebalancing. Bring in more small and medium customers so you are not so top-heavy.

10. Molly needs to plan her future. Most businesses are successful in their niches, and stumble when they go out of them. Do you want to have your dog biscuit and eat it, too? You can sell to both large and small markets with planning and care.

Chapter 27

The Five-Minute Solution to the Unexpected Death of an Employee

![5ive minute consultant logo] **Problem**

You own Jerry's Jerseys, a company with 200 employees that makes baseball uniforms and memorabilia on two shifts. Six o'clock this morning you receive a phone call that Milano, a valued supervisor on the wood products finishing line, died during the night. You know that he was an extremely heavy smoker. (*See Chapter 45 for a work-related death.*)

Possible Outcomes

- At work you call the first shift together and make the solemn announcement about Milano. You hold a minute of silence, a few people tell some stories about Milano, and sadly, everyone gets back to work. No one works very hard this day.

- You call Milano's widow and offer any help she needs. She tells you Milano definitely died of a massive heart attack and gives you the funeral arrangements. You call the employees together again and pass on the funeral arrangements and the cause of death.

- Alternately, after getting back to work, rumors fly about the wood sealants used, and seven people in the department complain about ventilation. You explain the finishes are water-based with no harmful chemicals. You go over the Material Safety Data Sheets (MSDS), but no one really is listening.

- The second shift comes in, learning of the death before you can even call them together. All ten people on the second shift in the finishing department ask for a transfer to another area of the factory.

What Jerry Should Do on the Morning of Milano's Death

1. Get to the plant as quickly as possible. When you make the announcement stress that the family has not released the cause of death. Offer every employee a chance to speak about Milano.

2. Spend extra time with Milano's closest co-workers. Don't worry about an hour of lost production now. Let his department slowly go back to work; most people find solace in returning to a familiar routine. Even though it may cause production disruptions, let his department work to its own rhythm today. If you have a fixed-time production line, let Milano's co-workers take frequent breaks by rotating in other employees. People who have tears in their eyes or who are thinking about Milano will make mistakes and be accident-prone.

3. Stay in touch with Milano's widow. Ask her permission to tell co-workers the cause of death. Honor her wishes.

4. Learn about the rituals of death in Milano's culture. Wikipedia is a good source. Honor these rituals throughout the plant.

5. Many employees will want to go to Milano's wake or funeral. Announce the plans as soon as the family tells you. Jerry doesn't have to pay people who take the time off (and it may set an uncomfortable precedent), although the time should be recorded as an excused absence. Announce the plans to both shifts.

6. Other employees may be on vacation or traveling on business. Have someone call them with the news.

7. Jerry should quickly respond to the rumors of bad chemicals by going over all the product labels and MSDS info sheets with every interested employee. This is key in keeping the employees comfortable with their environment.

What Can Jerry Do to Improve His and the Company's Reactions to a Death?

1. Death happens in every business at some point. Depending on your size it may be a regular occurrence, but to most businesses this is a rarity. Our company had three plants employing 250 people, and a death like this only happened once in 25 years.

2. Death, sadly, is one of the things that you should think about every couple of years. Does your group health insurance cover grief counseling for your employees? Most do, and you should understand the coverage so you can explain it.

3. In your emergency book (*see Chapter 23*), keep the name of a grief counselor who can come to your location or visit with the family.

4. Periodically look at the ethnic make-up of your employees and the rituals that would be part of their lives. In addition to death, you should know what to do for a birth or a wedding, and which days are special holidays.

5. Did Milano mentor younger employees? They will need special care during the grieving process.

6. A minimum of once a year, go over MSDS sheets with employees who use the covered products. Not only is this a very good business practice, it also is part of OSHA regulations. Work hard to replace hazardous products. Accept that replacement products may be more expensive. It is a small price to pay.

7. When a death occurs, ensure the company's response is the same for all employees. Don't do more for an executive than for a plant worker. If the employees take up a collection for the grieving family, match it if you can. Let everyone know their contribution has double the value.

8. Within a day, compute Milano's salary and vacation due. Find out from the family to whom to make the checks. You may have to write the check to the "estate of" the person. This will certainly delay the family getting the money, as it will take time to establish the checking account. Wherever possible, avoid this complication. One large check from your payroll service will have large tax impacts. Either do a manual check figuring the withholding tax, or cut separate, smaller checks.

9. If the deceased employee has company materials, computers or even a car, wait a week before setting up retrieval. Cancel credit cards and check-signing privileges right away.

10. Have a friend of the family come in to help clear Milano's personal effects. Don't ask his widow to come in.

11. As the leader of the company, you should attend all funerals. You can't force others to attend, but attendance at funerals should be discussed during interviews of incoming senior management.

12. Many families will need money more than flowers. Ask the family what they would prefer and let your company know. If there is a favorite charity, make a donation in memory of Milano. Some companies will place a picture of Milano in a special place

at the company as a permanent memorial.

13. The immediate family may never have gone through a funeral. Offer to assist them with arrangements. Dealing with a funeral director may be intimidating to someone from another culture.

14. If you offer employee life insurance, contact your broker so they immediately begin the process of helping the family. Once every three years, have employees confirm or update beneficiaries on company life insurance.

15. After a death of someone with customer or vendor contact, a thoughtful letter should go out. Don't leave it up to the new person to make the announcement. It will wreck that sales call and demoralize the new hire.

16. There will be people at your company who didn't know Milano. They will want to keep working and doing their jobs. If you close the company for a day, allowing coworkers to attend the funeral, are you going to pay those who want to come to work? Employees will be upset if they lose a day's pay for someone they didn't know well.

17. If the death is not sudden, such as one that occurs after an employee's illness, your company will be less shocked and not in need of as much care. If the death is because of something senseless, like drunk driving, honor the memory of the dead person, but make it helpful by donating to Mothers Against Drunk Driving.

18. Since Milano was a supervisor you need to replace him, but wait a couple of days. The new supervisor should have superior people skills. When introducing the new supervisor openly discuss Milano's contributions to the company and the department. Talk about the new supervisor's skills and discuss how each employee can help the transition.

19. Your goals include helping the family, helping your employees grieve, and still run your company.

The Five-Minute Solution to a Large Increase in Medical Insurance Costs

Problem

You own Cal's All-Star Cleaning Company, which does office and residential cleaning and maintenance with 53 employees. Employees receive medical insurance after three months of employment, costing you an average of $7,000 per employee. Over the last couple of years you have cut back on some of the benefits and coverages as costs have increased. This year's renewal is 15 percent more than last year's. You talk with your insurance broker and he says that you have more covered people than he has seen at similar-sized companies.

Possible Outcomes

- You absorb all of the increase, more than $55,000.

- Currently employees pay 20 percent of the cost of insurance, via payroll deduction. You raise this to 30 percent, covering the increase, but gain a very upset workforce.

- You try hiring part-timers, who won't get benefits, but they are just not as reliable and hard-working as your regular crew. You get complaints from regular customers.

- Your broker shops different insurance companies, but there is nothing cheaper available without significantly dropping covered benefits. You decide to cut benefits so your increase comes in at 5 percent. Just about everyone is upset.

- You remember what your broker said about the number of people on your plan and ask for more information. Is this the cost-saving miracle you need?

What Should Cal Do?

1. Cal has a couple of choices to reduce costs: reduce benefits, raise co-pays, and/or drop services, all of which will hurt his employees and leave them upset.

2. Two important suggestions are brought to Cal's attention:

   a. Weed out any "extra family members" on his insurance plan; and/or

   b. Reduce the number of employees who sign up for insurance at Cal's.

3. Cal looks at the sign-up card for each employee and sees children's names who don't match the parents. Also he sees a spouse on a couple of cards where he thought the employee was single.

4. In an informal survey of his staff, Cal learns that some of his employees don't use his company's insurance as they have better coverage from a working spouse. They keep Cal's insurance, though, to pay

the co-pays and deductibles the spouse's insurance doesn't cover.

5. Remembering what his broker said, Cal begins the task of reducing his insurance load.

How Can We Help Cal Reduce His Insurance Cost?

1. What can Cal do? He can reduce the number of people on his plan. Cal has wonderful employees, but the odds are that a few of them have extra people on Cal's insurance. Sometimes a family will place a relative on their insurance. Maybe a niece doesn't have insurance, has the same last name, and she is added. At my company we had this problem, and it took me by surprise. We asked all employees to bring in birth certificates, wedding certificates and immigration papers. In the end, we reduced our head count by 6 percent, directly lowering insurance costs.

2. Cal has to do this with tact. You do not want to call an employee a "cheater." Some people may feel that it is okay to cover extended family members on a family plan and not realize the mistake. And some people are trying to help a family member who may be out of a job. Unfortunately, extra family members who really need insurance almost always use the plan to its fullest extent and impact Cal's rates.

3. Announce the verification program two months in advance. Give people time to gather the documentation. Some may have a hard time; give them help to apply for copies of birth certificates or wedding licenses. Stress that this is not an immigration matter. Have your insurance broker at the initial meeting when this is announced, and let him take the heat for this new requirement. A good broker will stand by you.

4. You may consider back-charging employees for improperly covered members, but I do not recommend this. It is not worth the morale issue, and, if people can't pay you, a good employee may resign.

5. The next step is encouraging employees to voluntarily drop their insurance with you. At my company we had more than 15 percent of the employees do this. People who have alternate insurance can be persuaded to use that as their primary insurance. Maybe their spouse has family coverage, or they served 20 years in the service and are covered by the Veterans Administration, or are old enough to be covered by Medicare.

6. The most common scenario is that the spouse is covered. Cal needs to create a system that rewards his employees for dropping their insurance. Cal's average cost is $7,000 per employee. His actual cost is $3,000 for a single person and $9,000 for a family plan. Cal can offer a buyout plan that looks like this:

	Singles	Family
Current Cost	$3,000	$9,000
Employee Portion	$600	$1,800
Cal's Cost	$2,400	$7,200
Buyout Option	$900	$1,800
Cal's Savings	$1,500	$5,400

7. Cal needs to clearly explain this to his people. A single person saves his $600 employee cost and earns $900. A family saves $1800 and earns $1800, for a $3,600 swing. If this is more than the costs of the employee's alternate plan co-pays, the employee is ahead and so is Cal. The loser? The insurance company. The other employer does not increase its costs as it was paying anyway.

8. The buy-out money Cal pays has to be included in taxable income, so Cal will pay FICA and Medicare and pension if applicable. The employee will pay income tax, but it still is a winner for everyone.

9. This will work in any organization that provides medical insurance. The numbers will be different for each company based on

what insurance coverage it offers and the cost. But the concept is the same. If you offer your employee a big enough incentive, he will drop your insurance.

10. One thing to look for is an employee who drops your insurance and doesn't have other coverage. We made sure employees had insurance by asking for proof of coverage from the other plan. You don't want to be responsible for a person not having coverage and then getting sick. This is a moral obligation, not a financial one.

11. Make sure your employees understand they can come back to your insurance if their spouses lose coverage. Have your broker explain this clearly. If there will be a delay because of enrollment date timing, Cal should pay the COBRA costs of the spouse's plan until the employee is eligible for his plan. This will probably cost about what Cal is paying now anyway.

12. If Cal uses both of these options, he will save about 20 percent of his costs this year, and every year in the future. This adds up to big bucks.

13. I know some business people who only hire single people because the insurance is lower. To me this is very short-sighted. Hire the best people you can and make a better company, allowing you to provide good benefits.

14. There are very good options in other areas:

    a. Create a Health Savings Plan (HSA) for your employees.

    b. Offer a high-deductible plan.

    c. Keep your employees healthy.

    d. Join a local group, such as the Chamber of Commerce, which may offer you the option of buying group insurance in a larger group.

Chapter 29

The Five-Minute Solution to Choosing a New Supervisor

5ive minute consultant

Problem

You run a medium-sized business manufacturing and servicing widgets with 90 employees. Fred, your field service manager, told you he is moving because his wife, Ethel, received a job offer 200 miles away. You have two great people to choose from to replace him, Ricky and Lucy. Both, you feel, could do the job. How do you decide?

Possible Outcomes

- You spend time with each, choose Lucy, and Ricky understands (or vice-versa).
- You choose one and the other, upset at being passed over, gives you a two-week notice.
- You chose Lucy over Ricky, but she doesn't work out, so you ask her to go back to her old job. Ricky steps in and does a great job (or vice-versa).
- You couldn't make up your mind and don't want to upset either, so you bring in an outsider; Lucy and Ricky both quit a month later.
- You decide to get out of all personnel decisions in the future and to hire a human resources person to make these decisions and become your buffer.

What to Do When You Have to Make This Decision

1. Think it through before you start talking with Lucy or Ricky. Weigh all possible outcomes. Once you start the process, you are going to disappoint someone. Have plan B ready with an alternate offer to give your second choice new responsibilities and an alternate career path.

2. Can you split Fred's job so both have responsibilities? Doing this, you have two supervisors in an area where you used to have one. If you have further expansion in mind, this works. If not, you will have increased your payroll for no apparent reason.

3. Get Fred's input before he leaves. He will give you good advice on each person's skills.

4. Get the advice of others on your management team. That's what a team is for.

5. Read Lucy's and Ricky's employee reviews carefully. If you have a good review system, you will gain solid information about

how each works with co-workers.

6. Take the time to think about what you would like the position to be in six months or a year. Is your company changing? Bringing in new products? Expanding your geographic reach? Learning new technologies? Ponder if either Lucy or Ricky would be better in this role at the company you will become in a year.

7. You are down to the point where the pros and cons of each are the same. How do you make the final decision?

   a. Take the one with the best people skills. Both should be able to learn new technical areas.

   b. Take the one who cares about people more. A supervisor's job is about motivating others to get work done properly. A caring supervisor will gain more loyalty and respect.

   c. Take the one who shows more basic respect for your company in all aspects of ethics.

   d. Evaluate Lucy's and Ricky's basic aptitude for the job at hand. A learned person may not be good for this "in-the-field" job, but may be perfect for another job in your company. Base your decision on the best person for the job, not which person may be smarter.

   e. Don't feel trapped by the "all promotions come from inside the company" rule. It is generally better to promote from within, but not all the time. Every company needs fresh ideas occasionally. If you don't have the right candidate in-house, don't do the promotion.

   f. Often, it comes down to your gut feeling. Trust it. This is what made you a 90-person company. Be prepared for a rough conversation with the one who isn't chosen. Discuss specific things Lucy or Ricky can work on to improve. Give identifiable goals and set up a rewards system when goals are met.

Here Are Some Tips on What to Do Before Fred Gives His Notice

1. Expect this to happen—and, like Murphy said, at the worst possible time. New boyfriends or girlfriends, an unexpected inheritance, moving to be near the kids or grandchildren, or winning the lottery will all mess up your plans.

2. Once your company employs more than a dozen people, your job is more about managing people than actually working the business. Accept this fact and concentrate on your people's skills and work.

3. Every couple of months, ask yourself the question of who will replace whom when lightning strikes. If you can't name a person in-house, your bench is too weak. Tilt your hiring more toward people who have the capacity to grow.

4. Keep a file on possible outside hires. Hold on to business cards of anyone who would be a good leader: someone who takes care of you at a vendor's company, works for a competitor, or did a good job leading a work crew where you also worked. Join and be a part of social media networks like LinkedIn, especially in groups that pertain to your business. Anywhere you come across talent, remember the person. It may be years away and the person is not looking for a job, but you never know. It's only a phone call.

5. Cross-train in your company. See who responds best to new situations. See who adapts well. See who has the respect of others at the widget factory. Provide education and training courses that are open to all employees—but not required. The ones who attend are your future leaders. Plan a year or two ahead, identify promising candidates for promotion, and start a mentoring program.

6. It is by far less expensive to promote in-house than hire outside. Spend your money sending current employees for advanced education and training. Your company morale will be higher if people see opportunities. The biggest reason outside hires don't make it

is because they don't fit in with the company culture. You don't have this problem going in-house.

7. Are you a family-dominated business? If your nephew will be the next vice president of service, not too many people will want to be in a department where they see no path for advancement. It is still okay to bring along your nephew; after all, family comes first. Understand, though, the impact on other employees and be prepared to offer alternate career paths.

8. Look at the person's stability in his work life. Yes, there are studies that show a married person is more reliable and those with kids are still more stable. On the other hand, I would rather take a work-stable person with an interesting personal life than a guy who won't work late.

9. See who is a natural leader at the company picnic—who was the captain of the softball team or organized all the food? The person with you the longest may not be the best supervisor; longevity does not qualify a person as a supervisor.

10. Look for a person who occasionally works with a charity. Who brings in a raffle ticket that might help a local college? Who brings in Girl Scout cookies? (The Tagalongs are the best!) Who is a big brother or sister? These are the people for you to watch and train in the technical aspects of your widgets.

11. Watch for people who have been in the military. They know how to follow orders, how to give orders, and understand chain-of-command.

12. Look for people who are multi-lingual, and can easily speak with employees and customers in an ever-changing America.

13. The most important trait for a supervisor is the ability to make decisions. This person may not always be right, but is always better than someone with no decision.

14. Don't let age get in your way. A 55-year-old may have the perfect wisdom for the job at hand. Other than the senior managers, don't

think beyond a seven-year window. Few people know what their businesses will be like that far out.

15. Have a super employee review system in place. It should emphasize the future and what an employee can do, not what mistakes were made six months ago. A well-written, well-executed review system will pay dividends to you and your employees. (*See chapters 41 and 42.*)

16. Just because you promoted someone on Monday doesn't mean he/she is a qualified supervisor on Tuesday. Training is important, and it's better done before the promotion than during it.

Chapter 30

The Five-Minute Solution to Firing an Employee During Initial Probation

Problem

You own Rocky C's, a food service company with 40 long-term employees, which sells to restaurants, corporate cafeterias and caterers. Business is okay and you plan to hire two new people this year, one in the office and one driving a truck. The truck driver works out fine, but you are having a problem with Marge, the new lady in accounting.

Possible Outcomes

- Marge wakes up tomorrow and turns over a new leaf. Sure, and I will find the baseball cards my mom threw away when I left for college.

- You challenge Marge to be better and lay out a program for her to improve. She improves enough to keep her job, but never becomes a standout.

- You speak with Marge and tell her that she is not working out; pay her two weeks' severance and she leaves.

- She leaves, but goes to the Department of Labor claiming you didn't give her a fair chance. Your lawyer takes a desk in your back room.

What Can Rocky Do When He Tries to Salvage or Fire Marge?

1. Let's talk salvage first, as it is always better to salvage an employee. Rocky should bring her a specific plan to improve performance. The plan should detail her weaknesses and where she needs to improve. Rocky should give her a week-by-week plan of benchmarks she needs to reach in order keep her job.

2. This should not happen as the 90th day of Marge's employment approaches. After 30 days, Rocky should have a good feel for Marge's work and begin this program.

3. Each week Rocky should meet with Marge, going over her work output and giving suggestions and corrections where necessary. A few minutes each day looking over her shoulder also helps. After all, Rocky has invested in salary and training expense already. It is better to get a return on this investment.

4. Rocky can assign a more senior employee to help Marge with her job and interpersonal skills, both of which need help. The senior employee, though, reports back to Rocky that Marge has a bad attitude about work.

5. Rocky needs to make sure Marge is aware that her job is on the line. This should be in writing, in simple language, with a witness present when Rocky discusses this with Marge at about 45 days into her career. Hopefully, this will be the wakeup call that Marge needs.

6. If this doesn't wake up Marge, then Rocky should let her go. Rocky's employee manual doesn't address severance payments, but he decides to give her two weeks of severance, easing his own conscious. Marge applies for unemployment and contacts the department of labor; she claims she did not get a fair chance.

7. Fortunately, Rocky has a good record of his weekly meetings with Marge, and the case is quickly closed. Marge does get unemployment, but no other settlement.

What Could Rocky Have Done Better in Working with Marge?

1. Rocky should have a 90-day period that allows him to evaluate new employees as part of his employee manual. Since the word "probationary" carries a negative connotation, many companies are changing this to an "introductory period" with a more positive emphasis.

2. The average job interview runs an hour. Maybe Rocky does two or three interviews. In this short window of time you get an impression of the person, but Rocky cannot be 100 percent sure until actual work has been done for a period of time—thus the need for introductory periods.

3. Rocky needs to place this in his employee manual. Here are the steps to take:

   a. All new employees, at any level, should be hired for an introductory period. Some managers prefer 60 days; I am most comfortable with 90 days.

   b. All new employees need constant feedback and mid-course corrections. Assign a work buddy to give daily input on Marge's progress. Since Rocky is her direct supervisor, he should have a scheduled weekly meeting with her, during which he goes over her work output and answers questions. Rocky should set goals for Marge's progress and check the results.

c. Prepare a written report at 30 or 45 days and give Marge a clear vision of her status at that point. Tell her what still is expected of her. You may feel she is excellent and doing a great job ... tell her. Build up her confidence and push to teach her more. A review isn't always about solving problems.

4. If someone is not working out, you can still fire before the 90-day mark. When you write your manual, give yourself the option by stating that a full 90-day period is not guaranteed and that underperforming workers may be terminated at any time.

5. Rocky must create a "new employee checklist" of points to be covered during training. This should include items such as how to use the company's email system, where to get information needed to do a task and which people to ask which questions. Many new employees fail because they have not been taught well, not because they are weak employees. Rocky thinks he is only hiring two people this year, but with average turnover, he will probably hire six people, with just two new positions.

6. Rocky's goal should always be to salvage Marge and make her a productive employee. Nonetheless, at the end of the introductory period Marge can leave or Rocky can end the employment with no strings attached. Simply stated, at the end of the period Rocky can say, "I just don't feel you are working out," and end the relationship. But, Rocky cannot use an introductory period to terminate someone illegally, such as for race, gender or other discriminatory practices.

7. In many states you can still fire someone at any time anyway. So, what is magic about passing the 90-day mark? It means that full

benefits begin, and that both Rocky and Marge will bend over backwards to help each other.

8. In situations where employees wear uniforms, hard hats, name tags or other means of recognition, they often wear pins or badges showing they are introductory employees. This gives others a chance to introduce themselves and offer assistance to a person who looks lost or may need help. This identification is a great way to start a conversation and get a new person acclimated.

9. Some companies will start benefits at 30 days due to competitive hiring situations, but still reserve the probationary period for 90 days.

10. What happens at the end of the 90 days if you still are not sure if the employee should stay? You can extend the period for another 30 days, or whatever you and the employee agree to. But, if you are not sure by the time the employee has worked 90 days, you have not done your job as a manager. If the employee is marginal and you hope they can make it to just being better than marginal, do you really want them on your team? I think not. You want employees that will excel at your company. The only time to extend a probationary period is when an employee misses quite a bit of time during the initial period, maybe due to military service or illness.

11. Can Rocky have different probationary periods for different types of jobs? Yes, to a point. Truck drivers may learn their jobs more quickly than a knowledge-based worker, or, depending on the company, visa-versa. Rocky then may be tempted to create different programs. I don't recommend this. It may cause ERISA problems if you have a retirement program and may conflict with the terms of your benefits program, which usually states that all employees begin their health insurance on a certain date after employment.

12. There is one place where different programs do work! If you take a current employee and transfer or promote him, give him a 30-day look at the job. See if it fits. You already know the person has a good work ethic or you wouldn't have given him the new opportunity. At the end of 30 days, he can go back to his old job without any question. Maybe your great employee isn't a great supervisor. You want this 30-day option, too.

Chapter 31

The Five-Minute Solution to Someone Fraudulently Falling

The Problem

You own Deb's Debutantes, a chain of seven stores specializing in prom and wedding dresses. You have a manager in each store. Martha, the manager of store number three, just called saying that a woman slipped and fell in the store and claimed she hurt her back and needs to go to the hospital. As you head over to the store you speak with Martha and learn that the customer didn't come in with a young girl who might need one of your dresses.

Possible Outcomes

- Cathy Customer gets an x-ray and nothing out of the ordinary is found. Cathy goes home and you never hear from her again. Call your broker and buy the market, because today is your lucky day.

- Cathy calls back after going to her own doctor and says she is going to be out of work for weeks, and asks what you are going to do about it. As you hang up, you quickly look for your insurance agent's number.

- Cathy doesn't call you—but her lawyer does, and he says that Cathy will be in physical therapy for three months. He says he will simplify things for you by sending a settlement offer now. Your insurance agent and lawyer are going to be busy.

- Two years later, after hundreds of hours of time, you enter a civil trial. You think back—should you have accepted that first offer and been done with it?

What Should You Do When Martha Calls You?

- After Martha calls 911, she should make Cathy as comfortable as possible. When you speak with Martha, ask her to write down whatever she remembers. After Cathy is taken to the emergency room, Martha should take a lot of pictures of the floor and the general area where Cathy slipped. Put something in each picture for reference, like a ruler or a newspaper.

- Call your insurance agent immediately. This is the single most important thing you can do. He will send an investigator to your store and to the hospital.

- If you have video surveillance of your stores, get the tapes or disks and make copies. If these reside on a hard drive, make a duplicate copy on a portable or thumb drive.

- Advise Martha to speak with no one other than the ambulance EMTs or police. If strangers come into Martha's store taking pictures or asking questions, she should insist they leave right away. If they don't, Martha should call the police. If possible, she should take pictures of them. Tell Martha not to speak to any news media and explain that you will handle media inquiries.

- Follow up with your insurance carrier. The carrier will provide all the legal details for Deb's.

How Can We Better Protect Deb's Debutantes?

1. You have seven stores with a lot of traffic. Incidents will happen. Go over how to handle these incidences in detail at manager meetings. Have a written procedure listing the steps to take, the phone number of the local ambulance, and the 24-hour phone number for the insurance company. Always have a decent camera available, weather a cell-phone or a regular camera; keep the batteries charged. Practice taking the pictures at your managers' meetings.

2. The most common legal complaint today is the "slip, trip and fall" in a commercial establishment. It is very hard to prevent someone who has fraud in mind, but there are things to do to lessen the impact.

3. If you work to maintain a safe environment, your employees will have fewer accidents and fraudsters won't be able to point to a deficiency in your store!

4. Some interesting statistics from the National Floor Safety Institute (NFSI.org) are:

    a. 55 percent of slips and falls come from poorly prepared walking surfaces;

    b. 24 percent come from careless use of footwear, such as untied shoe laces;

c. 10 percent come from slippery surfaces without hazard warnings;

d. 8 percent come from lack of training for employees on hazards; and

e. Only 3 percent come from fraud, **but** these cost the most for business owners.

5. When a case comes to settlement, and the other side has pictures of your improperly maintained floor, you are going to lose.

6. Keep your floors spotlessly clean; no exceptions, and no trip hazards like extension cords or loose area rugs. Make sure the aisles are wide and well-lit. You may have to display less merchandise, but balance the decision of how much clutter you want, the potential risks and your sales volume. Don't over-wax your floors and create an ice rink. Make sure all stairs are very well lit, and have railings, non-slip surfaces and rugs tacked down. Check your emergency lighting once a month. Close bottom drawers on display cases.

7. Wipe up spills immediately. Place yellow hazard signs near the area of the spill until it is dry. Every store in Deb's chain must have a mop, a wet-dry vacuum and employees who know how to use them. Inspect your bathrooms hourly.

8. Don't wait for your landlord to shovel snow or melt ice in front of your store. Do it yourself and then complain to the landlord. In rainy or winter weather, place a water-absorbing mat at your front door for customers to wipe their feet. During inclement weather, assign one employee to monitor the door areas constantly and keep them dry.

9. Many slips, trips and falls come from an unexpected change in the walking path; maybe your floor has a 1-inch step in the threshold, or there is a bump-up due to an underground pipe. Get this fixed. It is just an invitation to a problem.

10. Train all store employees to understand who your typical customer is and is not. When an "is not" walks in, stay close and

offer service and help. When he realizes you are conscientious, he will likely leave.

11. If a customer asks for any medical help because he fell, be suspicious. Always report this to your insurance agent right away. Remember, your insurance agent is a pro at this; let him do his job.

12. Have long, straight aisles that allow you to see the whole store. Convex mirrors placed at the end of aisles let shoppers see who may be coming around a corner. These mirrors are not just to prevent shoplifting.

13. Put up a video surveillance system that will cover your entire customer area. Make sure the cameras are visible and place signs at your door stating that cameras are used. This will scare away fraud seekers. Some store owners place dummy cameras up. This can work, but it is not very expensive to have real cameras hooked up to a PC. If an accident occurs, don't give the tapes to anyone but your lawyer and only after you have made a copy.

14. Deb has told me that a parent who tripped over her own kid once sued the store; Deb won that one with video evidence. People will look up at cameras, and then fall down and call for help. Others will drop merchandise on the floor themselves, and then fall over it. Nothing will help your case like video documentation.

15. If there are spaces your cameras doesn't cover, like dressing rooms, try to have an attendant in the area at all times.

16. If your business has obvious shortcomings in floor set-up, fraudsters will take advantage. They will come in for a minute, and, if they spot weakness, they will come back in teams of three or four, take your attention to one side of the store, and the slip occurs in another area where you can't see what has happened. This is also true of shoplifting. Watch for a group of

customers arriving at once, who don't fit your normal customer profile. If this happens, bring as many of your employees onto the floor as you can.

17. In most cases, your insurance carrier will have the right to settle a case, even though you are 100% right that the case is fraud. Their decision is strictly a financial one; it will be cheaper to pay a small settlement that fight for no settlement. We had a suit where a drunk climbed over our fence to steal something from our dumpster. He hurt himself and sued us, and the insurance company settled, totally upsetting us. This affected our rates for a couple of years, and we couldn't do a thing about it.

Chapter 32

The Five-Minute Solution to Properly Exhibiting at a Trade Show

 Problem

You own Lou's Locks. You have invented and patented a new lock that you feel is a sure winner. You want to display it at the national lock-and-key trade show. How do you plan for going to a trade show, setting up a booth and drawing customers into it?

Possible Solutions

- Lou calls the show's sponsor and asks for advice. They give him the names of local exhibit companies near the show, but Lou is a thousand miles away.

- Lou talks with a local company about building a custom exhibit. They have great ideas but the final cost is $14,000 and Lou doesn't have this in his budget.

- Lou does this simply—with just a table-top display and the re-markable lock. Many people look at the lock, but few follow up with orders.

- Lou sets up his own exhibit and goes to the show, but he doesn't hold a candle to the big exhibits for the national companies. Lou is stuck in the center of a long aisle and few people stop at his booth. Lou has now invested a lot of money and doesn't see the return he expected.

What Could Lou Do Better with His Trade Show Set-Up?

1. At the trade show, make sure you have literature describing your product, and the path for ordering. Your phone number, website, email and other contact information should be on the flyer and should be easy to find. If your pricing is simple, place it clearly on the sheet. If you negotiate pricing based on the customer type and quantity, encourage people to call you toll-free for details.

2. You need a well-done booth. A new person in a second-tier booth will not draw attention. It doesn't have to be professionally done; Lou could do a bang-up job himself. Neat and inviting is better than glitzy.

3. Most trade shows have different pricing for booths. Corners carry a premium charge and are well worth it. Corner locations give more traffic and prestige.

4. At the show, you should be in the aisle, button-holing all attendees who walk the aisle, shaking every hand and getting every business card. You must draw people into your booth. You also should practice your ten-second pitch line. What 15-20 words will make people want to learn more about your new lock?

Let's Help Lou Prepare for His Show

1. During the year while Lou is inventing the lock, he should go to the show in anticipation of being a future exhibitor. Look at the customers walking the aisles. Are they buyers of his type of lock? Reading name tags, Lou can tell if there are buyers from big chains, or if it is local customers only. Also, see which exhibits are drawing the most attention.

2. Still not sure? Check out a regional show in your area. Most industries have a national show and smaller regional shows, which will be significantly less expensive. Give your exhibit a test run.

3. Most shows sell the names and addresses of attendees. Find out how much this costs; it is the basis for a future mailing list. Look at the attendees' companies and their positions within their companies. If they don't fit with Lou's potential market, be wary of going to the show.

4. Some trade shows don't allow selling on the floor! Ask before you go to prevent embarrassment.

5. Prepare a budget to do the show. Include the following:

   a. Cost of booth design and building;

   b. Cost to ship the booth to and from the show;

   c. Cost of the booth rental, carpeting, accessories, daily cleaning and lighting;

   d. The cost to unload the truck and set up the booth (considerable if the show is in a union work rule location);

   e. Lou's travel and hotel costs;

f. Preparation and printing of advertising; and

g. Advertising in the show program or sponsoring an event at the show.

6. You can possibly save money by using a local set-up firm to do all the loading/unloading and set-up. Ask the show manager.

7. You get ten seconds to grab an attendee's attention, and first impressions are key. Practice your 10-second pitch; have a 30-second pitch and a 60-second pitch as well. Booths reflect the image of the company. A simple one-person booth that provides a message is better than a multi-person extravaganza that makes outrageous claims. A trade show booth also gives you one great advantage over flyers and emails—you can demonstrate your product. Lou should have his lock operating in doors for customers to feel and see.

8. Most show operators ask potential customers if they want to be near or not near certain companies. Lou should ask to be near someone who is a good draw, helping him with visibility. Lou doesn't want to be near someone who has a competitive type lock. Don't be close to a booth with a noisy demonstration planned. It will hinder your conversations. Ask the show manager about this.

9. Keep your booth clean and organized at all times (i.e., no left-over coffee cups).

10. If you have two or more people working your booth, don't talk to each other while attendees walk by. Turn your cell phones off and don't wear a watch. Everyone who takes time to be at a specialized industry trade show is a possible customer, or reports to one, or recommends product or has an interest in Lou's industry. The trade press is especially important for the lock industry. Lou should be very eager to meet the press, pose for a picture with his lock, and send a press release for the after-show wrap-up article.

11. Don't, under any circumstances, have a pretty model with a short dress who knows nothing about your product. Lou should be well

dressed. Casual clothes indicate a casual business, and this is not good for a first timer at a show.

12. If this is your first show, don't be silly or try to pull off an inside joke. After you have been at a show for years you can get a little crazy.

13. Design your booth to be open and welcoming. If you have a large table across the front of your booth, people won't walk in, preventing in-depth conversations. Have your literature placed around the perimeter of the booth. Don't start a conversation with "How are you?" You'll only hear about their sore feet. Ask "What type of locks do you use?" Or, "Come in and see the greatest lock in the industry!"

14. If you have a computer or other device with a demonstration, make sure the volume doesn't hinder your ordinary conversation with a customer. A good video display does well at trade shows.

15. Smile all the time. No exceptions. Don't complain about how sore your feet are. No one cares. Wear comfortable clothing and shoes; no new shoes or high heels. No one enters a booth to talk to a frowning salesperson.

16. Make sure you collect a business card from every person with whom you speak. Ask each person to deposit his card in a fishbowl so you can follow up about the greatest lock in the world. If your product is so boring that you have to give away an electronic toy to get attention, start over at the inventing stage. Some trade shows are all about giveaways. Don't be tempted in your first show. Unless you can afford to give away something special, you will just be one of the crowd. Your products and your welcoming smile are better than a key chain.

17. Don't forget about buying the attendee list from the show producer.

18. If you have the budget, advertise before the show, inviting people to your booth with a promo about the greatest invention the lock industry has ever seen.

19. Call key customers and make appointments with them to meet at your booth. Give them a solid reason to stop at your exhibit, such as offering a show special.

20. Get to the show early and walk around the booths yourself. You will meet others who are displaying and can't get around to your booth. This is a great way to pick up a distributor in your industry. Be the last one to leave. If you are the only person on the aisle, the last customer will only talk with you.

Chapter 33

The Five-Minute Solution to a Work Emergency When on Vacation

The Problem

You own Joe D's Archeological Supplies, selling tools, equipment and clothing for outdoor and scientific use. The business is 25 years old, with 13 employees, and doing well. While you go on archeological digs as part of your product testing, your last family vacation was three years ago. Yesterday you flew to New Orleans for Mardi Gras with your wife and children. Your cell phone just rang and you were told of a work problem.

Possible Outcomes

- You have a trusted manager who can solve this problem and just about any other. Congratulations ... you pass the course on how to be good to your business and your family.

- You give twenty minutes of phone instruction to your staff and they attempt to solve the problem. Too bad they only heard every other word on your call and made the problem just a little bit worse.

- You spend three hours on the phone and then try to find your family among a million people. Your wife turned off her cell phone.

- You fly home, solve the problem, and get to the airport in time to pick your family up on their return. Your wife and kids give you an extreme case of go-jump-in-the-lake.

- The above outcomes are good; this outcome says that your family doesn't come home for three weeks and forgets to tell you where they are.

What Do You Do When The Phone Rings?

1. Figure out if this is a real emergency, or just someone panicking about making a decision. How? Quickly go through the range of options. If none of the choices will harm someone, put you out of business or land you in legal trouble, it's not a real emergency. Give a half-hour of advice and go about your day. If you can't explain the steps to take in a half-hour, plan on changing the manager when you get home.

2. If it is indeed a real emergency, then you must react. Your family will understand, provided you don't have real emergencies every month. If you do, plan on changing your management team, or change how you taught your staff! If they never have authority to make decisions when you are around, and suddenly they need to, it will not work. On-the-job training for emergencies is too little, too late.

3. Explain the problem to your family and why you need to react to it. Tell them how much time you will need, set a place to meet at the end of that time, and be there.

4. Ultimately, your decision is: Which is more important—Joe D's Archeological or Joe D's family.

What Can Joe Do to Prevent Making This Decision?

1. Hey Joe, learn to let go. Your employees have to make decisions on their own. Easy to say … hard to do.

2. Make up your mind. If you don't support the concept of letting go, it will never happen. Don't waste your time and the efforts of your staff if deep-down you know that you will never allow it. By the way, in surveys of entrepreneurs, one of the biggest problems is just this … learning to let your staff make decisions.

3. Don't expect your employees to instinctively know what to do in emergency situations. They have to be taught and need practice. Lay out each person's role in the company, including their duties and their responsibilities, and create a manual for each different position. Then if someone doesn't show up, the replacement person will have an easier time. Establish benchmarks for work to be done.

4. All this takes time, and you don't have enough of it because of the responsibilities you have. Duh! Start to off-load your repetitive tasks. Train co-workers. Give up all the basic work you do. This is what you have employees for. Let them grow and learn. If you don't, the good ones will leave you for a more enriching job.

5. Employees, for the most part, are eager to vary their daily routines. Let them take on responsibilities. Let them make small mistakes; don't jump in and instantly respond to small situations. After the fact, teach your team how the situations could have been handled differently. They will learn more this way than if

you just take over their problems.

6. Give specific instructions to your people and let them do the assigned tasks. Monitor on a scheduled basis, once a day for short tasks, or weekly for long-term projects. You will find that employees will do things differently than you did and, in many cases, they will do things better! As long as they get the results, it shouldn't matter what path they took, as long as it was within your general guidelines.

7. Delegate is a four-letter word to many entrepreneurs. During your slow times at work, hold training meetings with your leaders. Design problem situations and then solve them around your conference table. Don't interrupt. Let the ideas flow. Your leaders will start to mature.

8. Delegation is a skill that you can learn, just like every other skill you have developed. Give up small tasks first. Get comfortable with it. Don't give up on learning this skill after initial mistakes. The first couple of people you select for learning may not be the right ones. If you have never delegated before, expect to learn as you go along.

9. Start a program where you write down everything you do for a two-week period. Write down every little detail that you are involved with. Wait a week and then look back. You will surprise yourself with the repetitive nature of some tasks, and the absurdity of others. This will help you create the list of jobs to delegate.

10. You cannot wear every hat at your company. If you do, you will never have employees take a risk, nor solve a problem. Like all entrepreneurs, your business is your baby. It is hard to give up parts of it; but you must if you want to take a family vacation. Do not become the bottleneck in your own organization. You can spot this if you have more work to do than your subordinates, and they are waiting for you to get things done before they can start something.

11. You are the chief executive officer, not the chief everything officer of your company. You do many things well, but you are not the best at every aspect of running a business. Your first delegation project should be the areas you are not good at, or don't enjoy doing.

12. It is also okay to not get things done. Do the high-impact parts of your work first, and if you don't finish some low-impact items, go home to your family.

13. You will find that some of your employees enjoy doing their daily jobs and don't want more responsibilities. That's fine. Every business needs a balance of leaders and good workers.

14. What happens to your business if you get sick? What if you are in the hospital for a week? Your business will have to run. Even worse, what if your spouse or a child gets sick? I hate to tell you this, but you will get sick at some point and the doctors will not let you get stressed out using your cell phone or laptop. If you have taught your people to run the business, your sickness will not infect the business.

15. Reward your leaders with acknowledgement and praise of their successes. A little money and a lot of praise work well together.

Chapter 34

The Five-Minute Solution to an Angry Fired Employee

 Problem

You own Sandy's, a retailer of toys and children's furniture. You've been in business in Brooklyn, N.Y., for 32 years. You have 130 employees in twelve shops and a warehouse. Last week you discovered that Ralph, a three-year employee, has been loading trucks with extra merchandise that is being sold in the streets.

Possible Outcomes

- You fire Ralph on the spot. He pleads for a second chance. You don't back away from your stance; he leaves and you are done with him.

- You call the local police precinct. You meet a detective off-site and show her your evidence. She suggests they arrest Ralph and get the names of others who are helping. You want to prosecute, but if Ralph helps the police, you agree to cut him a deal.

- After Ralph is fired he blames you and promises revenge.

- The next day Ralph comes into the office with a tire iron, breaking up furniture and threatening people. You call the police and they subdue him.

- Ralph comes in waving a gun, sounding drunk. You have never been this scared in your life, even when you served in the Army.

What Can Sandy Do When He Fires Ralph?

1. When Sandy fired Ralph, he should not have been alone. Always have a second person present during a termination. If Sandy guesses that Ralph will be upset, ask a supervisor from the warehouse to "hang around" outside the door to his office. Leave the door open.

2. A better option is to suspend Ralph immediately and have a supervisor escort Ralph off the property. A day later, call Ralph into the office and go through the termination procedure. When he comes in, have him wait for just a minute or two. Observe his behavior. If you are the slightest bit uncomfortable, call 911.

3. If Ralph cooperates with the police in apprehending others, you don't have to worry. He knows his leniency depends on being helpful. This doesn't mean you give him a second chance, but you shouldn't be as worried about revenge.

4. Advise your employees that Ralph is no longer an employee, and, if he enters company property, immediately call 911. Make sure

this message goes to your retail stores, too, as they may not know what happened in the warehouse.

5. If you feel that Ralph will be out-of-control in a face-to-face termination, then call and terminate him on the phone. Have a second person listen in. It is not "business-polite" to fire someone on the phone, but so what? Ralph is a thief. If he threatens you, file a police report.

6. If Ralph comes in to pick up personal effects or get a final check, have your supervisors available near the office. If anyone detects a problem, call 911. If Ralph is wearing a coat, be extra-alert for something hidden underneath.

7. Millions of people are fired every year in the U.S., and only a small handful return with vengeance in mind. These cases get a lot of news coverage, but really are few and far between. Now, what do you do when someone walks in with a gun? Call 911 explaining the urgency of the situation. The police will send a professional negotiator to handle the situation. Let the police take charge and do what they say.

8. If you can't dial 911, now what? Keep calm yourself and try to keep your people calm, which is not easy. You don't want to further agitate Ralph. Talk softly and say whatever Ralph wants to hear, no matter what. As much as possible, do whatever he asks. Don't give him an excuse to get angrier. Yes, he can have his job back; yes, he can get his vacation or severance pay. A white lie here can be life-saving. Give him something physical or a future promise in exchange for letting specific employees leave. Never touch him.

9. Hostage-takers most often want to tell their side of a story. Let Ralph call the local newspaper or TV channel.

10. If Ralph comes in with a weapon drawn and starts firing, which is a one-in-a-million situation, follow your instincts. Duck down; if you are injured, play dead. Is it better to hide or attempt to disarm him? No one can answer that question for you. The situation will drive the options for you.

What Can Sandy Do to Reduce the Consequences or Prevent This

1. Don't try to make your facility a fortress. Your employees will not like it.

2. Fire laws require a second exit from all work areas. Keep these open and clear. Many companies keep their work areas restricted, where outsiders need to be "buzzed" in through a locked door. This will keep the casual problem outside but will not prevent someone intent on getting into your company. Former employees will know the back doors.

3. Many business phone systems require a personal code to make a call or only allow internal calls. Program your system so that any phone can always call 911.

4. Contact your fire/burglar company to do an assessment, and install wireless panic buttons under the desk of the receptionist and in a couple of other locations. Make sure to put one in your office. These are inexpensive and highly recommended.

5. Cameras can only record what has happened. They will not prevent an upset employee from coming in. An ex-employee doesn't care about anything but revenge and won't care if he is seen on video.

6. Don't get into arguments when you fire someone. Tell him he is being terminated, but don't debate the issues. You only aggravate the situation needlessly.

7. Sandy fired Ralph for theft, a fairly clear situation. If you are firing someone for poor performance, find out if he is under any outside stresses. If so, this firing may be the final straw. These stresses include:

   a. Financial problems;

   b. Medical situations; and

   c. Family or personal issues.

   It may be better to give the employee a leave of absence to work through these problems than to add the additional stress of losing a job. Not every company can do this; not every employee will share his problems, but, where possible, this may prevent a future serious problem.

8. Don't say "This is hurting me more than you" or "This is tough on me, too." After all, you still have a job. Let the fired employee leave with dignity. If he has a company car, let him drive home and then pick up the car. Let him come back for his personal items after hours, when he won't have to pack up in front of her peers. People who have been fired are in a mixed-up emotional state. Don't push them over the edge by being arrogant or non-caring.

9. Your employee manual should state that it takes two managers' agreement to fire someone. This allows for cooler heads. If an employee does something that deserves firing and there is not a concurring manager available, suspend the employee and tell him to come back tomorrow. Don't fire someone in front of a crowd; do it privately. This avoids the employee wanting to respond to you in front of the same crowd, which leads to problems.

10. It is always better for the company to take the high road. No public fights. The rest of your employees will respect you, and you will have fewer problems that can escalate into violence.

11. Set up a training program for yourself and your supervisors. Visit www.fiveminuteconsultant.com for assistance with this.

12. Drug and alcohol testing programs may help you hire fewer "problem people."

13. If you know the person you are about to fire wears or owns a firearm and is less than stable, call the police and ask if they have an officer who will visit your place of business for five minutes. Not every police department can do this based on its manpower availability, but it doesn't hurt to ask.

14. Review your employee manual and insert a section that says firearms are banned from all company property. This will lessen the chance of a serious incident.

Chapter 35

The Five-Minute Solution to Use When ICE Knocks on Your Door

Problem

You own Carl Coopers' Town Car Service, a limousine and delivery service. You have 298 employees, mostly delivery van drivers, bicycle messengers and town car drivers. On Tuesday morning, two gentlemen come to your office from the U.S. Immigration and Customs Enforcement (ICE). They ask to review your I-9 forms. They say they will come back in three days, allowing you to pull together relevant information. ICE may also send a letter called a "notice of intent to audit," and then show up three days later.

ICE is the principal investigative arm of the U.S. Department of Homeland Security (DHS) and the second largest investigative agency in the federal government. It was created in 2003 through a merger of the investigative and interior enforcement elements of the U.S. Customs Service and the Immigration and Naturalization Service.

Possible Outcomes

- The agents come back, find no problems, and leave.

- The agents ask to meet with 30 employees, but when you call them into the office, you find out that 28 of them have left, never to return. Your delivery schedules for the next couple of weeks are really stretched.

- The agents advise you that you have not kept your I-9s correctly, and that you may face civil fines. You thought you had done everything correctly ...OOPS!

Should Carl Have Done Something Different on the Day ICE Arrived?

1. No. He invited the agents in, opened his personnel records and cooperated. He could have been stubborn and demanded that they come back with a warrant (which of course they would, but with a bit of wariness). Immigration policy is set by Congress. It doesn't do any good complaining to the ICE agents.

2. The ICE agents are doing their jobs; they are not there to pick on Carl Coopers. Then why are they there? It could be that a disgruntled former employee said that Carl hires undocumented workers at low wages; it could be that a competitor dropped a dime on Carl, or it could be Carl's time was up in the law of averages. There are numerous "anti-immigration" websites that detail how to file complaints with ICE over companies that might have illegal immigrants.

3. ICE has a mandate to audit "critical infrastructure and key resource" companies in the United States. If your firm is a defense-related company, count on an audit.

4. Carl's job upon hiring a new employee is to verify information required for the I-9 form. For example, let's say he's hiring a new employee named Clem Roberto. He must check Clem's identity and employment eligibility. There are three lists to work with:

a. List A verifies both identity and employment eligibility. On this list are ten documents, including a valid U.S. Passport;

b. If Clem doesn't have a document from list A, he needs one from list B, which confirms identity; and

c. One from list C, which confirms eligibility for work in the U.S.

5. Clem has to complete his portion of I-9 form the day he starts working and Coopers' has to complete the form by the third day after Clem begins. Carl must keep the I-9 for either one year after employment ends or a total of three years—whichever is longer. The Department of Homeland Security has a very good employer handbook (available at http://www.uscis.gov/files/form/m-274.pdf), which Carl and all business owners should review.

6. Carl's job is to examine the employee's documentation and if it appears correct, accept it. If, in the audit, the agents find a well done fake, Carl will not be held liable. Carl will have problems if the documentation is so poor that a third-grader would have seen the difference.

7. The ICE agents have discretion in applying fines. If there is willful violation, the potential fines are shown here: www.ice.gov/news/library/factsheets/i9-inspection.htm, and can get serious for repeated events. Normally, if Carl just has some random mistakes, he will get ten days to fix them, avoiding fines and penalties.

8. The best thing Carl can do during the visit is to fully cooperate, learn from the agents, and promptly fix all problems they point to.

What Could Carl Have Done Better in His I-9 Record Keeping?

1. All business owners feel there is too much government paperwork and intervention. Why look for more? So that you won't be sitting on a time bomb, that will go BOOM at the worst possible time. Carl's personnel manager should be very familiar with all of the rules relating to I-9s.

2. Carl should participate in E-Verify, a free service of the Department

of Homeland Security. Go to www.everify.com to get all the details. E Verify will make life so much easier for Carl's office. This will, in less than ten seconds, confirm your applicant's eligibility to work in the United States. A positive report from here, along with a correctly completed I-9, will prevent problems down the road.

3. Carl should keep all I-9 records separately from the employee file for confidentiality purposes. Every two years, these records should be checked and any employee identification presented that has an expiration date on it should be recertified.

4. The Social Security Administration also has an easy to use website for verifying social security numbers. Go to: http://ssa.gov/employer/ssnv.htm.

5. Yearly, Carl receives a letter from the Social Security Administration (SSA) detailing employees' social security numbers that don't match up with an existing account via a letter entitled "Employer Correction Request," commonly known as "No-Match" letters. Carl should take reasonable steps to resolve the mismatch, and apply these steps uniformly to all employees referenced in the SSA letter. This may be due to a typo in sending in Carl's taxes, or it may be that someone has used a false SS number. Carl's personnel manager should go to the person, privately, and explain there is an error in their number. You don't want to cause a good employee to run if there is a problem. Help the employee get correct paperwork.

6. It is always better to help a good employee than train a new employee. So what if it costs you a couple of grand for an immigration lawyer or a tax accountant? Your retention of a good employee is worth way more than that. Not every employee will get the coveted green card, but for your better employees, it is worth trying.

7. When the ICE agents visit, they will know about these letters. While you don't have to respond to the letters, if you receive two annual letters noting the same problems, it can cause the agents

to say there is willful misconduct on your part, which can cost you serious money and grief.

8. A company the size of Coopers' should have an outside attorney or consultant perform a self-audit every couple of years. Finding your own problems is much better than finding out about them from ICE. If you find mistakes on I-9s, keep the original and attach the new form to it. If it is a simple mistake, cross out the erroneous info, write in the new data, sign and initial the change.

9. Illegal immigration is a political football. There are federal laws and an increasing number of states are setting more stringent standards. If you are intentionally hiring low-wage, illegal employees, someone will report you, whether for economic or political reasoning. You can't hide behind an "I didn't know defense" when you underpay workers` or knowingly hire undocumented workers.

10. Undocumented workers will run when they see the ICE agents. There is a justifiable fear of detention and deportation of your workers. Prevent this by hiring qualified workers in the first place, or helping those people that contribute greatly to your company.

Chapter 36

The Five-Minute Solution to Training Your Employees and Yourself

 **Problem**

You are the owner of Ernie's Banking Supplies, a 77-person company that manufactures materials used by banks, from imprinted pens to paper coin wrappers. Last week two employees retired after 30 years with Ernie's.

Possible Outcomes

- The two replacements learn the jobs quickly, and you go on as before. Of course.

- One succeeds, and the other screws up the imprint division so badly that you are now running two weeks late on orders.

- Ernie planned on only trained people taking leadership positions, but didn't follow through because he was just too busy. He revived his training plan for the third time when another manager gave notice.

What Can Ernie Do When the Two Staffers Retire?

1. Ernie should realize that the problem starts with him. If he was a proactive trainer, his people would be better trained and ready to grow. Ernie, it seems, kept putting this problem aside once the immediate emergency was solved.

2. Ernie knows the age of his employees and should anticipate retirements about a year in advance. It is perfectly okay to ask senior employees what their long-term plans are. Ernie picked out the replacements early, but it appears he did a poor job of training.

3. Wait, isn't it the job of the retiring employee to train his replacement? You may think so, but he may not be a good teacher, or may not like the replacement, or is just too busy, or the replacements are too busy training their own replacements. (There are 512 possible excuses.)

4. The right answer is that, ultimately, it is Ernie's responsibility to have his managers in place and ready to work.

5. Ernie needs to establish a permanent training program within his company. It may be easy to predict retirements, but that will cover only some of the situations that demand well-trained people.

6. A month or two before the actual retirement, the new supervisor should take control of the department, while the retiring supervi-

sor shadows and mentors him. Ernie should spend extra time with each new supervisor.

7. Ernie should retain the current print shop supervisor part-time to mentor the new supervisor. The current problem needs to be fixed before Ernie plans long-term educational programs.

How Can Ernie Implement an Effective Training Program?

1. First step, Ernie has to commit to this. Unhesitatingly. He cannot let people put off their training time. How can Ernie impress the importance of this on others? He has to lead and participate as well. His actions will speak louder than any written policy.

2. Ernie should make continuing education a discussion point at every employee review. Stress how important it is to learn and what the consequences are for side-stepping the training programs. Employees who know how to learn will grow at Ernie's company, which itself will grow the company.

3. "Proper training" does not mean that employees work in another department for an afternoon. (*See Chapter 47 for cross-training*). Employees should invest 4 to 5 percent of their time in learning, taking vendor courses, going to seminars, or going back to school, in person or on-line. Ernie should pay for this, provided the employee gets a least a B. Grades are important for Ernie to monitor employees' success. Courses should be approved by Ernie's HR department in advance and can be anything that will stimulate learning. Any course in English or another language that is used by Ernie's employees or customers is fine. All technology courses, law, finance or technical skills training will help Ernie's. Ask the employee what he will get out of the course and how it will help him grow.

4. Ernie can't force employees to go back to school, but he can reward those who do. Think of the pride someone will have by getting a GED or other degree. This employee will thank Ernie for life.

5. Halfway through the course have the employee write a two-page synopsis of the course so far. You will see his level of engagement and thank or encourage him. At the end of every course, each employee should give a two-hour training program to the rest of Ernie's employees who can benefit from his knowledge. This will help his presentation skills and help motivate others to take courses. Let him practice with your HR person in advance. Once an employee schedules a course, it should take precedence over daily work. Homework, though, is to be done at home, not at work.

6. Ernie's HR department can work with a local community college to arrange discounts for Ernie's employees. Many colleges will tailor specific courses to local business needs. For instance, if you are putting in a new computer system next year, ask the college to create a course that will fit your schedule and learning needs. This is fairly common and should not cost you more than the regular classes at the school.

7. How does this help an employee to take over the printing department at Ernie's? It trains him to learn and teaches him to keep an open mind. Going forward, at least half of the training should be completed at Ernie's, from veteran employees who understand how to teach. The practical knowledge is equally as important as the basic knowledge.

8. Employees have to manage their schedules of classes, both as teachers and students. Real emergencies will occur that force changes, but keeping to a schedule is a job to itself, which teaches time management skills. Ernie and the HR department should offer help whenever it is asked for.

9. There is not a business owner anywhere who "knows it all." Ernie may not need to know how to work a printing press, but he does need to understand law, finance, marketing, computers and much more. If Ernie started his business and didn't continue learning, the business would be frozen in time.

10. Ernie should commit a minimum of 5 percent of his time to self-education. This is about a day a month. He might go to a one-day seminar, or schedule an educational visit to a key vendor. At a trade show, he should spend as much time at the educational workshops as walking the display floor.

11. Ernie could take a graduate-level course at a local university or online. Ernie should not worry about his grade; he should just get the knowledge. This can be done on Ernie's schedule, evenings or weekends. Then, Ernie has to share his new knowledge with the company, and let everyone know how important it is to keep up with current ideas and technology. Even though Ernie's business is not very high-tech, his customers are. He has to be able to communicate with them at their level of proficiency.

12. A great training time creator is a "lunch-and-learn" program. Set up a series of once-a-week programs, each about 20 to 25 minutes. Employees can bring their own brown-bag lunches, or ordering pizza always works. This has to be totally voluntary. No attendance should be taken or it may be considered time worked subject to the wage and hour laws. Your vendors should be glad to come in with their training staffs.

13. Google "training new supervisors" for a long list of organizations that offer in-person and online training programs.

Chapter 37

The Five-Minute Solution to Hiring Someone Who is Taking a Pay Cut

Problem

You own Johnny's Bench, a company that distributes park benches and outdoor furniture. You have three warehouses employing 135 people. Your computer guru left. You are searching for a new chief technology officer (CTO), and the best candidate, Molly Fitzwilliam, approximately 30 years old, is willing to take a $15,000 pay cut. Should you hire her?

Possible Outcomes

- Molly comes on board, does a bang-up job, and within a year you raise her salary to her old number.

- You hire Molly; she does a great job for six months, and then leaves you for a higher-paying job. Looking back, you should have given her more money, but that would have upset the wage structure of your management team.

- You hire her under a guaranteed raise program, so that in two years she will be at her old wage. She doesn't seem to work as hard as you had hoped, though, and you are stuck giving her raises.

- You decide not to hire Molly for fear she would be unhappy with her salary. Your second choice comes in at the salary level you have budgeted, and does a very good but not outstanding job.

What Should Johnny Have Done on Hiring Day?

1. This is one of the toughest dilemmas of an entrepreneur. There is no absolutely correct answer. It depends on the circumstances at Johnny's that particular day.

2. Johnny's has six senior managers, all roughly making the same, around $90,000 plus benefits. Molly previously was making $110,000, and Johnny feels he can go to $95,000. In the interview Molly said she would take the pay cut because she is unhappy at her current job and knows that Johnny's is a great place to work because Molly has a friend who works at Johnny's. During the second interview, the discussion primarily concerned salary, and Molly insisted money was not the most important part of her job requirements.

3. Johnny has to weigh all of the factors. Molly would be great for the job, but not if she leaves in six months chasing more money. Johnny needs to understand what really motivates Molly. By now, Johnny knows her business capabilities are excellent. He needs to

ask questions about Molly's values and long-term goals:

a. What kind of car does she drive? How old is the car? What condition is it in? An expensive car says money is important!

b. Look at the jewelry and clothes she is wearing. Fancy means good taste, but may also indicate a need for money.

c. Discussing Johnny's 401(k), ask what Molly sees for her retirement—a house in the south of France, or a simple cottage in New Hampshire? She may say it is too far away to think about, but that is never true; everyone has dreams. Talk about your own plans as a way to stimulate the conversation.

d. What is her favorite vacation? Shopping on Rodeo Drive, or going to Wrigley Field for a day game?

e. Johnny can't ask directly about Molly's family—whether she has kids or if she is planning to. But Johnny can discuss where she lives and ask about the school system in that town. If she knows about it and thinks it is a good system, she wants to stay. If she doesn't know anything about it, she is not planning to be involved there. Maybe Molly's kids are in private school anyway, but this will usually come out in conversation about schools.

f. If Johnny's offers a flexible spending plan (*which every business in America should ... see Chapter 48*), gauge Molly's reaction to it. If she says the paperwork is not worth the money, then she is a free spender, and may like the big bucks. If she likes the program, it indicates a thriftiness, which predicts that a lower salary is okay.

g. Discuss your industry and the role Johnny's plays in it. Does it interest Molly? If she only cares about IT and says she can run a department no matter what the product is, then you should think twice. If she asks about your history and shows knowledge from research she did on the web before the interview, that's good.

4. Does Molly need corporate health insurance? Maybe leaving this out of her package will free up money to adjust salary!

What Else Could Johnny Do to Help Him Make This Decision?

1. Think about the job description before you begin interviewing. Is now the time to recast the job? What do you want this job to be in two years?

2. Are you better off hiring an inexperienced person you can train in your ways, or do you want a seasoned professional? What has been your hiring success rate in both scenarios?

3. Don't rush. Johnny doesn't have to make this decision at the current interview. Give yourself time to sleep on it. Gut decisions come out better after a good night's sleep.

4. Never make an important hiring decision alone. Have your number-two person join Molly and you for lunch. Ask a couple other senior managers to meet with Molly.

5. The most important part of hiring a management-level person is "the corporate fit." If Molly fits in, she will stay longer and will be worth a greater investment. If she is very qualified, but is a round peg in a square hole, she won't last and that will cost you big bucks for a do-over.

6. Do a serious job of reference-checking. Many companies only give name, rank and serial number from the personnel department. Try speaking with the owners; there will be a greater chance of good information. Did Molly leave previous jobs for money, or were there other reasons? By the time of the third interview, you should be sure that her job changes fit your idea of appropriate.

7. Your job application should always request personal references. Now, we all know that the references will be good friends and say good things about Molly. But, talk with the friends and ask them if they have ever taken a vacation with Molly and where they went. You can ask questions about the reference's lifestyle and family that you can't ask Molly. Most "friend" references will

speak way too much about Molly and you will learn about Molly's motivations.

8. Study the market for people who lead IT departments in companies your size. It is as easy as calling local head hunters and asking what they would do to get the job order at your company. They will tell you the market. You can Google "salaries of IT managers" and you will get active lists. If you have to readjust your budget, this will give you good direction.

9. Plan a meal with Molly. See how comfortable she is in a social situation with you and another manager. Ask Molly to drive; this is a good way to learn about her car. Let the other manager steer the conversation. Don't give her pre-set questions; just let it be a regular conversation and see where it goes. If Molly asks a lot of questions about the company and the people, that's a good sign. If she keeps the conversation on topics other than the company, this is a bad sign.

10. Before your final visit with Molly, decide how upsetting it would be to hire her above your other salaries. At most companies this would be fairly disruptive. Don't, for one second, believe her salary will not get out. Will your other managers understand that IT is the hot job now and Molly's numbers are average for this specialty? You really can't discuss this with them, but you can predict how they will feel.

11. The worse option is to hire Molly at a low number and have her leave after six months. You will have wasted a ton more money this way. Your goal is to really feel if she wants to work for you at the reduced number, and if you feel she is honest with you, welcome Molly to Johnny's Bench.

Chapter 38

The Five-Minute Solution to Too Much Overtime in Your Payroll

Problem

You own Chuck's Cheesecake Company with 13 stores on the East Coast. The company has grown since you took over from your father's one store, turning positive cash flow and profit consistently. This year, your CFO tells you that expenses are up, with a significant increase in overtime.

Possible Outcomes

- Chuck sends an email saying all overtime is stopped unless there's an emergency. Chuck's district managers write back saying they need a certain amount of overtime with their key employees. You don't budge.

- The cheesecake stores lose some key employees who counted on the overtime, but even with adding to the overall employee count, Chuck's costs are lower than paying overtime.

- Chuck's customer feedback shows a decrease in overall store quality starting when the overtime ban began. He doesn't know the cause; are the employees doing less as retaliation or is there not enough time to do everything needed?

- Chuck meets with the managers; ten are okay with the reduced overtime and three feel it is hurting the revenue and profit of their stores.

- Were there better ways to cut costs?

What Could Chuck Have Done Better in Attacking Overtime Costs?

1. Chuck did the right thing by listening to his CFO. In a company with few employees, overtime can't be avoided. In a business like Chuck's, significant overtime is the most expensive way to operate.

2. Chuck works as hard as anyone and has a difficult time with hourly people who manage to stretch work to fit expanded overtime hours. His managers all work on a quarterly profit-bonus system, and he thought they would be pleased with this reduction in costs.

3. Chuck's mistake was not getting advance buy-in. In announcing this program, he should allow managers a six-week period to revamp their schedules and allow employees to adjust for lower

incomes. Very few employees are happy with a reduction of hours; many will need to get part-time jobs. In tough economic times, this places a new burden on the employees and creates bitterness in a previously happy work force.

4. The managers should reward a handful of good employees at each location with up to ten hours of overtime per week. Up to 5 percent of total company hours, worked as overtime, can actually be beneficial.

5. Chuck should send mystery shoppers to visit stores at least twice per week and increase to three weekly visits in the first weeks of the overtime reduction. (Author's note: Being paid to shop in a cheesecake store is a better job than writing this book.)

6. Chuck should make a visit to all of his stores, meeting with the few people that retained their overtime, explaining that they earned a special privilege. Explaining the long-term health of the entire chain is in the best interests of all employees, he may avert some of problems.

7. Chuck needs to rally the three non-believing managers. They should come around when they understand the gravity of the situation. Those that don't are not team players, and unless they wake up, they will have to go.

What Could Chuck Have Done to Prevent the Overtime Problem?

1. Once a company gives a benefit or sets a wage pattern, it is just about impossible to successfully withdraw it. Workers will be resentful for years. The availability of overtime is taken for granted after three consecutive months. Employees will come to expect the income and increase their style of living accordingly. Then, when the overtime is taken away, problems occur. Employees will suddenly look toward unions, competitors and

other ways to supplement their incomes at your expense.

2. Chuck should ask his CFO to find out why the overtime increased. Was it at every store? Chuck needs to teach the managers to look for bottlenecks in production or shipping of cakes. Are these causing people to work late? Find inefficiencies that cause extra work and resolve them! Does your overtime start after eight hours per day, or 40 worked hours per week? This can have a big impact, so set your schedules accordingly. Be sure to check your state laws; California, for instance, requires overtime after eight hours per day.

3. Check your time and attendance system or your time clock punch cards. Are people punching in before their shifts and getting paid? If you pay based on quarter-hour increments, are people punching out at eight minutes past the hour and getting paid for the full quarter-hour, causing more overtime?

4. If you are going to be busy for three months because of a big contract or a busy season, explain the purpose of the overtime, and give dates when the overtime will end, preventing expectations. Unless you schedule overtime by seniority, spread the overtime across as many people as possible, with quality of work being the measuring stick to earn the extra hours. Make a clear statement: those who work hard will earn extra hours.

5. Avoid overtime in jobs that require heavy lifting, using sharp knives or tools, or handling dangerous substances. Employee safety concerns are more important. If workers in those categories earns overtime based on their good performance, give them an easier job after eight hours.

6. Except for a few key exceptions such as a foreman who has to set up and then work a full shift, never let overtime become automatic at your company. Consider putting these leaders on salary.

7. Forecast your employee needs accurately to prevent using overtime. This is one of the most important jobs of each store's man-

ager. Make this an important criterion of the manager's review. Scheduling personnel is a tough job. Be sure to control unexcused absences by reprimanding the offenders in line with your employee manual. Don't let people take off on your busy days. Spread vacations throughout the year, letting seniority take care of conflicts.

8. Overtime expense increases direct labor by 50 percent, plus taxes and workers' compensation. The overall cost of overtime is 60 to 70 percent, especially if impacting 401(k) plans or vacation.

9. If you are a union-organized company, bargain over how you assign overtime and avoid a strict seniority clause. Also, if you pay benefits by the hour, make the argument that full benefits are covered by the normal 40-hour work week and should not be paid on overtime. This will be a hard battle, but one that can be worked out. Don't accept the argument that your overtime benefit payments subsidize other employers who don't give 40-hour weeks. If you can't get this through, it may be the time to withdraw from multi-employer bargaining and negotiate one-on-one with the union.

10. It may be less expensive to carry an extra person on a second shift permanently than to keep a first-shift person over when needed. Ask your CFO to run both scenarios. If you don't have an accountant on your staff, ask your payroll company for some "what-if?" scenarios.

11. Many companies try to avoid overtime by giving employees "comp" time. Comp time must be used in the same payroll period as the original overtime worked.

12. Overtime during holiday and vacation weeks is a tricky issue. The wage and hour laws say that overtime is required after 40 worked hours. If you are closed for a Monday holiday and the employee works three ten-hour days, and one eight-hour day, does he get 38 regular hours and eight holiday hours, or does he get 46 total

hours, giving him six hours of overtime? Either way will be legal, but must be laid out in your employee manual so it is clear to all. You know which way the employees will want it.

13. You ask an employee to work overtime for four days, but on the fifth day, she is ill and can't come to work. She has worked 40 hours and then the sick day. You expected her to earn the overtime pay, and she expected to receive it—what do you do? If you don't pay it, people will be reticent to accept overtime requests from you. There is no right answer; just be consistent. Be very clear in your employee manual what the pay will be in this situation, I suggest you pay the overtime in this circumstance.

Chapter 39

The Five-Minute Solution to Your Child Joining the Family Business

Problem

You own George's Bush and Tree Service, a 41-person company that does commercial landscaping and tree-trimming along electric power lines. Your daughter, Barbara, just graduated from college and, surprisingly, wants to join the company. What is the best way to get her started at George's?

Possible Outcomes

- You are totally surprised by the decision. Previously, Barbara hadn't expressed interest in joining the business, but did work summers in high school. Is it because of the tough job market for English majors?

- You ask her for a three-year commitment to learn various jobs within the company. Barbara figures she can make her mind up after a year. You agree, but hope she will stay longer. It turns out her first year is a success and she plans to stay around for a long while. The perfect outcome!

- Barbara's degree is in English, with a minor in ecology. She is an outdoor person and wants to work with the tree crews. You are nervous about her climbing and the heavy lifting.

- Barbara's boyfriend asks her to move in, except he is 1,500 miles away. She says yes and gives you notice. You saw this coming, but didn't say anything. You're glad you didn't give her major responsibility.

- Barbara joins the tree crew and proceeds to upset everyone by telling the experienced foremen what to do. The foremen come to you and ask for help.

- After six months Barbara tells you this is not for her. She asks to go back to graduate school for an advanced English degree.

What Can George Do for Barbara's First Day?

1. First, be proud. Whatever Barbara's reasons, having your child want to work with you is an honor.

2. During her first six months, spend time with her teaching personnel matters, company finances and the role that each person plays. In detail, explain how your foremen have earned their current positions. Let her appreciate the hard work that's been done by others.

3. Before she starts, take as much time as needed to really understand Barbara's goals. You may think you know her goals, but you

should ask as an equal and not a parent. Tell her that she will often be caught in the middle. You will treat her like an employee at times and a partner at other times. Give her a valid timetable, at least six months to a year, of how long she will be "just a worker," reporting to someone other than you. She can't be a leader on her first day; make sure she understands this.

4. Teach her that some employees will be jealous of her. There is nothing she can do to prevent this. Barbara has to earn respect through her work ethic and civility in dealing with others. She doesn't have to lift the heaviest tree limbs, but she does have to work her full shift, be on-time and not gripe about anything. Set her up with a consistent work and training schedule.

5. Place Barbara with your most trusted crew. Let her learn from the best. Talk with the foreman and explain both his and Barbara's roles. Stress that he is in charge.

6. You have 41 employees. At least one is unhappy with you. Given the opportunity, people upset at you may take it out on your family. It is not brave to send your child to the roughest crew; it is foolhardy. Barbara's health is more important than anything, no matter what.

7. Will other employees feel threatened in their positions? Meet with them prior to Barbara's start date and explain what her job duties and responsibilities are. Do you have a policy of not hiring family members? If so, don't break it just for yourself. Shelve the entire policy and start fresh on hiring. To me, hiring family members of good employees is good business.

8. This will be hard on both of you, but you have to be the dad and always take the high road. Start this from day one. Don't place extreme expectations on Barbara. Let her grow at a pace you both are comfortable with.

9. Family tax and financial planning may indicate you give her a good salary. That's okay. But make sure her benefits and extras are the same as your other company leaders. If you buy her a car, put it in her name,

not the company's, unless all of your foremen get company cars.

10. Lastly, don't call her "Daddy's little girl."

What Should George Do After Barbara's First Day?

1. Have weekly training time with Barbara and teach her the business from your point of view. Work with her to lay out her career path at George's. This will change as it goes forward; be patient.

2. Plan on her changing paths a couple of times. Most people do.

3. If, after a year, Barbara still loves the business, start long-term planning. Does she want to go back for a graduate degree? Does her boyfriend live far away? Maybe you would open up a branch location there? Does Barbara think she can move the company into new areas like tree-farming or timber-cutting? Give her opportunities to shine on her own.

4. Let her fail at something without you stepping in at the last moment. She will learn more from that than using your checkbook to solve a problem.

5. If you are planning to work for at least ten more years, don't teach Barbara your daily work. Work on new ideas for her after she learns the basics. Ask yourself: what were the two biggest problems you had last year? Ask Barbara to solve these problems, or better yet, prevent them in the first place.

6. Right now, you are a labor intensive company. Maybe Barbara wants to move into selling tree-trimming tools on the Internet. Don't laugh; it could be the next big thing. Innovation is possible in every business!

7. Provide an expert's education by sending her to trade shows and seminars. Have your accountant, insurance broker and lawyer teach her. They will do a better job than you. If they can't, you need new professionals on your speed-dial.

8. Hook Barbara up with an outside mentor, maybe a respected leader in a related industry, who can take her under his wing. You

can't be her only teacher. Many family businesses insist their children work for three or more years outside the company, in the same or related industries. Ideally, it should be the type of and same size company you expect to be in five to ten years.

9. Your long-term job is training her as a leader. After she has the basics down, let her shadow your meetings with vendors and employees. You are teaching her to be successful more than you are teaching her the tree business.

10. You should have a monthly "family business" meeting with all members of your family and discuss any issues that come up. Listen to everyone and work out solutions to problems. At work you are the boss; in the family meeting, you are just one among equals.

11. Give Barbara a job performance review just like every other employee. This will help her, help you, and teach her the process of reviewing employees, one of the most important jobs of a leader.

12. If, after a reasonable period of time, maybe five years, you and Barbara decide she is not going to be the next president of the company, she still can be the owner. Hire a strong business professional who will team up with Barbara, but let the professional run the day-to-day operations. If you and Barbara disagree on whether she should be the next president, you need a family business coach; only an outsider can help you down this road.

13. You'll have to have a plan for Barbara's husband, in case he ever wants to join George's. Will he report to Barbara? Can they handle this?

14. What if you have two or three kids who join the business? Who will be CEO? You don't answer this on the first day, but in your personal retirement planning this will be the thorniest question you will encounter. A consultant whose first name begins with "P" is a good source for advice.

15. How do you affect the financial transfer to the next generation? Your tax advisor has a big role here, planning between gifting and selling your stock.

Chapter 40

The Five-Minute Solution to Planning a Company Picnic

5ive minute consultant™ ## Problem

You own Bill's Gates and Locks, a big-city company that installs gates and security products. Bill's employs 140 people, mostly field service techs and locksmiths. Many come into the office only when they need spare parts. You want to build greater camaraderie by having a company picnic.

Possible Outcomes

- You have a great day! Just about everyone comes with their families, the food is delicious and the weather is perfect. For months following, everyone at work seems happier.

- You have a pretty good day. Unfortunately, at the company softball game, a couple of guys have too much to drink and get into a dust-up over an umpire's call. This puts a damper on the rest of the day.

- You were conservative on the food estimate, and midway in the afternoon you run out of food. Your guests start to leave early.

- Some people gripe about the day chosen as they can't be there.

- You wake up that morning to pouring rain not knowing what to do. At 11 a.m., you cancel, but are responsible for the food and the park rental. Some employees don't get the word and wait at the park for an hour before going home upset.

What Could Bill Have Done Better on the Day of the Picnic?

1. First, three cheers for Bill in setting up the event. A picnic or similar event absolutely builds employee morale. This transfers directly to improved workplace performance. There's no doubt about it.

2. Bill placed a big bet on the weather. Could he have found a place that had open spaces and a roofed pavilion? Yes. It costs more for rental, but is wise planning for a one-day event.

3. If there is a weather problem, make the decision very early in the day. Don't leave people hanging around. Put a message on the company phone, email or twitter for everyone to check. Phone trees are okay, but they never hit 100 percent.

4. In your catering contract, negotiate an opt-out fee based on the amount of time given before the cancellation. One day or one hour before the picnic should have different cancellation fees. You're going to pay for the food, but try not to pay for the staff. Make

arrangements to take the perishable food to a food pantry. Ask the caterer to store the frozen food for your make-up day.

5. Figure on each employee bringing three people. So, 140 employees could mean upward of 560 picnic guests. It is okay to ask employees if they are going to attend and how many people will join them. Make the caterer responsible for the food, and, if they run short, make it their job to get more ASAP.

6. You won't please everyone on the date. Sorry.

7. Alcohol is the biggest problem at a company event. You may have responsibility if someone gets drunk and has an accident on the way home. If the picnic ends at 5 p.m., close the beer taps at 3:30. Some companies give each person two drink tickets, hoping to reduce consumption. Ask those who don't drink not to give tickets to others. Also, it's hard to restrict people from bringing their own booze to a picnic. Have key leaders of your company on the lookout for problems and attempt to solve them quietly.

How Could Bill Have Planned This Better?

1. Start planning next year's picnic the day after this year's. Discuss what went well and what didn't. Try having a theme—maybe a safari, out-west or a country fair. This points you in the right direction for food and decoration. Some companies hold their picnics on a weekday, so employees don't have to give up a weekend, but this will reduce family participation. I favor weekends.

2. There may be limited locations for your picnic; reserve as early as possible. Avoid Memorial Day, July 4 or Labor Day weekends; too many people travel. Set your plans now for a make-up date.

3. Avoid having the picnic at your home, even if you have the land and can save money. Odds are you have a nicer home than most of your employees. This will cause resentment by some people.

4. Avoid amusement parks for company picnics. People wander all over and don't stay together as a group. Parents have to stay with

kids on the rides and may consider this a burden.

5. Mail invitations to each person's home. This brings the family into the planning!

6. Appoint a committee of employees to run the picnic. Don't have too many supervisors in the group. Let the committee meet on company time. Give the committee a realistic budget. Plan on $12-$15 per person for food. Add $10 per person for extras, like t-shirts, hats, volleyball nets and baseballs. Alcohol is additional. If you have a lobster bake or special foods, you can double the food cost. Be sure to have vegetarian fare and appropriate ethnic dishes.

7. The committee should set up volunteers for babysitting, set-up and clean-up, refereeing, prizes and transportation for people without cars. Make plans for handicapped family members as well. Many people feel it is okay to bring pets to outdoor parties. Make this decision up front and state yes or no on the invitations. If yes, be sure to provide water bowls and plastic clean-up bags.

8. If you have employees who live far from the office, set up hotel space so they can join the party. Remember, your goal is to build company goodwill.

9. Supervisors should stay sober and be friendly to everyone. Owners have to look forward to a pie-in-the-face and yet be friendly to everyone. Husbands and wives of leaders do the extra work. If you set up a dunk tank, take a turn in it yourself.

10. Some companies have employees bring potluck dishes as a cost-savings idea and to get people involved. I recommend against this. Make this a party where people don't have to get up early to cook. People who are not good cooks won't attend. Also, do you reimburse people for the food they bought and cooked? This only ends up with confusion. Let employees know what they should bring: blankets for the lawn and sunscreen or towels if there is swimming.

11. Decide on who can attend. Is it the immediate family or can kids bring friends? Single employees should be okay to invite a friend or

significant other. Be tuned in to the cultures of your employees. It may be appropriate to bring parents or grandparents. If you have signs or a printed schedule, print in languages your crew will understand. It is tempting to invite customers; don't do it. It is okay for vendors to sponsor part of the picnic and give them credit, but their sales reps should not be there. For instance, Acme Lock Company can sponsor the soft drinks. Don't let a vendor sponsor the beer.

12. Let the committee decide which games to play; soccer may be more important than softball. Have games like chess and checkers, or horseshoes and croquet, along with the big field games. Have games for all ages. Team games help build employee relationships. Team scavenger hunts are great!

13. Bill's is a 24/7-type company and someone may have to answer a service call. Ask for volunteers to be on standby duty, and make sure they don't drink. If someone goes out, give an extra bonus.

14. Limit speeches to just a few minutes, if at all. The only thing to announce is the "thank you list" of the volunteers. If this is an annual event, announce people with significant company anniversaries. Don't discuss company financial results or business issues. Bill's time is better spent meeting each family than giving a speech.

15. Bill doesn't have to give any special gift like a key chain or pocketknife, although if you have the budget, do it. A typical summer item like a T-shirt works. The single best gift Bill can give is his handshake and smile.

16. Be sure to have a first-aid bag available at all sports events. If it's a hot day, bring extra water and juice drinks.

17. If you are really concerned about weather, contact your insurance broker for information on event insurance. Confirm with the broker that your liability policy will cover the event and find out if you need an alcohol rider.

18. The most successful kids' event is face painting. Hire a local artist to come in for a couple of hours. Don't hold contests for coming in costume; people with money will come out ahead.

Chapter 41

The Five-Minute Solution to Giving a Bad Employee His Review

Problem

You own Miss Julia's Child Care Centers, LLC, a chain of daycare facilities that employs 90 people. You are due to give James, your accounts payable person, his annual review. For a couple of years, James' job performance has gone downhill. He does okay paying the bills, but is a real jerk in dealing with co-workers and vendors. In planning this review, you decide to place James on probation.

Possible Outcomes

- You do a great job speaking with James. Over the next couple of months James becomes a great employee. Your preparation was worth it.

- James disagrees with your assessments, but says he will try your ideas. Two months later he is back to the same old James; you have another meeting and give him 30 days to shape up.

- Before you are finished, James storms out of the review session, goes back to his desk and starts working. You call him back in and give him the 30-day warning.

- James starts shouting at you during the review and you respond by suspending him for three days and placing him on 30-day probation.

- James quits during the review, blaming you for all of his problems. He says he will get even with you.

How Could Julia Handle the Review Session Better?

1. Let's look at Julia's preparation. She reviewed her notes and wrote the sections giving numerical grades in the review form. The most important part of a review is the program to improve the grades; just giving James a grade hasn't improved him previously. Julia needs to write a step-by-step program to encourage and monitor James' performance. Always start out with good comments on James' work. If you can't come up with anything good, it's time to let James go.

2. Don't place James on the defensive. Smile as he comes into your office; your body language sets the tone. If you are nervous and foreboding, he will pick up on it and respond in kind. Julia should not comment on James as a person; she should only speak to specifics about his work and communications at work. Never make it personal!

3. Is James a good employee in the wrong job? If he were in a position that had no interpersonal contact, would he do better? In Julia's company, such a position may not exist, but keep this in mind in your company.

4. Julia should not talk about herself or what she has done in similar situations in her own career. The whole conversation should be about James and his career.

5. Julia should ask James how his year is going. She should let him speak first; he may bring up his problems and ask her for a path to solve them. Most employees who get bad reviews know they have problems and may be trying to solve them. If you help James from this point of view, you are a hero!

6. Specific milestones are needed for James, like going a month without yelling at a co-worker or vendor. Last year, Julia received six complaints from co-workers. This year's goal is zero. There should also be positive goals, like taking more on-time payment discounts.

7. Julia can require James to take steps to improve. Google "anger management course" and dozens of offerings appear. The online courses look good, or there may be a live course in your area. They run from a couple of hundred to a thousand dollars, based on the number of hours in the course. If James is making $50K, spending a thousand or two to retrain him is a smart investment.

8. James may have personal problems and could be taking them out on his coworkers. Speak with your insurance broker to understand the mental health options in your health insurance. It is uncomfortable to suggest an employee should get professional counseling, but, at this point, outside help may be the right approach. Go over your insurance plan's option with James, suggesting that he takes full advantage of the plan.

9. Julia should ask another manager to sit in with her and take notes. Always have a third person in the room when there will be an antagonistic employee meeting.

10. Rehearse prior to a tough meeting. Have another manager play the role of James while you go through the entire review. Ask the stand-in to become aggressive so you practice responding to the outbursts. Never raise your voice during a review. If you end up in court, it may be construed that you egged James on. More importantly, be the big kid, and don't lower yourself to the level of a yeller.

11. When giving 30 days probation, be very specific on the reasons and remedies that James needs to apply. Define the remedies and make them measurable. Also, describe the plan as "up to 30 days" to observe James' improvements. Schedule meetings weekly to update James on where he stands. After ten days, if James has gone downhill even further, he should be fired.

12. When James quits in a huff, escort him from the office. If you have the slightest fear of retribution by James, call the local police and ask them to drive by your home on a regular basis. Make sure everyone at Julia's knows James is not allowed on the premises. Call your bank immediately and change your account passwords.

How Could Julia Have Addressed the Problem of James Better?

1. Julia chickened out on James' previous reviews. This should have been addressed last year, but Julia hides from confrontation. This is common among entrepreneurs; we are constantly trying to please people. If you feel the same way, hire a strong vice president to handle your people and related problems. Everyone has strengths and weaknesses. Know yours and work into them. When you delegate certain responsibilities, be sure to give the authority to go with them.

2. When Julia received the employee complaints she should have addressed the issue. The annual review should be about looking forward, improving James and the company.

3. If James has been a jerk for two years and you just now tell him it

is unacceptable, it will take him time to accept your thoughts and create change. Don't expect change overnight.

4. Three months before this year's review date, reread last year's review. Were there goals established? Are they being met? If not, it is your fault for not following up and motivating the employee. If the goals have been met, start thinking about what's next. You don't have to wait for three months to come with plan B. Do it now, and then review at the scheduled employee review meeting.

5. Many companies use the annual review as a report card on last year. The most successful companies use the review as a tool to motivate employees for next year. Annual reviews of the employee should be staggered throughout the year, usually on the anniversary of employment. Wages should not be a topic at the annual review, but should be a separate discussion based on both the company's and the employee's success, scheduled after the company's fiscal results are known.

6. In the review, Julia placed James on 30-day probation. Now, he passes the 30-day period okay. What happens if he reverts back to yelling? Place him back on probation with a very tight leash. One more incident in six months and he is terminated. His motivation now is to keep his job. If he completes the six months, then start working towards improving other skills.

7. Julia should have talked with different supervisors to get their opinions on how to motivate James going forward. She doesn't need to hear their take on his problems; this she knows.

8. Why all the effort for James? Maybe you should just get rid of his negative impact on the company. But a reformed and improved employee is a great asset. He will be a poster child for the caring atmosphere of Julia's. You may help him solve a personal problem, for which he will be eternally grateful.

9. Writing and giving a bad employee review is one of the toughest things for a business owner. Your first ones will not be easy.

Chapter 42

The Five-Minute Solution to Giving a Good Employee Review

5ive minute consultant **Problem**

You own Muddy's Water Company with 59 employees. Business has been good in the bottled water industry and your employees are happy. Henry has been with you for six years and has risen from a laborer to foreman. His annual review is coming up and you understand Henry is looking for a big raise. You want to give it to him, but you worry about continuing to keep Henry motivated and growing.

Possible Outcomes

- You plan the meeting well, outlining a three-year growth program for Henry. He is excited about your offer for the job growth and potential earnings. You tell Henry he is one of your best employees and are proud that he is on your team. You treat him like a son, and he respects you.

- Henry comes in with a great idea to expand production with low investment. You feel Henry is a great employee and tell him so. Nonetheless, Henry is not happy with your salary offer. You plan a meeting in two weeks to review his salary again.

- The review is okay. Henry is disappointed by the salary you offer and says he's worth more. You give him ideas for the future, but he is not listening and is still thinking about the salary. You are not sure of Henry's feelings at the end of the meeting.

Could Muddy Have Done Better in His Review With Henry?

1. Muddy (his real name is Manny, but his kid brother always called him "Muddy" and the name stuck) needs to carefully plan the future for a great employee like Henry. They don't come along often.

2. Henry has been a great bottling factory employee. It's time to teach him more, letting him meet customers and learn the office. Also, Muddy could offer Henry a tuition reimbursement program. Henry could learn more about mechanical engineering or business. Both are good options. Make the offer, showing your support for Henry and ultimately improving Muddy's.

3. Two weeks is too long to wait for the next meeting. Henry will be nervous and worried about the meeting. So will you. Give yourself time to think about the situation, but don't overanalyze. You know Henry wants to stay with you, so create a program where he will grow, giving him opportunities to earn more. Do this within three or four days and get it behind you.

4. Muddy violated the biggest rule of reviews: Once you mention money, the rest of the conversation is foggy. If you give a good raise, Henry is spending the money in his mind. If you give a raise that Henry doesn't agree with, he is fuming and not listening to your great ideas. If you must do the financial and monetary review together, make money the absolute last part of the meeting.

How Could Muddy Better Handle Employee Reviews?

1. It is extremely important to separate the financial and employee reviews. Have the employee review on the anniversary of employment and the financial review 30 to 60 days after the end of your fiscal year. If you give Henry a great review, he'll expect a great raise right away. If you give a weak review, he will say it is because you're offering a small raise. Separate the two reviews! How can you set raises until you know the general health of the company? Henry's raise should be 60 percent based on personal work and 40 percent based on Muddy's financial results.

2. Everyone loves praise. Be generous with yours. Discuss two or three incidents of Henry's good work throughout the year, not just in the last month. Focus this in the direction of where you want Henry to grow. For instance, if you want Henry to be a mentor, praise a time that he helped others at Muddy's.

3. Have Henry mentor weaker employees in his areas of strengths. Give Henry help learning to be a teacher. Check with your local colleges about courses in education or teaching English as a second language. Create time in his schedule to do mentoring; don't overload this on top of his regular workload.

4. Even a great employee like Henry can do better in some areas. You don't want to ever say an employee can't do better; everyone can. If you give Henry a four out of five, lay out the steps Henry can take to bring his grade up!

5. You are going to give Henry a good raise. You don't want to offer a percentage of profits or sales, but you can tie a bonus to specifics under Henry's control. Try an incentive for reducing employee turnover, reducing workers' comp claims and reportable accidents, or a reduction in waste. Instead of giving Henry more money, you are letting him earn it. He will feel better about it!

6. You are doing a lot of preparation, but it can go out the window when you ask Henry what his goals are. Not everyone wants more dollars every year; he may want extra days off instead of a raise. Be prepared to adjust your thoughts. Listen to Henry's ideas and work to satisfy his as well as your needs. At the review's end, ask Henry for feedback. Don't let him leave the room upset or confused. Make sure he understands the program you created to help him improve and get his buy-in right there. If he is not sure, meet again in a couple of days. Let him discuss your ideas with family or a friend.

7. Structure Henry's review as a teaching tool. As he grows, Henry will write and give employee reviews. Explain why you have written certain things, and not others. In one section of his review, tell how he did a poor job on something, and then do the same section again, using a positive tone—about how he could have improved the situation. Let him feel the two approaches and help him understand his feelings in both paths.

8. Look to non-cash incentives as well. Can you give Henry a company car? This is a lot better than an equivalent raise. You both save on taxes.

9. Many owners and managers put off employee reviews of their good employees and instead focus on the problem people. This is a major mistake. Muddy didn't fall into this trap, but many do. It is the good employees who keep the business running. While you have to do all the reviews, giving your time and input to the stars is more valuable than worrying about the weaker employees.

Let's go over some employee review tips, for all employees:

- **Set a firm schedule for the review meeting and keep to it.** Make sure you are in a room that is sound-proof. Don't allow any interruptions; turn off your phone.

- **Set clear targets and goals for all employees.** Confirm with each person that he understands the goals, the rewards for reaching them, and the possible consequences for not reaching.

- **Review your goals for each employee quarterly.** If he is on track, give praise. If not, give advice and help.

- **There should be no surprises in a review.** If an employee is doing poorly, you should discuss this during the year and start an improvement plan ASAP.

- **The employee should fill out the same form as you.** Compare your forms and discuss the differences. Start your work at least a month before the review, and discuss the review with another manager. Give the employee a month as well. If the employee does write out a growth plan, try to use that one. The employee already has buy-in!

- **Perception trumps reality, unfortunately.** The quiet guy in the corner, doing the job, is better than the friendly person who doesn't get the job done. Recognize this.

- **Spend the bulk of your review planning time on next year.** Last year is done. Stress improvement going forward, not rehashing the problems of yesterday.

- **You may have disagreements with the employee on the review.** This is okay. Let the employee make his case. There is nothing wrong with you changing a grade or acknowledging his point. In the long run, you are the boss, but keep an open mind.

- **The review should run 30 to 45 minutes.** As you rehearse, keep this in mind. If you have more than that to cover, schedule a second meeting.

- **Many employees are nervous in reviews.** Make the room comfortable. Don't sit behind your desk; sit as equals. Keep the room temperature cool.

- **Let the employee talk!** This is an old trite (but very true) statement: You have two ears and one mouth, so you should listen twice as much as you talk.

Chapter 43

The Five-Minute Solution to Managing a Seasonal Business

Problem

You Own Deb's Levee, a marina and boating supply business. Weather dictates that you are only open nine months a year. Your employee turnover is 60 percent, as most people want full-time work. How can Deb grow the business while so much time is spent on training her new staff each year?

Possible Outcomes

- Deb finds workers who like to ski in the winter. Her problems are solved!

- Deb hires a full-time training person so her spring can be spent growing the business. The trainer does a great job, and the turnover drops to 40 percent.

- Deb tries paying salaries over twelve months. Only a few take this option; most want their full pay so they can travel during the off-season.

- Deb has always been perplexed on the issue of giving seasonal employee health benefits. Would it be a year-round cost? Would the cost offset her costs in rehiring and training?

- Deb keeps things as they are, rehiring each spring, and enjoys a comfortable living.

What Can Deb Do This Spring to Help Hire Long-Term Employees?

1. According to the Department of Labor, Bureau of Labor Statistics, in 2010, 35.7 percent of the non-farm U.S workforce changed jobs, the lowest number in 10 years. In 2005, 46.5 percent changed jobs, totaling more than 62 million job changes. All-in-all, Deb's numbers are not bad considering her seasonality.

2. Deb can search out companies that need a work force opposite of hers, and create a workforce alliance. Where? Companies that service heating systems and retailers that are busy during the holidays, snow plowing, ski areas and winter sports retailers are candidates. UPS and FedEx hire huge numbers of people around the holidays. She can promote these businesses to her employees and vice-versa.

3. Every state has an unemployment office. Deb should go there in January, anticipating her March hiring needs. Many employers think people who get jobs from the unemployment office are at the bottom of the barrel. Nothing could be farther from the truth! A good

job hunter will access all means of getting a job. Deb can speak to a job counselor, who will help her write advertising and give advice on current employment trends. During the current economic slow-down, the federal government and many states are offering tax incentives to hire through unemployment offices. These savings could help her pay a good employee the extra three months!

4, Deb should ask the seasonal people who have stayed with her year-to-year to bring their friends in for interviews, offering an incentive—maybe $25 for each interview and $500 for each person hired who works through the season. The new hires will have a mentor and will know the company before they start working. This will reduce turnover.

5. Are there customers who love boating so much they would work at the Levee? People who put their boats in the water the first day and are the last ones out are candidates. Customers are also great sources to create word-of-mouth interest in Deb's. There is no need to give them an incentive; they want Deb's to operate smoothly so their boating time is perfect.

6. Deb's busiest time is when school is out. Teachers make great employees; they are eager to learn, teach others easily and work well with people of all ages. Even though teachers are only available for about two months, this fits Deb's peak demand. Contact the local school department or the teacher's union for referrals.

What Can Deb Change in Her Business Model to Attract Employees?

1. Deb should look at starting another business whose operation would nest well with the Levee. Deb could create a new part of her supply business as a winter sports outlet. This would allow her to hire people for year-round employment. It would use her facilities to their fullest advantage, twelve months a year. She already has the infrastructure. What's needed is a good manager who knows

the winter sports business and is willing to work for a start-up. Deb will supply needed capital for inventory, initial promotion and advertising. After all, is there really much difference between water skiing and snow skiing?

2. Her crew has experience in fixing boat motors. Fixing snowmobile motors fits in. How about anything else with small engines? She could have people drop off their lawn mowers for winter storage and tune-ups. This would require very little investment on Deb's part and she can keep her mechanics working all year.

3. In our economy, benefits are as important as wages. At the low end of the wage scale, benefits are more important. Under the Affordable Care Act, Deb is going to be offering some sort of medical insurance to her employees. Her costs will go up, but hopefully, she will get better employees, whose productivity and retention will save her more than the insurance costs. During the winter the employees could pay the full cost of the insurance or go on COBRA. She needs to work out numbers with her insurance broker.

4. Job sharing would work in Deb's company. She could hire two people for the same job, letting them coordinate who works when. Giving more flexibility would attract certain people who can only work part-time, but have a full-time work ethic. Job sharing requires more communications, employee cooperation and some extra bookkeeping. This is not hard to do.

5. U.S. military vets are fantastic employees. Contact your local state veteran's office to set up a job fair. They also have regional job fairs that you can attend with other employers, where Deb can find another employer that complements her needs. Current vets may only want part-time or limited-length work as they readjust to civilian life—just perfect for Deb. Vets have great work ethics, leadership skills and are all team players.

6. Deb can expand her job search reach by using Facebook, Craig's

List or Monster, or her own website. The "help wanted" section in the daily paper is just one part of today's formula for hiring.

7. Deb might want to look at opening another marina in a more southerly direction that has year-round boating weather. There is risk and more capital is needed. This is an expensive option. The object, though, is to think of every idea, and then eliminate the ones that don't fit.

8. Working with seasonal and part-time workers has many advantages, and Deb should factor these into her considerations:

   a. Lower hourly and benefits cost per worker;

   b. In some states, lower unemployment insurance costs; and

   c. Fresh employees with energy coming on board each year.

   Even though Deb thinks she might be better off with more permanent employees, there is a greater cost.

9. Here is a great website with tons of information about unemployment insurance costs in each state: http://www.ows.doleta.gov/unemploy/uifactsheet.asp

10. Spending the money on a good employee training program is probably the best option for Deb. She has to remember her goal is not to change her employees, but to have time to manage her growth.

Chapter 44

The Five-Minute Solution to Raising Prices in a Retail Store

 ## Problem

You own Brad's Bar-B-Que Pit, a retailer with four stores selling outdoor furniture, grills, special sauces and party supplies. Your accountant, Stan, just gave you last quarter's financials, and you dropped from being profitable to a losing year. Stan says your expenses are well controlled, but margins are thin. He recommends raising prices.

Possible Outcomes

- You do an across-the-board price increase of five percent and don't receive any negative feedback. Good for you, Brad.

- You go for selective price increases and charge more for some items, but hold prices on the everyday purchases like the sauces and party supplies. This seems to work well.

- You raise prices and your biggest competitor starts an ad campaign touting low pricing on patio furniture. Your products are higher quality than his, but in the current economy it seems that low price trumps good quality.

- You raise prices and sales go down across the board. You are right back where you started, losing money.

What to Do When Stan Tells You About the Decreased Margins

1. This is not a problem to solve in one day. You have to raise prices, but take time to look at your competition, customers, vendor costs and overhead. Unless you are going down the tubes fast, take the time to create a pricing program that works for your clientele. Don't have a knee-jerk reaction and raise prices by five percent on everything. Pricing strategy isn't that simple. Talk with your customers and ask how they feel about the prices of your products. Why do they come to Brad's? This information will help you decide which areas have price flexibility.

2. You never want customers to have a reason to shop around. Don't do a flyer or ad announcing "Price Increases—Buy Now!" You're not big enough to dominate the market, so your competitors may not follow your lead, but they will promote their prices at your expense given the chance.

3. Have you squeezed your vendors hard enough? This is the time that you ask for special pricing for the rest of the season. Other-

wise, you have to go shopping—the same thing you don't want your customers to do!

4. Have a friend visit your competitors with a shopping list and buy a whole party's worth of goods. Check the prices yourself from the cash register receipts. You'll often hear about a one-day sale down the street and then lower your prices for your every day products. The goal here is to see where you can raise prices and still be in line. If a competitor is under-selling you on a staple product, go to the vendor and demand the same costing as your competitor. Amazingly, you can get a better price by asking for it. Be assertive!

5. Reduce your high-maintenance items such as those with a high return rate or items that have poor packaging where you get ten percent breakage. Keeping your overhead down reduces pricing pressure.

6. Don't confuse cash flow with profit. You may be selling inventory that you bought last quarter, so the cash registers look good. Listen to Stan. Cash flow is today … profit tells you what will happen tomorrow.

7. Raising prices is risky, but far less risky than losing money.

Let's Look at Various Pricing Strategies That Will Help Brad's

1. Your pricing strategy is just as important as your advertising or store layout strategy. It has to be consistent and easy to understand.

2. It is tough to be the lowest priced retailer. The companies buying multiple truckloads of barbecue sauce will get lower pricing than you. They also have automated warehousing, which reduces their costs. Don't try to compete with them. You will lose.

3. You can, though, sell in larger quantities. If you sell sauce at $1.99, sell three for $5.75. If your store layout allows, set up a case section where you sell full cases of sauce and other basic products. This lowers your handling costs, which allows you to sell lower and still make money!

4. By now, you know you need to raise prices. Avoid across-the-board increases. It takes effort to focus on items and brands, but it's important to know the overhead on each type of item. Which items take up more floor and warehouse space? Which have more returns? These require higher margins.

5. Raising prices takes time. Raise the price on an item, and send out a coupon covering the increase, valid for one month. This gets people used to seeing the higher price before they begin paying it. If you do an across-the-board increase, give out a five-percent discount coupon on all orders totaling more than $100, driving people to make larger purchases. When you send this coupon mailing, don't announce the price increase.

6. In Brad's industry, he should raise prices about three months before seasonal demands begin.

7. Do you have store-brand items? Customers can't price-shop these. You don't have to set store-brands lower. In fact, they can be higher, due to your high-quality ingredients or your superior quality control. Most consumers identify low prices with lesser value. (Think Mercedes and Chevrolet.) What is your store image? Are you closer to a dollar store or high-end?

8. When Brad raises prices, he can experiment. Since he has four stores, he can raise the prices in one store and measure the results. The commodity items, such as sauce or charcoal, will always carry lower margins. Brad can raise pricing more easily on gift-type items, which show less price resistance.

9. Brad can create affinity group price specials. As he raises pricing, he can distribute coupon plans to local churches, military organizations, unions, teachers or just about any group in his area. This allows higher public pricing, but can bring a dedicated core group of shoppers. Giving a donation back to a non-profit group that comes in on a special night is a great way to gain customers at every pricing level.

10. Take your top ten items and ten mid-level items and raise the

prices. Follow them for three weeks and check the sales results. You will see where price changes have had an impact. Maybe you will roll back one or more items, but you will see which types of items hold up at higher prices.

11. Work to make your store a destination shopping event, rather than a commodity store. Brighten up your displays, give samples, and make sure your on-floor salespeople are the best. With these changes, pricing becomes less important as a decision point.

12. Try different pricing points for mail order or on the Internet. Set up quantity price breaks for these shopping channels. Most people who shop on the Internet look for ways to cover shipping charges, and getting two or more items for the same shipping charge is a winner. Internet shoppers are much more price-conscious than in-store shoppers.

13. Why do big retailers place impulse items on the corners of aisles and near registers? Because people pick them up without looking at the price. Do the same thing for your shops. Also, even though it looks corny, always price at $5.99 or $5.97 rather than $6. You would think that every consumer would see through this trick, but it still works.

14. Experiment with the packaging size of products you sell. Ten years ago, coffee was sold in one-pound cans. Now the cans are 13 ounces at roughly the same price. Customers look more at price than size, and have not felt the increase created by the decrease.

15. Generate buzz about your store, using publicity, Twitter and Facebook. Customers coming in through these social media outlets will not be as price-sensitive as those who look for pennies. Make a charitable donation of your new private-label brands to a local food pantry or shelter and get positive press attention.

16. Remember it is tougher to raise prices than lower them. Put the time and effort together to raise prices that will impact your bottom line positively.

Chapter 45

The Five-Minute Solution to Handling a Work-Related Death

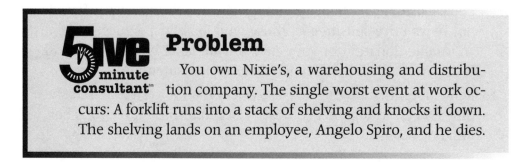

Problem

You own Nixie's, a warehousing and distribution company. The single worst event at work occurs: A forklift runs into a stack of shelving and knocks it down. The shelving lands on an employee, Angelo Spiro, and he dies.

Possible Outcomes

- There are no good outcomes. The only way to go is from bad to worse. A death at work, like anywhere, is awful.

- OSHA, both federal and state, starts an investigation within hours. You had good record-keeping and a solid safety record. Nonetheless, they shut you down for a couple of days. Morale at Nixie's becomes non-existent. You wind up with a heavy fine, lose 10 percent of your customers, and don't sleep well for a year.

- Your insurance company investigates and discovers the forklift driver has two previous DUIs on his record. A blood alcohol test of the driver, done an hour after the accident, fortunately, is clean. Your insurance company cancels your policy anyway, though, because you were required to vet all drivers with them prior to hiring. OSHA discovers that the brakes on your forklift didn't work properly. The maintenance logs show you knew about this, but told the mechanic to hold off on fixing it until next month. Your fine will now jump up to about a million.

- You get arrested for accessory to manslaughter when it's discovered that you bought a couple of beers for the forklift driver at lunch (and all of the above occurs as well).

What Do You Do Immediately After the Accident?

1. Call the fire department or an ambulance. Make sure every phone in the building can dial out for a 911 call. Clear the debris and get to Angelo as quickly as you can. Have your first aid kit ready; clear out all unnecessary people.

2. As soon as the professional first-responders arrive, they are in charge. Do exactly what they tell you to do. Cooperate fully with no questions asked.

3. Talk with the local police to decide who is going to notify Angelo's family. If it is you, do so promptly. Don't let another employee call

them, or worse yet, a news organization broadcast the details.

4. As the situation stabilizes, call the following people: your insurance broker; your lawyer; the union business agent, if you are unionized; your business partners; your key managers; and your family—you won't be home for dinner.

5. Don't try to cover up anything at this point. It is too late. I promise you that the OSHA investigators are smarter at uncovering problems than you are at trying to hide them. This will only backfire on you in a big way. OSHA will take a couple of hours to get there. Speak with your attorney to get direction about speaking with OSHA.

6. Assign one person to speak with the media. Make it clear this person is the only official representative to speak on the record. You can't prohibit others from talking, but you can strongly encourage all of your employees to speak only with OSHA investigators, your attorney and insurance investigators.

7. You may want to hire a grief counselor to visit with all of your employees, in small group meetings, or individually. I recommend this to help Nixie's move forward. This website, http://www.therapytribe.com/therapy/Loss_Grief_Counseling.html, is one source to find a local grief counseling service.

8. Have your sales manager make calls to your key customers and explain the situation to them. She should be honest about what happened and should stress that Nixie's service will not be impacted.

9. Have your CFO or accountant explain your benefits package to Angelo's family. If you have a life insurance component, get the paperwork started for the family. Give the okay to advance the funeral costs to the family, up to a preset amount, usually around $5,000.

10. Don't admit blame to anyone at this point. Be very consoling to the family and to your coworkers but don't, under any circum-

stances, speak about the accident details to any outsiders. Stress this same thought to every corporate officer and manager.

How Can You Prevent This Horrible Tragedy at Nixie's?

1. First, accept the fact that all fatalities and accidents are preventable. If you believe that "accidents happen" and don't want to take action to prevent them, please drop me a note with information about your company. I want to open up a company that competes with yours as you won't be in business long.

2. Preventing accidents is good business. It reduces workers' compensation insurance. It keeps employees happy and keeps productivity up. It saves you untold grief and complications. Your first stop is your liability and workers' comp insurance carriers. Contact each one's loss control team and ask for an assessment of your plant. It should be a no-charge part of your coverage. Next, do what they tell you to do. Yes, it is an expense now, but it is better than an injury or a death. You might not do everything they suggest immediately; take a couple of months and implement slowly. But, don't take two years either.

3. Set a culture of safety at Nixie's. It starts with you. Don't look the other way when you see a safety rule being ignored. Wear your own hard-hat wherever required. You should always use your safety glasses in a work zone. Don't quibble over costs of safety. Don't go half-way. It sends the wrong message.

4. Next, stress safety when hiring. Do drug and alcohol testing before confirming employment. (*See Chapter 20.*) When checking references, ask about the applicant's safety record. Begin safety training on the first day of work.

5. Empower your managers and employees to be pro-active on safety. Take yourself out of the loop except for setting the annual budget. Give someone the responsibility to make Nixie's safer, and then let

him or her do it. If an employee breaks a safety rule and gets suspended, don't override your own supervisors, saying, "Come on guys, let him work, it was only a small rule." (I have made this mistake, and looking back, it sure was stupid on my part!)

6. Safety practices will change your business. What used to take four minutes may now take five. Go with it. It seems silly to put a lock-out tag on machinery when you only take two minutes to replace a filter. Placing this safety tag for even small projects gets everyone at Nixie's in the habit and that is what is important.

7. There should be ten-minute monthly safety meetings with all employees. Have a predetermined agenda for managers on all shifts and departments. There are great programs on-line at the National Institute of Safety and Health, www.cdc.gov/niosh, and at www.osha.gov. Don't be afraid to contact these agencies for information and ideas. They are there to help you. Yes, they can bite you in the tail if you screw up, but their primary goal is to help you prevent injuries and deaths.

8. Look at jobs that you take at Nixie's. Sometimes a customer comes to you with a tough project because it is inherently unsafe. Be careful. Sure, you can charge more for the risk, but you rarely make more than the risk is worth. Have your safety manager look at the project and estimate what it will take to change your process to do this job safely. If you get the job with this add-on in place and you change your process to make it safe, then good for you.

9. Make sure your safety records are updated continuously. You will detect your own injury patterns and can work to prevent them. Don't wait for an inspector to point out that you have had three truck accidents where the driver was not wearing a seatbelt. Learn to treat some events as local first-aid situations rather than sending someone to the emergency room. This will reduce insurance costs.

10. Create an in-house investigative committee and completely empower the committee to do its job. There should be an accident

report after every accident or near-accident. The report should find what caused the accident and how it will be prevented in the future.

11. Creating a safe environment starts with housekeeping. Keep your place eat-off-the-floor clean. This creates an attitude of reducing waste and caring for your products. Get rid of half-filled, unmarked chemical containers. The big pile of junk in the corner that you might use someday will be a fire hazard (or a trip hazard) before it actually will be used.

12. Train all employees on every chemical you use. Besides being the law, it makes sense. People will get the job done more quickly using the right product the first time.

13. Specify first-responders within your own company. Have a trained first-aid person on every shift; go to www.redcross.org/en/takea-class for info from the Red Cross. Have first aid kits, eye wash stations and a defibrillator available for easy use.

14. There are actions for every industry and company. The common theme is that it starts at the top. If you want a safe environment, you will benefit from it. If you don't care about the safety of your employees, it will hurt you.

Chapter 46

The Five-Minute Solution to the Law of Unintended Consequences

Problem

You own Richard's Bacon and Pork Stores, a chain of nine stores that sells meat, groceries and food specialties. Times have been good and you are planning an expansion to include pre-made dinners and catering. You sign new leases, buy equipment and hire chefs. Suddenly, though, the bacon grease hits the fan.

Possible Outcomes

- The economy tanked just as you were expanding. Same-store sales fell nine percent last month after you invested in upgrades. You didn't plan on national economic problems to impact your chain. You didn't respect the law of unintended consequences.

- The chefs have to start three hours earlier than your regular staff, and also stay later cleaning the ovens and kitchens to keep sanitary standards. Payroll is 20 percent higher than budget. You didn't pay homage to The Law.

- Your insurance costs go up 45 percent because of the ovens, sharp knives, increased hours and more footage under roof. Remember, The Law is The Law.

- You thought you were adding more choices for your customers. It turns out your customers loved to cook and didn't take to the prepared meals. You have to find a whole new group of customers who buy prepared foods. You fought The Law and The Law won.

What is the Law of Unintended Consequences Anyway?

It was first clearly defined by Robert K. Merton in 1936. There are three broad types:

1. Good consequences—also called a windfall! You buy a car, decide to leave it in the garage because of the high price of gas, and when you finally decide to sell it, it is a valuable antique and you make a fortune.

2. Neutral consequences—you invent email and the world is a better place; then along come computer viruses buried in spam mail. One thing good and one thing bad, you break even.

3. Bad consequences—more cars and power plants help economies grow, but the 95 percent of us who acknowledge science know that global warming is a worse outcome. (And for the 5 percent of you

who deny it, take your heads out of the sand!)

Another definition of The Law is: a simple plan goes haywire in a complex environment.

We are going to talk about definition number three and how it affects businesses like Richard's Bacon ... and yours!

How Could Richard (or You) Work With and Respect "The Law?"

Huh? If all the geniuses at the BIG corporations and the government economists can't beat The Law; then how can I?

Actually it is easy.

1. First, acknowledge that The Law is real. It is even stronger than Murphy's Law. The Law covers every action you will take as a business owner.

2. Plan on it happening, and work to gain all of the good consequences and few of the bad. In other words, plan for the worst and hope for the best. (This is an old phrase ...I don't know who created it, but I didn't ... I am planning for the copyright infringement letter I will get.)

3. The next step might be to think of every possible scenario, have a plan to address each, and waste so much time planning that you never do anything. Remember you are in business to add value to a product or provide a service and then sell this to customers! Respect The Law, but it is not the most important law in Richard's business. The Law of Economics stating Richard must make a profit to survive still trumps The Law of Unintended Consequences.

4. Richard should stay abreast of local, regional and national economic news. A few good, free websites are available; these include Bloomberg.com, money.cnn.com, and my favorite for iPhone/iPad users, Zite.com, where you can create your own news magazine. I use this daily to keep updated with my areas of interest. Your trade publications and/or association always will have a good industry

outlook. Check with your key vendors as to how they feel the business will be in the coming 12 months. Travel to another city and scope out similar stores listed in the Yellow Pages. Learn from them by observing where they place their emphasis.

5. Start small. Try a new idea in part of your business, and then expand as success sets in. Set up stop signs in your project. Set your goals and define points where you pull the plug, where you hold steady and where you add more dollars and efforts to increase the project. You don't have to necessarily wait for a stop sign date either. If the project starts out like gangbusters, you may move up more implementation, or may pull the plug early if you see problems. But, at the stop sign presets, do your serious review of the project. It's good to have a second opinion from someone you respect. You may be so caught up in the project that you can't see the forest for the trees.

6. Is this decision a "bet-the-company" situation? Spend plenty of time studying the strategy. If Richard had redone one store he wouldn't be in trouble. Decide if the worst possible results will sink your company. If so, unless you are the ultimate gambler, don't do it. Some bet the company decisions create huge, successful results, but many don't.

7. Don't know who to turn to for advice? Try a local college for a professor of business; go to score.org, a free resource of retired business people; your local banker may suggest a local, successful business person who can become a mentor. And, of course, any consultant whose last name starts with the letter "B" surely is a great source of help.

8. If you hire a new person and that person doesn't work out, it's probably not a big deal at Richard's. But, if you are a three-person company, it is a big deal. Check references carefully when hiring where it will have a big impact. This doesn't mean Richard shouldn't check all applicants; just that the impacts are different for different employee levels.

9. Your business is along a river that has never flooded. Your insurance broker reminds you to carry federal flood insurance. You ignore the warnings about a hurricane coming up the coast. While you are swimming away from your front door, you realize that the small investment would have been worth it. Remember to look out for the worst possible consequence of an action and prepare for it.

10. Richard brings a new line of imported hams into his store. They sell great. Three months later the importer gets shut down by the Food and Drug Administration for rats in its warehouse, and Richard runs out of product and customers go to his competitor. He calls his old supplier, and they laugh at him. Richard would have been wise to carry both suppliers. It costs a little more in inventory, but a small investment here would prevent a major problem!

11. When The Law smiles at you, say thank you, make a donation to your favorite charity and move forward. But always be prepared for the tumult that will come if you don't respect The Law.

Chapter 47

The Five-Minute Solution to the Flu Virus That Stops Production

Problem

You are the owner of Fred A's Stair Company. You build custom staircases for residential and commercial use, both decorative and simple fire escapes. Your busy season is the fall. Fred A's employs 45 people, 30 in manufacturing, and the balance in sales, engineering and admin. Last week, there was a flu virus floating around and ten people in manufacturing called in sick. Also, two people were scheduled for vacation.

Possible Outcomes

- Your company continues without missing a beat. You realize you are over-employed and could save quite a bit of payroll.

- Your output falls by 50 percent and you fall behind on every job, spend a ton on overtime, and feel like beating your head against the wall. You can't afford to hire extra people, just on the off chance you need them for fill-ins. Contractors are calling for delivery every day.

- You bring in some temporary workers, but they don't have the skills to work on the decorative stairs but do help with the steel fire escapes. Unfortunately, it is the decorative stairs that make you the most money.

- You dust off the cross-training program presentation you heard at an industry trade show and vow to start implementing it January 1.

What Should Fred Have Done When His Employees Called In Sick?

1. Prioritize what work will get done. Call the customers whose work won't be on time. Let them know why and what you are doing to get the work caught up. When Fred calls six customers, four are okay with it. He tries to jam the other two into the schedule. This is the time that Fred should remember who pays bills late, who back-charges the most, and who always cooperates. Fred decides to take care of his cooperative customers. Good for you, Fred.

2. Is it too late to get flu shots for the whole company? Fred calls his doctor and is told, "Forget it." He buys gallons of chicken soup.

3. Checking with the available supervisors on which employees can jump to other jobs, he focuses everyone's attention on the correct projects.

4. Should Fred ask the sick employees to come back before they are completely healthy? If they are 75 percent capable, isn't that better

than nothing? But, wait, what if they infect more people? Fred can't take that chance.

5. So, there is not much Fred can do. His only course of action is to better prepare for this. And that preparation is cross-training throughout the whole company.

Here is a Cross-Training Program for Fred (and for Any Business)!

1. You have read this before … it starts with Fred. He has to commit to a cross-training program, understanding the costs and not waiver from supporting it. Unless you are a one-person company, cross-training should be on your agenda.

2. The next hurdle you will face is getting the folks who have been there for a while on-board. They will see this as giving away their special skills to younger people who make less money. They will assume you are trying to cut costs, when in fact, it is the opposite; you are going to spend more money on training!

3. So, start with these "old-timers." Explain the program and ask each one which job they would like to learn as an understudy. They will begin to realize you are serious when they earn overtime to work on a different production line. You will want to train most of the workers on regular time, but for this first crew, spend the bucks. For how long? Since these are experienced folks, between 40 and 60 hours, spread over two months, should do. In effect, senior people will be teaching each other, so the overtime is actually doubled, once for the teacher and once for the student. Believe me, this is worth the cost.

4. Get a bi-weekly, short report from the teacher and the student assessing how the training is going. You will want to set up training for the senior person on how to be a mentor/teacher. Not sure how to do this? Check your local community college for a mentoring course, or call your local office of SCORE. (The Service Corp of Retired Executives) Schedule a half-hour review with both people

half-way through the program, seeing what needs to change and what else is needed to help the program succeed.

5. Ask the senior people who they would like to train as their fill-ins. This makes it personal to them and will improve the success rate of the teaching greatly. They will understand this training will make their jobs easier when another employee shortage occurs.

6. Next, you have more junior people starting training, and they will be eager to learn new skills. Schedule a half-day per week of learning for three or four people. This should not cripple your schedule. It may take a year for Fred to train his whole staff; that's okay. When someone finishes his training, he is more valuable to himself and to Fred. Is it worth a .25 per hour raise? You bet it is. Have a small ceremony when a person graduates from his training, give a certificate and the raise. If you are uncomfortable with the raise, then give a gift card that can be used with a local merchant.

7. Now that people are trained, have them switch into their new jobs for a day or two every quarter to keep their skills sharp. When vacations are scheduled, make sure the student's schedule allows for stepping up. Does the student make a higher wage for the week at a different job? Yes, if the other job carries a standardized higher wage. If there is no discernible wage difference, then a small gift card at the end of the week is a great way to say thank you.

8. You will begin to recognize the folks at your company who want to learn more and grow with you. These are the ones to help you start a new production line or to send to night school for management training. Cross-training takes away the "my-job-is-a-dead-end" approach. Cross-trained folks will stay with you longer, cutting your turnover.

9. Some positions have a built-in second-in-command. There are two options here:

    a. The designated second goes to a different department to learn a new skill area; or,

b. The senior manager lets the second-in-command absolutely take over for a couple of days per quarter, letting him/her get the full feel of being in charge.

10. R-E-S-P-E-C-T ... a great song, and even more important in the shop at Fred A's. When someone works in another's job, he will realize it is just as hard as his own and mutual respect will flourish. No one will be upset thinking everyone else has an easier job.

11. What about the office? If your phones are not answered, you are as out of business as if the paint line out back is understaffed. The key areas in all offices are: payroll, accounts payable and receivable, and the big one—computer operations. It might be hard to cross-train in computers. You should have a backup company or an outside consultant available to step in when needed.

12. How about for you? Do you have a back-up person? You could get the flu, or you might even want to take a vacation. You should appoint a definitive number-two person who takes charge when you are not around. A lot of entrepreneurs don't like to do this as it sets a hierarchy and the people not picked might want to look for another job, thinking they are not going to grow. It is a tough position; nonetheless, sometimes life isn't under your control, and if you break your leg, you'll need that number-two well trained.

13. By the way, look at your vendors. Are they well cross-trained and able to supply your needs? If they are, ask if you can study their programs before you start yours. If they are not, look for another vendor.

14. A successful business will have a culture of job-switching about every five years. It prevents boredom and helps retain people. It is completely worth the investment.

15. You will train some people who will shop their new skills in the employment market. Yes, you will lose a few after their advanced training. Don't fret it; don't let this derail your program. The gains you earn cannot be measured.

Chapter 48

The Five-Minute Solution to Starting a Flexible Spending Account

Problem

You own David's Butler Service, a residential cleaning service. You have 25 part-time and 18 full-time cleaners and staff. You want to give additional benefits, but frankly, you don't have enough profit this year to increase benefits. What can you do, at little or no cost, which will hit a home run with your employees?

5ive minute consultant™

Possible Solutions

- You decide to give employees one extra Friday afternoon off with pay. Your nomination for the boss-of-the-year gets lost in the mail.

- You offer to reimburse employees for 30 percent of their gym memberships. Since most of your employees physically work hard all day, they don't need a gym. Someone places a dumbbell with your picture on it in the front window of your office.

- You introduce a plan of giving each family four tickets to a New York Mets game. Seven New York Yankee fans and four Boston Red Sox fans threaten to quit if they have to go.

- Finally you come up with it: You discover Flexible Spending Accounts and think this is the greatest idea you've ever heard of.

What is a Flexible Spending Account?

1. A medical Flexible Spending Account (FSA) plan is a tax-advantaged plan that allows employees to use pre-tax dollars for healthcare expenses, dental and vision costs, prescription medications, medical equipment and more with a $2,500 maximum benefit per year.

2. A dependent FSA can be used for child or adult care necessary to allow you or your spouse to work or attend school full-time. This plan has a $5,000 maximum benefit for a jointly filed tax return, or $2,500 for a single return.

3. A transportation FSA is used primarily for mass transit or van pooling expenses. It can be also used for parking at your primary worksite or to park where you get transportation to work, such as at a bus or train station. There is a yearly maximum of $2,760.

4. How does this work? Dave's employees contribute pre-tax dollars to a fund set-up by Dave's company and administered by a professional FSA company. This is usually done by regular, equal

payroll deductions. Here's how it works for a Dave's employee making $50,000 per year:

	Without FSA	With FSA
Gross Income	$50,000	$50,000
Deduct FSA Contribution	0	2,500
Taxable Income	50,000	47,500
Less: 20% Income Tax & 7.65% FICA	13,825	13,134
Take Home	36,175	34,366
FSA Funds Available to Spend	0	2,500
Total	36,175	36,866
Dave's Employee Saves	0	691

5. Each employee just came out ahead by $691. Very little hassle, very easy for Dave. If the employee had signed up for dependent or transportation programs, he would save even more.

6. This is one of the best gifts our government has ever given us. And "us" includes Dave. Dave is going to incur a thousand or two in startup costs and probably a $5 to $10 per month/per employee cost. But (and this is a BIG but) Dave is going to save on his share of the FICA taxes as well. Here's how:

   a. Let's guess that Dave will get 15 part-timers to sign up at $1,000 each and 12 full-timers at $2,000. This comes to $49,000 in wages deferred.

   b. Dave now saves his share of FICA at 7.65 percent, which is $3,748.50 per year. This more than covers his upfront and ongoing costs. He can save more by getting more employees involved.

7. So, the employees and the company win, both supported by Uncle Sam.

How Can Dave Implement This Program Successfully?

1. There are definite pluses and minuses from both the employee and Dave's point of view. Dave needs to understand both so he can emphasize the positives and overcome the negatives.

2. The employee pluses:

   a. Employees save real dollars now;

   b. An employee commits $150 per month. In February, she needs dental work costing over $800. She will get totally reimbursed for this from the plan even though she has only contributed $300 so far;

   c. If an employee takes full advantage of all three plans he can get tax preferences of:

      • Medical - $2,500;

      • Dependent Care - 5,000

      • Transportation - 2,760; and

   d. Total eligible - $10,260.

3. The employee minuses:

   a. Employees have to spend their full amount each year—"use it or lose it." Dave has to explain this clearly, encouraging employees to look at their needs carefully. In the first year Dave should encourage employees to be cautious in their deferral amounts. An employee who doesn't spend all of her money will be upset at Dave, not at Congress where the rules were written;

   b. As November comes into view, each employee should look at his account balance and see what he has left to spend. Dave can search for a plan that gives employees up to 60 days after the year's end to submit claims or he can go with a plan that ends December 31, without the extended-time option;

c. There may be some bookkeeping and paperwork on the employees' part. Dave can select a plan that gives an employee a debit card, which can be used as cash, up to the amount the employee has scheduled to defer. Or he may get a plan where employees have to submit claims and then get reimbursed. If Dave is as smart as I think he is, he will opt for the debit card plan, as this will make his employees happier; and

d. Employees who quit forfeit their current balances if the plan has no delayed filing time option. Again, this is up to Dave, and whatever plan he chooses, David must explain clearly to his team.

4. Dave's pluses:

a. He is giving a benefit, which will create happier employees. No question about it. A plan like this helps employee retention and recruitment; and

b. Dave has the opportunity also to come out ahead financially. More than likely he will!

5. Dave's minuses:

a. He will file a slightly more complicated tax form at year end. The startup paperwork will take a dozen hours;

b. Dave needs to shop around for a supplier of this plan. There are hundreds of companies out there. Dave should ask his insurance broker for advice;

c. Dave keeps all of the forfeited money, but also is responsible for the money that is spent by employees before their full contribution is made. Congress placed these two parts of the bill together, estimating that, on average, this will balance out and Dave will not make or lose money in this section; and

d. There is the risk that an employee will spend a large amount in January and then leave. It can happen, but should not be a big enough concern to scare Dave away.

6. Dave's vendor for the plan should meet with all the employees, teaching the plan and answering questions. After that, the personnel people at Dave's need to understand the program and introduce it to new hires.

7. The plan may change from year to year. His personnel manager has to stay on top of the changes. She should meet with the vendor every six months.

8. Start training for the plan in October, giving all employees plenty of time to figure out how much they want to allocate. Remember, it is important for Dave to urge people to be conservative in their first year's allocation.

9. The bottom line ... this is the best, low- or no-cost benefit available in the country today.

Chapter 49

The Five-Minute Solution to Questions You Can Ask in an Interview

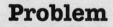 **Problem**

You own Paul's Pumpkin Pickin' Patch, a large retail store with 20 full-time and 45 part-time folks. Paul is slowly reducing his role in the Pumpkin Patch, and has promoted Peter to the Pumpkin Patch personnel position. Is Peter going to produce for Paul's?

Possible Outcomes

- Peter does a great job and continues to hire great people.
- Peter does okay, but a rumor surfaces that Peter makes off-color jokes in the interview process. One lady storms out of an interview.
- You get a letter from the Equal Employment Opportunity Commission office asking for information about questions Peter asked Pedro, whose first language is not English. Peter asked, "What would Pedro do if a customer didn't buy something because of not understanding him clearly?"
- When you discuss these issues with Peter, he gets very defensive and upset that you are questioning him. He thinks he has done a great job.

What Plan Could Paul Implement for Improving Peter's Personnel Performance?

1. Paul relied on Peter's previous positions and assumed he knew what he was doing. Paul should have screened Peter, just like every other job applicant. Even when you promote from within, interview the person. Peter may be a great salesperson on the Pumpkin Pickin' Patch floor, but Paul has never seen Peter act as a personnel person; he should have been extra-careful in this sensitive position.

2. Paul should help Peter prepare by practicing the interview sessions, by bringing in resumes of people he interviewed previously and posing as the applicant. Peter and Paul should do at least a dozen practice interviews. After each session Paul should critique Peter's presentation of the Pumpkin Pickin' Patch programs and his interviewing style. If Peter doesn't take well to constructive criticism, he is not the right person for this job.

3. Paul should remind Peter that open-ended questions are the best for learning an applicant's strengths. For instance, "Did you like

your last job?" is weak compared to "What did you like about your last job, and why?" Avoid questions with a "yes" or "no" answer or hypothetical questions. Ask questions about circumstances that have happened at the Patch and how the applicant would handle the events.

4. Paul can, and should, sit in with Peter on interviews. This is no different than shadowing a salesperson or working with a shipping clerk who is new to his position. Paul should remain silent, except if Peter makes a gross mistake.

5. How long should Paul work with Peter? If Peter doesn't have the basics and the legalities in place within a couple of weeks, Paul should think about putting Peter back in his previous position. It may take a year to develop the keen senses to spot a winner right away, and that can be learned from experience. Peter should follow up with the people he hired. If they were successful, what were their attributes? If not, then correlate these characteristics as well.

What Are Legal Questions You Can Ask?

1. Let's start with a negative answer. You can't ask about age, race, sexual preference, religion, pregnancy, disabilities, marital status or national origin. I, for one, totally agree with these restrictions. These are absolutes and you can find yourself in some serious trouble if your company exhibits a pattern of violating these restrictions.

2. So how does Peter ask questions that will help him to hire and promote folks at Paul's? By asking questions that relate directly to the jobs available at Paul's. First, Peter and Paul have to establish "Bona Fide Occupational Qualifications" (BOQs) for the positions. A salesperson on the floor has to be able to stand on his feet for up to two hours at a time; lift a 50-pound box of merchandise; work a computerized cash register, process a credit card sale; and make change from a one-hundred-dollar bill.

3. Legit questions for these BOQs would be:

   a. Can you stand for up to two hours without taking a rest break?

   b. Can you lift a 50-pound box?

   c. Can you make change? (Computer and math skills are not a protected right. You can go directly to these questions.)

   d. What are your skills on a computer using Windows?

4. If Pauline Applicant answers these questions with a simple yes or no, she probably doesn't have the social skills to be in sales. This is an answer unto itself. By far the vast majority of people will tell you the answers you are looking for. All you have to do is listen. Don't jump in with a comment after her first sentence. Let her ramble. Odds are she will.

5. You can set the tone for this by asking the questions in a conversational way. Instead of question 3b above, you might say, "We sell a variety of products, including 15 types of bird seed. Our best seller is sunflower seed in 50-pound bags. Would you be able to help a customer by taking one to his car?" Perry may answer with a yes, or may ask if this happens often, or if he can get a stock boy to do this. These are cues that he will have a problem with lifting. Again, let Perry speak until there is a distinct silence in the room.

6. Let's ask Pauline about her children, which, of course, you can't ask directly. But you can say that during special sales and around the Christmas holiday shopping period, Pauline will have to work longer hours, coming in early and staying late. Ask if this fits her schedule. You are not being underhanded or sly. You have a BOQ that certain times of the year require extreme flexibility in hours and scheduling.

7. Along the same lines, don't ask whether she prefers Miss, Ms., or Mrs. This confirms marital status, which is something you can't ask. But you can look at a person's hands. Does she wear a wedding ring? Ask yourself is this is important to you ... and then understand that it shouldn't be.

8. So what really is the best question? Here it is: "Patrick, tell me about yourself." Patrick knows this subject best and more often than not will tell you everything you want to know. Patrick may respond with, "What do you want to know?" You say, "Anything about yourself that will help me know you and your skills." Let him ramble. Keep throwing in, "That's interesting," or "Wow, I enjoy baseball, too!" If Patrick plays it close to the vest, that is a warning sign. Patrick may not have something to hide, but his personality may not fit your culture.

9. You can't ask, "What church do you attend?" but you can ask what hobbies Priscilla enjoys. If she has no hobbies, is she dull and boring? Ask what her favorite TV show is. Ask if she follows women's basketball. Ask if she follows any sports. If she likes team sports, that can be a plus. People who play softball on a team are better in a working team environment than someone who plays singles tennis (though that tennis player may make a great leader).

10. You might ask Pedro, "What did you do on your last vacation?" This is an open-ended question that will tell you a lot about him.

11. You can certainly ask about Pedro's last job with open-ended questions:

    a. How did you overcome obstacles?

    b. What did you like about working there?

    c. If you were in charge, what would you have changed?

    d. What did you learn there that will help you with the job we are offering?

    e. What are your life goals? And, what are your career goals? Were they met at your last job?

12. Ask the same questions about Pedro's previous jobs as well.

13. You can't ask, "Have you ever been hospitalized?" or "Do you have any disabilities?" You can't ask "Have you ever been treated for drug addiction or alcoholism?" You can clearly ask about gaps in

time from a resume or application, though, and you should get full answers here. Pedro may just say he was looking for work, but you can pick up on a hesitation or pause before he answers.

14. If the job requires Patricia to drive her car or a company car or truck, you can ask about her driver's license and tickets or suspensions on the license. But don't ask this question to someone whose BOQ doesn't include driving.

15. You can ask about criminal convictions that are related to the job. For instance, an accounts receivable person would answer a question about fraud or stolen cash, but not about a conviction for drunk driving. Phrase your questions based on the job position!

Please note: It is a Department of Labor regulation that you retain all employee job applications and resumes for at least one year after they are received at your office. The purpose of this is to show, during an audit, that you did not discriminate against a class of people. This is your source of information for the training scenarios.

Chapter 50

The Five-Minute Solution to Should You Buy a Competitor in a New Area?

Problem

You own Arthur's Ice Cream Cone Company. Or at least that is the way it started 30 years ago—just ice cream cones. Now, you are a commercial baker in a city of a million people. You have 45 employees. Your CFO, Danny, has told you that last year was the best ever; you have plenty of liquidity, no bills unpaid and a very stable workforce. You decide to grow. What should Arthur do?

Possible Outcomes

- You decide to start Arthur's II small, just as you did with your first bakery. It takes five years to make a dent in Lowell, your new city. For the first three years, Arthur's II becomes a pit into which you pour money and time every day.

- Danny suggests you start big, make a splash with new trucks, new equipment and a big advertising campaign. Six months in, the economy tanks and you have to sell two trucks and lay off a third of your workers.

- A business broker comes to you with an offer to buy an existing bakery. It seems to have all the financial numbers in line with your expectations. But what about the company's infrastructure, quality standards and the stability of its workers?

- How does Arthur make the decision as to whether to grow a new business or an existing business and switch it to Arthur's norms?

How to Start This Decision-Making Process

1. Arthur has to do some soul-searching. The two extremes are starting anew or buying an existing entity. If Arthur is dead-set for or against one option, there is no need to go further. If Arthur is in the middle, or gently to one side or the other, it is time to start weighing the pros and cons of each option.

2. Arthur's Ice Cream Cone Company is privately held and run by Arthur. Whatever decision he makes, Arthur has to be comfortable with it. It is not like Arthur has to do this expansion.

3. Arthur remembers how he started and grew. He liked the work and thrived on the successes and even the stress. But, does he want to go through that again? He knows he can do it; the question is, does he want to?

4. Buying an existing, similar company appears easier, but Arthur has

never done this before and doesn't even know how to look or where the land mines are. It would be a lot easier in many ways, but it also has the potential to be a bigger flop if the acquisition doesn't work well.

5. Whatever Arthur does, he needs good advice. He must get an accountant, lawyer and industry consultant familiar with mergers and acquisitions, especially the tax and legal consequences of different ways to structure the deal.

6. It all comes down to this: Arthur needs to make a list of the pros and cons of each decision. If they end up equal, then Arthur's gut feeling will take over. Until then, though, let's look at these pros and cons.

7. What is Arthur's generational plan? Does he have children to leave the business to? Will they want to have the extra chore of a second location? Arthur has to think ten years down the road for this one. Leadership transition and tax planning are important issues.

The Start-Your-Own Business Option—the Pros

1. Arthur will have complete control over the path of the business and will grow it to meet his standards. He can nurture the growth, putting in more funds as he feels comfortable.

2. Promoting current workers to Lowell and filling the open jobs at Arthur's is good for business. This keeps people excited about their work and builds team morale.

3. Steve, a great bakery manager on the second shift, would be interested in moving to the new city and taking on the general manager's responsibility. Arthur can train Steve for the new position before starting the new business and he is confident Steve will do a great job.

4. Arthur can set his standards high and expect they will be maintained, not hurting Arthur's good reputation.

5. This takes much less cash up-front, but requires a longer time to earn a return.

6. Arthur can set his own goals and decide when he meets them.

The Start-Your-Own-Business Option—the Cons

1. Arthur will have to delegate most of his authority to Steve as it is a two-hour drive to Lowell. Sure, they can work via phone and email, but it is not the same as looking at the dough.

2. Arthur just doesn't have enough time to teach every new employee. Will he be comfortable with Steve doing this?

3. Pulling his second-shift supervisor could hurt his current bakery. Has his replacement been properly trained? Arthur is not sure.

4. Does Arthur really want to work this hard? He says yes to his team, but isn't sure when looking in the mirror. He has to be sure before the decision is made.

5. If Arthur's II sinks, will it hurt the main plant?

The Buy-the-Existing-Business Option—the Pros

1. Placing Arthur's name on the existing company guarantees customers will be there, excited about Arthur's legendary good service and quality.

2. Arthur doesn't know much about buying a business. He is smart enough to get a qualified consultant, a top-notch lawyer and an accountant on his team. He also is smart enough to take their advice. He knows he can't do this on his own.

3. Everything is in place on day one—the plant and equipment, the trucks, the customers and the staff. Arthur and Steve only have to train the existing staff to their standards.

4. Why is the business being sold? Is it for a good reason, like the

current owner retiring? If he is staying, will he work well with Arthur and Steve? Will he work well as an employee when for many years he was the boss? Or is the sale because of problems? If this is the case, Steve has to come in shaking things up from the first day.

5. The current staff knows local business regulations (in this case the health and food inspectors). This is a real asset.

6. The company Arthur wants to buy has been in business for a while. Its management must have been doing some things well. Arthur can expand their best practices to Arthur's I and benefit both companies. There assuredly will be some good employees who can help the base business, too! The business may have products that Arthur doesn't bake now, which he can expand into. Cross-pollinating brands and best practices really helps both companies.

7. By structuring the deal with ownership by Arthur's heirs, creative tax advantages can be explored. There are options, such as buying the full business or only the assets, which are best left for discussion with Arthur's legal and tax advisors.

The Buy-the-Existing-Business Option—the Cons

1. Can Arthur's culture be successfully implanted? Since this has never been done by Arthur, he is not sure. But he does know that his work culture is the most important reason for Arthur's Cone's success. He reads about companies that are very successful in buying others, but also hears about deals that cause both companies to spiral downwards.

2. Does Arthur want to invest 30 percent of his net worth in the new facility, when he can start from scratch with a low investment? He realizes this type of investment is not for the faint-of-heart.

3. Does he have to hire everyone at the current place? What if he

doesn't feel there is good current management? No, he doesn't have to hire everyone, but it is probably good business to do so for a trial period. It is inevitable that some folks will not meet his standards, but Arthur should invest a couple of months to review all staff. He should move Steve there from the beginning and ask him to be the teacher and mentor to his new workers.

4. Expenses are much larger starting on Day 1. There is not an easy exit option when buying an existing operation.

5. Starting small is easy. When purchasing an existing business, you have to hit the ground running and there is less margin for error.

6. It's a good thing he has a team helping him. He discovers a pending lawsuit that wasn't declared in the buyer's presentation. His accountant questions how inventory is valued, and the consultant thinks the buyer is asking 15 percent too much.

7. No matter how hard you try to keep negotiations private, things leak out. Arthur doesn't feel comfortable side-stepping questions from his current employees, but it is necessary until the deal is firm.

This will be the toughest business decision that Arthur will make and he should take his time and decide at his own pace. He shouldn't be pressured by artificial dates created by the seller's advisors. The only reason to move more quickly is if the other bakery is going to be shopped to other buyers or sold at auction.

The Five-Minute Consultant

Chapter 51

The Five-Minute Solution to Johnny Come Lately

Problem

Bill owns Texas Bill's Taxi and Limo, Corp., with 20 cabs, 20 Town Cars and six high-end limousines. Most cars run two shifts per day, seven days a week; Bill has about 150 full- and part-time drivers, six mechanics, and ten in the office staff. If a car doesn't leave the garage on time, Bill loses money, but more importantly his customer service fails. How can Bill keep drivers motivated to start on time each day?

Possible Outcomes

- You hold a driver's meeting explaining how important being on-time is for your customer service program. Unfortunately, 30 drivers show up late and miss the meeting. This is the "walk softly" approach.

- Working with the rules in your employee manual, you suspend the worst offenders, and end up firing 15 people. Attendance really doesn't improve, but morale goes down the gas pipe. This is the "carry a big stick" theory.

- After the firings you hear talk of joining a union to prevent you from firing more people. You know you would win a certification election, but the time lost, cost and grief will be overwhelming. You want to avoid this.

- You think about hiring ten drivers on a stand-by basis to cover the late drivers, but your CFO crashes this idea.

- Wait-a-minute … Bill is about to try an approach new to him … working with the drivers to develop ideas that might eliminate on-time problems.

How Could Bill Set This Up with the Drivers?

1. The first step for Bill is defining the problem. Is the lateness confined to just one shift? Is it the same drivers or does it spread across Bill's Texas Taxi? What steps have already been taken by the shift leaders? Have any worked and, if so, why? Is it real or a computer-generated problem? Bill gets a report from his payroll service that lists late punch-ins. What is late? Is it one, five or thirty minutes?

2. What time is reasonable for Johnny Driver to be on time? In my book, (and I guess this is!), on-time means just that. There is no reason to be five minutes late every day. This is just sloppiness on the Johnny's part and will be evident in his other work.

If Johnny is on-time every day and one day there is a highway accident on his way that delays him an hour, to me that is excusable. Life happens.

3. Bill has to define on-time two different ways.

    a. For payroll purposes, when does the employee lose pay? Bill pays by the quarter hour. Does Johnny get docked at five minutes late, or seven? I recommend no more than five minutes be allowed for payroll purposes.

    b. The second definition is work-related. If Bill ran an assembly line where each job was dependent on the previous position, one person being late is a disaster. The tolerance for lateness would be zero. But in this case, there would have to be spare workers available because life does happen. Texas Taxi can survive with an occasional late punch-in.

4. Bill has to decide what his late policy is. My recommendation is allow one late punch per quarter. On the second late, Johnny gets a verbal warning with a note to his personnel file. On the third, a written warning, on the fourth a three-day suspension and after the fifth within a quarter, Johnny should go looking for a new job. Bill's Texas Taxi and Limo, Corp., also needs an annual definition. Three late days per quarter equals twelve per year and is not acceptable. Bill should allow no more than twice the quarterly limit in a rolling twelve-month time period.

5. Bill should allow his supervisors some discretion. During a major snowstorm, expect many people to be late. But then again, this is the exact situation where Texas Taxi would be the busiest and Bill should expect his drivers to make every effort to get in on time. Bill, should remember the drivers that made it in on time during the storm, when writing annual reviews.

6. The shift foremen and the supervisors are key as they motivate drivers. Bill needs meetings with each shift leadership group, getting them on board to any solution. One leader suggests pay-

ing a bonus to those who come in on time. Bill rejects this, feeling this is their basic job.

7. So, now Bill meets with the drivers and gets their input. Surprising Bill, they agree with him. They don't like customers who complain about other drivers, or having to pick up customers who are late for an appointment. It cuts into their tip money to deal with unhappy riders. Ninety percent of the drivers agree that employees should be penalized if they arrive late to work. The other ten percent wouldn't agree with management if they received a gold-plated invitation to discuss the problem. Bill learns a big lesson. He should have trusted his drivers long before.

8. Six drivers volunteer to work with Bill to set on-time standards. For a business setting up new standards, having the employees help set them is priceless. Here are the fundamentals they came up with:

    a. Customer service is important. Being on-time with pick-ups is second only to the passengers' and the driver's safety;

    b. What really is on-time? Should there be different definitions based on job duties at Bill's Texas Taxi? What should Bill do about salaried staff?;

    c. On-time starts are more important in the Town Car and Limo business;

    d. Town Car and Limo drivers make the most money. For promotion to these jobs, taxi drivers must have an excellent safety and on-time record;

    e. Being on time is more than just punching in on time. It includes coming back from breaks and lunch on time; and

    f. After finishing a run, drivers should immediately check in with dispatch for their next run. They can't take 15 minutes here and there. As all cars are equipped with GPS units, the committee agreed that supervisors should check all periods of ten minutes or more without movement. Bill had wanted to do this, but feared there would be backlash. Working with the committee is great!

9. Bill meets with his payroll service provider and finds he can save more than $50,000 annually by putting in new time clocks that communicate directly with the provider. His staff can now approve generated reports rather than creating them for transmitting to the provider. Payroll goes from two people to one with a strong back-up. No more buying and storing years of time cards either.

10. The drivers offer suggestions to make the whole company more efficient:

   a. Create an in-house traffic coordinator, creating constant updates on construction delays, traffic and weather;

   b. Fifteen percent of customer complaints are due to looking for the pickup address location. Computer screens in each car could transmit pickup points and directions rather than using radios. This technology is very inexpensive today; and

   c. With these computer screens, drivers can accept credit cards. Carrying less cash gives drivers a greater sense of safety.

11. Bill's Texas Taxi implements a new start time for the taxi drivers. Instead of 6 a.m. to 4 p.m., and 4 p.m. to 2 a.m. shifts, Bill staggers the start time into four different times, 15 minutes apart. This creates less confusion when all the drivers come in, and allows a few folks who might be late to take the later start times. As simple as this sounds, it is a major breakthrough for Texas Taxi and is successful right away for Bill and the drivers.

12. Bill buys the new time and attendance payroll package, which has a two-year financial payback. It takes a couple of weeks for the supervisors and drivers to get used to it, but is only a small hiccup.

   a. The committee agrees that being at work means being ready to work at the scheduled start time. It does not mean swiping in, and then going to your locker and starting to get ready.

   b. All of Bill's employees, including Bill, swipe in and out. This significantly reduces paperwork for the mechanics and salaried folks as their time has been tracked manually in the past.

c. The committee decides that employees who are late more than three times in a quarter should start the disciplinary chain with a written warning; the fourth, a suspension and the fifth, termination. They agree with Bill that twice this amount in a year is also cause for discipline.

13. It turns out the employees are as tough as Bill wants to be. They feel a strong loyalty and pride in Texas Taxi and want it to be successful. All of the care that Bill has paid to his company of the years is now returned.

14. With everyone's support the plan works. A handful of bad apples quit; ten are written up in a month and five more are terminated three months in. On-time performance rose from 95 percent to 98 percent. The drivers, the customers, the supervisors and Bill are happy.

This sounds like a storybook ending. After I left college, I drove a cab in Boston for a year. While we didn't have the technology issues, the rest is real-life from my career.

Chapter 52

The Five-Minute Solution to Deciding to Let People Work from Home

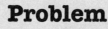

Problem

You own Guy's Medical Supplies, a 20-person company that sells, rents and services medical equipment. You have four people in the office who do insurance billing. Filling out the myriad of forms from each company is critical as insurance companies look for perfection in the form before they will send payments. Robin, one of your billing wizards, asks if she can work from home. Her husband just had major surgery and she needs to stay home with him. She says she will work her full eight hours, but not necessarily from 8 to 5, like the rest of the crew.

Possible Outcomes

- You don't have anyone working from home and think it would be a big disruption in the office. After you say no, Robin, regretfully, gives notice.

- You agree to try it for a month, but your heart's not in it. You don't feel that people will work as hard at home as when you are around. You don't set up any metrics to measure Robin's success, and using your gut feeling, decide the experiment hasn't worked. When you ask Robin to come back to the office, she gives her two-week notice.

- You talk to your neighbor, Krista, a business consultant, and she tells you about success stories where she assisted companies in setting up home work programs.

- Guy listens to Krista, sets up Robin, and much to his surprise, Robin's output actually increases. Guy kicks himself because he didn't do this sooner.

What Should Guy Plan Before Committing to a Work-at-Home Program?

1. Is Robin the right person to create this program around? If she is not, and the program fails, Guy will never try this again. Robin, being the trail blazer, has no guidelines in place so Guy and Robin have to work together closely.

2. What land mines are there in picking people to work at home?

   a. The person has to work well on his own and doesn't need constant help and encouragement from his supervisor;

   b. She has to be technically competent to manage her own computer, printer, fax and phone/Internet connections;

   c. She has to work well alone. There is no one to talk with at the coffee pot; and

d. An at-home worker must be a top-notch time manager. She can't blame others for her problems or work output.

3. Most companies consider work-at-home to be an earned privilege. Guy can reward his best workers and motivate the slackers.

4. What are the advantages to Guy's business?

   a. A work-at-home program will retain good employees, reducing a company like Guy's biggest expense—hiring and training new personnel;

   b. An office worker needs about 200 square feet of office space, considering their 8-foot by 10-foot work area and common space allotment. If Guy's office space is tight, work-at-home is a real saver. Parking needs also are reduced;

   c. There are no thermostat wars; less office politics; fewer interruptions in the work office; less chance of illnesses spreading to all workers; and

   d. Guy's carbon footprint will shrink as will Robin's. Every little bit helps.

5. What logistical problems will Guy need to clear before starting the program?

   a. Is Guy covering the cost of Robin's home office? She needs an ergonomic chair, desk, computer and peripherals, and a data line. Spending $5K or so is a small investment in a good employee like Robin. Guy should do it;

   b. Guy should not let Robin use her own home computer. This can lead to problems if their business relationship breaks down;

   c. Guy has to configure an excellent fire wall and should get a computer genius to help him. He has to decide about cloud computing, arranging a virtual private network (VPN) or using the Internet. Listen to the genius; and

   d. There should be a continual back-up running on Robin's computer. I use Carbonite and it works fine. Whatever Guy uses for his back-up system at the office should work. If Guy is not using a continual back-up, then someone please step up and hit him in the head with a baseball bat.

What Are the Day-to-Day Plans That Will Help Robin and Guy Succeed?

1. Guy has to be supportive of this idea, just as he is of any other new program that starts at his business. If he feels it will fail, it usually will. Still, a good program has scheduled stop signs. At three months there should be a thorough review of the success or lack of for the program—then again at six months and then a year. After that the program is now a regular part of Guy's.

2. There are two types of general programs—one where someone is a full-time worker at home and one where a person works just one or two days per week at home. Let's look at each.

3. The full-time program is easier to manage and causes less office interruption. People know how to contact each other rather than wondering who is in the office on which day. Robin still needs to come to the office if you have a weekly staff meeting or training session. Also decide if Robin will come to the office to cover during vacations or sick time. Since Robin's work-at-home program is based on her husband's health, this might be tough; if you have employees working at home just for convenience, they must come in to cover vacations and other needs.

4. Employees working full-time at home need contact with the office. Encourage them to come for an occasional lunch with the crew. Be sure to include them in all company announcements and events. Assign a work buddy who will help Robin with all follow-up details that need to be done at the office.

5. How will Robin get her work assignments? Does the paperwork need to get dropped off to her every day? Will it be faxed? E-mailed?

6. Robin has tasks to do as well. She has to set up her office at home. It should be a dedicated space, not one that she sets up each morning in her dining room. She needs storage space for supplies—paper, ink, etc. She should have a dedicated phone, either a cell or a separate office line. Her toughest task is to train her family and friends. When she is at work, she is not to be disturbed. It will take some time and gentle reminders teaching that when she is at work her family and friends shouldn't stop to visit with her. In Robin's case, her husband's health is an overriding aspect and that will still come first.

7. All work-at-home folks should keep to a firm schedule. Their offices and customers need to know this schedule and should be able to contact them during these times.

8. Robin will actually be saving quite a bit of money.
   a. She may have less dry cleaning and new clothes cost;
   b. She'll be eating in restaurants less. Also, she will have the chance to eat healthier by preparing her meals at home;
   c. Her commuting costs drop from five trips to one per week; and
   d. Using a dedicated space, she qualifies for the home office deduction on federal income tax.

9. Robin won't be late for work on bad-weather days or get caught in traffic jams. In fact, Robin will be more productive than the rest of the office. How much time does the rest of the insurance billing team spend at the coffee pot?

10. For the occasional work-at-home person, more problems can pop up. Do you invest in their office when it will be used two days per week? It takes an extraordinary employee to continuously switch between the office and home—select carefully. Avoid Mondays and Fridays for the occasional worker's home days. Keep to the same weekly schedule.

11. Don't allow people to work from home on request. This will usually be because they have to be home for something, like a repair per-

son coming, and that will interrupt the work day. The very special employee will be able to work around this interruption, while the average employee will not.

12. Setting up the occasional worker requires more management attention to results on a day-by-day basis. Be sure to train your managers for this.

13. Studies show that a work-at-home situation, when well-managed, is really beneficial for the company and the employees. It tends to work better for larger companies, but small companies can make it work with the right combination of management attitude and employee selection.

Chapter 53

The Five-Minute Solution to Creative Hiring

Problem

You own Cathie's Private Duty Nursing Service. You employ 30 nurses who work with home-bound patients. Last month you received a contract to cover a new county and you need to hire 20 new nurses in the next three months, but have received no qualified responses from your help wanted advertising.

Possible Outcomes

- You spend a ton on overtime for your current staff. They love the extra money, but you are losing dollars for every shift. This can't go on.

- You call the local nursing school, but they have no one until the June graduation.

- You try to sub out some of the work, but your competitor is charging you an outrageous price because you took the work away from them.

- As you begin to pull your hair out, you think you may have to return the contract ... but wait … you call your brother, Bill, and he shares many creative ideas with you. Not all worked for Cathie's business, but they might work for yours.

What Did Bill Teach Cathie That Helped Her Recruit More Nurses?

1. Placing ads in the paper used to be the top way to reach job seekers, but this is changing. Even in a slow job market, Cathie must stand out from the crowd. Place a border around your ad, put your logo in, and leave plenty of white space in the ad. Brag about your benefits more than the salary, especially flexible scheduling. Nurses are a highly educated group; describe your education benefits in your ad or how you'll help them get certified in your state.

2. Make it easy for applicants to reach you; list your website in the ad. Place a job application form on the site and on social media sites. List your office, fax and cell phone numbers. Show applicants you care by speaking with them yourself. If applicants don't have a resume, encourage them to send a homemade video describing their work background.

3. Describe the culture and style of your company. Highlight diversity when describing your company. Many ethnic minorities are afraid to switch jobs because of paperwork and cultural fears. Advertise in non-English media. If you receive a resume from someone who is not a native English speaker, have a translator available

for the phone or personal interview. While the nurse may speak English, an interview is stressful, and speaking in a native tongue may relax the candidate better, making it easier for you to hire.

4. The cover letter is more important than the resume. You can teach skills, but not attitude. You'll discern a good attitude within a well-written letter. Don't worry about grammar. You are not hiring an English teacher.

5. Use alternative advertising:

   a. Rent a couple of billboards. It is surprising how quickly an ad can be produced;

   b. Create your own "YouTube" piece. Have some fun with it, and it may go viral, reaching a huge audience;

   c. Place an ad on search engine sites. These can get expensive, so limit your search words and geography;

   d. Place ads on web-only job sites (visit www.fiveminuteconsultant.com for a list.)

   e. Create a web page with "Success Stories of Cathie's Nurses." Get permission from your current nurses to share their stories about working at Cathie's. Give some ghost-writing help to those who need it. People like reading stories with happy endings, and working at Cathie's certainly should qualify.

6. Cathie's current nurses are her best hiring resource:

   a. Ask your current nurses for referrals. This is the best hiring program for Cathie. Give a nice bonus; let's say about two weeks of pay after a new nurse has been employed for 90 days;

   b. Ask your current employees where they meet other nurses for lunch or for happy hour. Put a flyer up at those restaurants;

   c. Ask what websites they visit for nursing information. Place an ad there;

   d. Same thing ... ask which newspapers are most read;

   e. Put a flyer in the store where they buy uniforms; and

f. Is there a central dispensary for medicines and supplies? Another great place for a flyer, or a paid ad.

7. Can any of the work positions you are hiring for be filled by someone with a handicap? If so, I promise these people will become your best employees. Go to http://www.sba.gov/content/hiring-people-with-disabilities for info.

8. Take a strong look at people who have been out of the workforce for an extended period of time. Maybe they lived in another state, were out of the country or were raising a family. Job-sharing is a great way to reenter. Does your company's environment support job-sharing? Cathie's certainly does. Plan on hiring some nurses part-time, with a 90-day review and a plan to take them full-time after that period.

9. Have an open house at your company to discuss job opportunities. Call the business editor at local papers with your story of how you're trying to hire people. In times of high unemployment, this is news. Call the radio and TV stations offering to do an interview. Contact the local unemployment office to list your job openings. They will give you good advice on running a job fair/open house.

10. Look at all of the job applications and resumes you have received over the past couple of years. (Yes, you did keep them … actually you are required to keep them for at least a year.) People who were good but may not have fit in the opening you had then might be just perfect for one of these 20 slots.

11. To me, some of the best workers in the United States are former military folks. Whether they have been in for four years or a full 20, they are well-trained, respect organizations, are good learners and good teachers and will really appreciate getting a civilian job. Try one of these websites to start hiring a vet: http://www.hireheroe-susa.org/about/hire-a-veteran, or http://www.mynextmove.org/vets/. Companies with more than $100,000 in federal contracts are obligated to "take affirmative action to hire veterans."

12. You can always spend money to hire. Employment agencies will

be able to bring you candidates, but at a cost. Cathie found out she would need to pay between 33 percent and 50 percent of the first-year wages. She decided this was just not in her budget. If she was looking for a single specialist or a key second-in-command of her company this would be a good route to travel.

13. Check out your competitor's websites. See how they list their job openings. Check out nurse-hiring websites from across the country and meld their best ideas into your site.

14. Look at the Facebook pages of your current nurses. See what they like, and use that as a direction to place advertising.

15. The most obvious place to look, graduates of nursing schools at graduation time, just never seems to fit your hiring schedule. But it is a good idea to network with the leadership and placement offices at all the schools in your region. They often get calls from alumni or people who move into the area.

16. When you have a booth at a local health fair or trade show, hang a sign stating you are accepting resumes. Have applications with you and hand them out liberally. If the timing is right and you are hiring now, place an ad in the trade show journal about hiring.

17. Go to every event where you can hand out a business card to health-care professionals. Attend lectures at local hospitals, lunch-and-learn programs, or awards and recognition events honoring local nurses or doctors. Reach out to alternate health care providers—physical therapists, mental health workers, laboratory workers and X-ray technicians. They all know nurses and would be pleased to pass your card on to their friends, provided they are sure you are reputable and would offer their friends an improvement in the job.

18. Contact other nursing service companies and see if they are looking to out-place any staff. Maybe they had a lay-off and would refer people to you. You have to be a little careful here that you are not just getting their cast-offs. If you know the company as reputable, you should be okay.

Chapter 54

The Five-Minute Solution to Firing an Employee Over Forty

 Problem

You own Karl's Baseball Card Shop. It's a nice business, with 15 employees (some of whom are part-time) who help you stock shelves, sort baseball cards and talk baseball with customers. Your store is open seven days a week during baseball season, and four days a week during the winter. Danielle, your cashier, is 43 years old. For the last six months her attendance has been unreliable. You have discussed this with her four times, and she tells you that nothing is wrong. Last week, she called in sick both Monday and Thursday. What do you do now?

Possible Outcomes

- You speak with Danielle first thing on Monday morning, warning her that any more unscheduled absences will be cause for suspension and then termination. Unfortunately, you don't put this in writing, but she improves her attendance.

- The following week Danielle doesn't come in on Tuesday. She tells you wasn't feeling good, but didn't call in until 10 a.m., when she was due in at 9:30 a.m. You suspend her for one day when she comes back to work on Wednesday.

- The following week, Danielle calls in sick on Thursday and Friday. On Monday morning, when she comes in, you have a heart-to-heart talk with her about reliability, give her severance pay of one month, let her go and replace her with a recent high school graduate.

- Three weeks later, you get a letter from Danielle's cousin, Thomas, who just graduated from law school, saying that you have violated the Age Discrimination in Employment Act (ADEA). He wants to meet with you to discuss a settlement. Who threw this curveball?

What Is ADEA and How Did I Violate It?

1. The Age Discrimination Act, passed by Congress in 1967, states that employers cannot discriminate against employees because of age. Employees over 40 years old qualify for protection. Employers also cannot retaliate against someone who has filed a complaint, and in most cases, cannot set mandatory retirement ages.

2. Now, Karl was nervous. As a small business owner, he never bothered much with all of the government "stuff." He paid his taxes on time, paid his people well above minimum wage and never had a problem like this. "What did I do wrong?" he wondered. He didn't know.

3. What he did wrong was that he didn't keep a good record of the problems with Danielle. He was certainly correct to let her go. She let him down, consistently. But Danielle is over 40, she was replaced by a much younger person, and that is the trigger that

caused interest by the attorney, Thomas. After all, Thomas told his cousin he could get her big bucks because Karl violated the law.

4. STOP! This is not supposed to be suspense novel. Let's go to the finish and work our way back. Danielle had no cause to sue and Thomas was stopped in his tracks. The ADEA law only applies to employers who have 20 or more employees. Karl lost sleep for no reason. But, what if Karl had 22 employees? Would he have been on the hook? Probably not, but he would have had a tough time proving it without documentation. Karl would have to be interviewed by an agent from the EEOC, and possibly go before an administrative hearing. In the long run, Karl would have won; his payroll records would show Danielle's spotty attendance.

5. Many states have similar laws, and some states cover employers with different levels of employment. Karl still should call his attorney to ask what his state laws are.

6. It sure does sound silly that Karl would have been in trouble for firing a poorly performing employee. What is the government thinking? Well, there is good cause for such a law. It used to be very common for companies to lay off their most senior employees, those who probably made the most money. This disproportionally impacted older workers. And that is wrong. It is a pain-in-the-backside to keep up with all of the government programs. But these programs protect all people, and most commonly, those in the most need.

What Should Karl Have Done If He Had 22 Employees?

1. Since spring training is more important than knowing federal regulations, I wouldn't expect too many folks to know the hard details of this regulation. Is Karl lucky that he was below the line? Sure, but that is pure luck and not part of a sound business practice. Karl needs to do better. How?

2. There are basics to the discrimination laws in the U.S. This is in other chapters, but is so important, here it is again: An employer may not discriminate because of:

   a. Age
   b. Race
   c. Religion
   d. National Origin
   e. Sexual Preference
   f. Gender
   g. Marital Status
   h. Pregnancy
   i. Childbirth
   j. Physical Disabilities

3. To learn more, visit www.eeoc.gov and start reading. This website is easy to navigate and will help all businesspeople understand the basics.

4. But back to Karl, what can he do that will help his business grow, keep his employees happy, and prevent this problem from popping up so easily again?

5. **Karl needs a consistent feedback program, to and from his employees.** It really is this simple. One sentence of consulting genius will solve all of the problems in Karl's baseball card world.

6. Karl would have easily answered an investigator's questions if he had an employee review system, showing when and how often he had communicated his displeasure with Danielle. He did provide progressive discipline: warnings, suspension and then termination. He was perfectly within his rights, and it was good business, too, to terminate Danielle. This lack of documentation was Karl's only mistake.

7. A proper review system is key to every business's growth and retention of good employees. You don't need fancy forms or computerized scoring. Write out a half dozen key metrics for your business and rate each employee accordingly. The most important part of the review is to plan tomorrow rather than complain about yesterday. If Karl has a problem with an employee, he should take care of it when it occurs. Don't wait for the review.

8. The review is to encourage employees to grow, hear their ideas, and share your vision of where the business is going and how each person fits into this vision.

9. What would some review topics for Karl's Baseball Card Shop look like?

    a. Is the employee reliable?

    b. Does the employee do their assigned job well?

    c. Does the employee work to further the goals of Karl's?

    d. Does the employee cooperate with other employees, acting as a mentor when appropriate?

    e. What are the employee's goals?

    f. What are Karl's goals for this employee?

10. Karl is whispering in my ear right now. Most of his employees are high school kids who stock shelves and clean up. How can they have goals? Of course they can! They may be very simple relative to the business world: Get a good reference for a full-time job, or for college admission; teach baseball to younger kids; or earn a consistent income. His full-time employees' goals would include learning more about the business, possibly helping Karl to open a second store, computerizing the inventory and just about anything else that can be thought up.

11. Employees who communicate with their managers stay at jobs longer. Karl will have less turnover if he develops this communication format.

12. So, what else does Karl need to know about age discrimination?

    a. You can't force a retirement age on most employees. The exception is generally for senior management in a large organization.

    b. Discrimination can be relevant in current employees and job applicants. If you say to an applicant, "I can't hire you because you are too old to stock shelves," you are leaving yourself open for problems. You should ask the question, "Can you stand on your feet all day, lifting boxes of baseball cards to the shelving?" If the candidate says yes, then, unless you send all applicants for a physical before hiring, you should consider this applicant.

   c. Lastly, Karl cannot retaliate against an employee who files a complaint. This will cause more headaches, which you just don't want.

13. By the way, I believe that older workers bring wisdom, skills and, most importantly, patience to many jobs. Who better to discuss the heroes of yesterday on all of those baseball cards than someone who grew up listening to ball games on their transistor radio? Get the youngsters to do the heavy lifting and you will have well-balanced team.

Chapter 55

The Five-Minute Solution to Setting an FMLA Leave of Absence Policy

Problem

You own Malcolm's Cats, a company that publishes and distributes books about animals. In the last couple of years you have grown from 40 to 70 employees. With this growth has come confusion, created by you, over who can take extended leaves of absence, for what reasons and for how long. And, of course, you have been putting off a rewrite of your employee manual. Phillip has just walked into your office asking for a 12-week leave of absence because his mother-in-law is very sick.

Possible Outcomes

- Phillip is a key person at your company but has not done a good job in training his second-in-command. You tell him the printing department will fall apart without him. You agree to let him work two days a week, and extract a promise to start more cross-training. (*See Chapter 47.*)

- You grant Phillip the leave, but insist that he pay 100 percent of his insurance premiums. He tells you he can't afford this, especially since he won't be working.

- Phillip reminds you that Jessica asked for a similar leave last year. It was during a slow period and Jessica's work load was easily spread around. Since you said yes to her, how could you say no to Phillip who has been with you five years longer?

- Phillip is upset with your negative answer. He starts talking about the Family and Medical Leave Act (FMLA) and how you will get in trouble for not following the guidelines. You thought the Family Leave Act is a new entertainment group at the Friendly Family Nursing Home.

What Should Malcolm Learn About the Family and Medical Leave Act?

1. The federal law, enacted in 1993, guarantees most employees 12 weeks per year of unpaid leave for designated circumstances, which are:

   a. Family illness for yourself, spouse, children and your parents;

   b. Participation in military service;

   c. Participation in a family military leave, such as when a service member takes a leave and the spouse wants to spend time with the service member; and

   d. Pregnancy, adoption or beginning foster care of a child (adoption and foster care must take place within one year of the child entering your family).

2. In 2007, there were approximately 141.7 million workers in the U.S., and the law covered 94.4 million. Which companies are covered?

   a. Those with 50 or more employees within a 75-mile radius of the worksite; and

   b. Most, but not all governmental offices, regardless of size.

3. Which employees are covered?

   a. Employees on your payroll for twelve or more months; and

   b. Employees who worked at least 1,250 hours in the last twelve months.

4. Many states have individual mandates and Malcolm will need to speak with his local attorney. These include:

   a. Some states include civil union partners;

   b. Some cover events of children's education, such as taking time off to see a school play or attend a graduation;

   c. Domestic violence or sexual assaults are covered in some states; and

   d. There are different minimum company sizes in various states. For instance, a company in Maine with 15 employees is covered by FMLA.

5. What about medical and other insurances? Malcolm is responsible for maintaining his share of existing insurance for the duration of the leave; Phillip is responsible for the balance. Malcolm can receive Phillip's share any way on which both agree, i.e. payable over a long period of time. Malcolm also can cancel the insurance if Phillip does not make his payments. While legally correct, this is a morale destroyer.

6. What's not covered?

   a. Your parents are covered, but your in-laws are not (sorry, Phillip);

   b. Pet illness is not covered;

c. Companies may deny leave for a "key employee." This is someone whose absence would cause "substantial and grievous economic injury to the company's operations." To qualify, an employee has to be salaried and among the top 10 percent of all earners at Malcolm's. If Phillip applies for leave, Malcolm has to notify him that he is a key employee and not eligible for leave. This can be appealed to the Department of Labor or civil courts; and

d. If spouses work for the same company, there is a maximum of twelve weeks of FMLA leave for a new child, not twelve weeks for each spouse.

7. There are complete books written about FMLA. They are more valuable to your HR person, if you have one, or your lawyer. Malcolm needs to know enough about FMLA so his leave policies for Malcolm's Cats are handled properly.

Let's Help Malcolm Write His Leave Policy

1. Let's define "employee leave." It is whenever an employee voluntarily asks for an extended time away from work and plans on returning to work. It is up to Malcolm to decide what is correct for his company.

2. Does Malcolm want to be generous or cautious? Does he want to issue strict rules or general guidelines? Does he want to follow the minimum guidelines or be super-employee-friendly? Each of these answers dictate Malcolm's costs, the frequency and duration of work interruptions, and also his employees' love of the company and their desire to help out when the company is in need.

3. At Malcolm's there will be a few people who milk Malcolm's kindness. It is tough to remember, but these rotten apples will not spoil the barrel.

4. So, Malcolm has decisions to make. Here are the questions, and my recommendation to my buddy Malcolm:

   a. Should he require that all vacation time and sick days be used up prior to granting leave? No, a family may have a summer vacation already planned and paid for. A broken leg in January could force the employee to give up his vacation. If an employee has more than four weeks of vacation or accrued sick days, at least two weeks of these should be used first.

   b. Should Malcolm let non-FMLA eligible people get leave? Yes, set a guideline that employees with six months' tenure qualify. If they were good enough to be hired and made it through six months, consider them one of the team. If someone works 1,000 hours (say, two people are job sharing) I would honor the leave request. Set 800 worked hours as the floor for future requests.

   c. Should Malcolm cover the employee's portion of the medical costs? No, set up a plan where the employee pays back his share.

   d. Should Malcolm extend the conditions where a non-medical leave is acceptable? Yes, depending on the reason. If someone wants to take a vacation, say going back to a home country for eight weeks, I would say yes, but they have to pay 100 percent of their medical costs. Employees know when the busy periods are and should not ask for time off during these periods.

5. When Jessica returns to work at the end of her scheduled FMLA leave, Malcolm must return her to the same or equal job, with the same hours, benefits and pay. The only exception is if Malcolm has changed the entire department that Jessica worked in. If Malcolm has laid off the department and can prove that Jessica would have been laid off, then she does not have to be returned to a job.

6. If, while on leave, Jessica works for a competitor or starts her own business, Malcolm's call should be to his lawyer for guidance in his location.

7. If Jessica doesn't return as scheduled, Malcolm can terminate her retroactively and ask her to pay the company's share of the medical expenses. It's not likely Malcolm will get this money.

8. Employees are required to give Malcolm a 30-day advance notice when asking for a leave, where possible. If the leave request is for an accident or an unplanned situation, the employee should request the leave ASAP. This guideline is in the law to help companies plan their work schedules.

9. When another employee wants to take an extended vacation, he can't ask Malcolm to guarantee his job or to maintain his benefits. (Actually he can ask, but Malcolm doesn't have to guarantee anything.)

Chapter 56

The ~~Five~~ *TEN*-Minute Solution to the Dangerous, Disgruntled Employee

(Note: One of the most vexing of all problems a business may face, requires a longer conversation.)

Problem

You are the owner of Steven's Wiener Factory, a 360-employee company with 18 retail outlets, selling 20 varieties of delicious products that fit in a bun. Your office is behind your first store and has been expanded a couple of times as you've grown. Last week, one of your store managers, Harry, was let go because of "creative bookkeeping." He said money was due him for all of the long hours he put in. In fact, he didn't work any harder than the rest of your team. At 2:15 p.m. this afternoon, he rushes into the main office with a handgun and demands to speak with you.

Possible Outcomes

- You calmly walk out of your office, speak with Harry for a few minutes and when the police arrive, he is taken away peacefully. You go back to your office to change your pants.

- Your receptionist screams, "He has a gun!" The 12 people in your office panic, not knowing what to do. Should they run to the back door? Most jump under their desks as Harry walks toward your office. Diane, who is in the restroom, hears the screams and luckily has her cell phone. She calls 911 and the police arrive, talking Harry into coming out. It turns out his gun wasn't loaded.

- Hearing the screams, you run out of your office. You divert Harry's attention, asking him into your office and allowing your staff to run out. They call the police. Harry and you talk for ten minutes with the police in the outer office. He breaks down crying and the police take him away. You have saved your office crew, defused the situation and the President of the United States calls the next day commending you for being a hero.

- This outcome is not pretty. Harry shoots you; you are wounded and the emotional scars will be with you for life. When the police arrive, Harry kills himself. Was this preventable? Could it have been less severe?

Was This Foreseeable? Preventable? How?

1. Yes and no. It is impossible to fire someone and be sure there will or won't be a problem. It's like a weather forecast: Harry's upset with a 40 percent chance of returning with a gun.

2. You don't have to fire someone to be at risk of a problem. Steven may have given a raise to Jim and not to John, and John can be upset. Or if Bill's wife left him because he was working too hard, will Bill blame this on Steven?

3. Does Steven need to have each of his employees undergo a com-

plete psych evaluation? Sounds ridiculous and expensive. But, with proper training of senior managers and a well-written and administered employee review/feedback system in place, many problems can be found and handled.

4. Will you find every problem child? Never. The overarching goal of an employee review system is to benefit the employee and Steven's Wiener Factory. Not every employee is a happy camper, but you cannot expect managers (even senior managers) to analyze an employee's thoughts and definitively point out the ones that will commit workplace violence. In fact, if this becomes your focus, you will quickly run Steven's into the ground.

5. What should Steven and his senior managers look for? Don't wait for the annual review to take notice of events that can be a precursor to a bigger problem. If Steven sees or hears about an event, action should be taken quickly to ascertain the facts. It is trite, but true: An ounce of prevention is worth a pound of cure. Look for an employee who:

   a. Has been upset recently over something, work-related or not, which is having an impact on work productivity;

   b. Has undergone a major change in behavior, appearance or demeanor. What is major? Significant enough for Steven to made aware of it by his own observation or from a manager;

   c. Has begun to challenge authority at any level;

   d. Has started blaming others for large or small problems, or perceives others to be causing problems where none exist;

   e. Abuses drugs, alcohol or prescriptions. Your employee manual should cover this and give you the right to test an employee showing signs of abuse;

   f. Has an obsessive romantic interest in another employee or non-employee, and has been rebuffed;

   g. Constantly talks about weapons, carries a concealed weapon or carries one with high visibility in his car or truck. Define a weapon fairly loosely—knives, hatchets, pipes and chains. (Even my cherished baseball bat can be a weapon.);

h. Talks about other events of workplace violence;

i. Is a bully. Most bullies tend to act this way out of a perceived or actual weakness in their own lives, which may explode in the workplace when their bullying target stands up;

j. Acts morally superior to others at work. Someone may resent this, openly causing conflict; and/or

k. Feels he is entitled to special rights that others have. These rights may have been earned by others, but this employee feels left out or feels the opportunity to earn the rights wasn't given.

6. Steven and his managers need to listen more than they talk. This is true of every successful business leader. As it relates to the dangerous employee, these phrases should draw your attention:

a. "You'll be sorry" for something, real or made-up;

b. "You better watch your back;"

c. "This isn't over yet;"

d. "My turn is coming;" and/or

e. "You take care of the other guys, but I never get the overtime."

7. Watch for specific events that indicate potential growing problems, like:

a. An employee who throws things around your office, warehouse or plant;

b. An employee who pounds on his desk, loudly enough to draw a look from everyone in the room;

c. Any act of an employee touching another where the other is upset. Sometimes it is only horseplay, but once someone pushes another it can escalate quickly;

d. Any report of vandalism to a person's property. The problem will multiply itself under revenge;

e. A shouting match loud enough to cause disruption. The one who is shouted down may harbor a grudge;

f. Graffiti on someone's locker, personal things, car or work area; and/or

g. Mean or malicious emails, correspondence or phone messages.

8. Once you see or hear of a situation that may be a precursor to violence, you have to take some action. There are many times in Steven's business that taking a wait-and-see approach is valid; a precursor to violence is not one of them. Letting a situation fester only makes it worse. When an outburst occurs where the whole office hears it, you have to take definitive action; this is where you earn your leadership stripes. Sure, it's not easy to be the peacemaker, but no one ever promised you that running Steven's would be easy.

9. Steve and his management team must set a policy of calling the police and advising the victim to file a complaint with all cases of violence.

10. In many businesses you need an access code to make a phone call. This can delay or stop a call to 911. Program your phone system to allow a 911 call, without interference, from every phone in your company.

11. Now that Harry has everyone's attention, what do you do? It's too late to start planning. You have to make an instantaneous life-and-death decision. Maybe you served in the armed forces and have a feel for this, but most Americans have not. Steve walks right up to Harry and says, "Let's talk; come into my office." He hopes Harry will do this so that the others can escape. In fact, this is the first test to check if Harry is rational. If he does accept Steven's offer to talk, it generally means the situation will settle itself without bloodshed. It may take hours of talking and a professional negotiator from the police department will most probably get involved. If that happens, precisely

follow the negotiator's instructions; he has done this and knows how to safely end standoffs.

12. Don't argue with Harry; agree with him. You are not trying to win debating points. Don't escalate the tension. Stay calm. Speak in an even voice and don't contradict Harry. Even if he is wrong on his facts, now is not the time to teach him. Your calm demeanor will keep the situation in check until help arrives. Ask him, as a show of good faith, if he will release the women in the group. His beef is with you; you are willing to stay there and work it out. Give him something in return, like letting him make a phone call to a local media outlet, which also will bring the police.

How Does Steve Prepare for This When It Is Such a Remote Possibility?

1. Good question. Do you discuss this every month? Every quarter? My recommendation is to discuss this every year in a company Steven's size. Spend maybe an hour on it and remind all involved not to be heroes. Invite an officer from the local police department to go over basic procedures.

2. The best way to prevent this type of episode is to be aware it can happen. Managers should be aware when an employee is hostile and/or threatening. Don't wait for an employee review to realize this. When a manager senses a problem employee, that is the time to get advice from other managers. What do they see? Do they have any experience with this employee?

3. The current phrase is "zero tolerance." And it is the correct answer in dealing with the threat of or actual violence. Many managers will feel they are making a mountain out of a molehill. Strongly encourage your managers not to feel this way. It is by far better to discuss than to ignore and hope the problem employee gets better. Every incident of potential violence must be recorded and discussed to find a way to counter the problem. Should the manager

discuss this with the employee? Yes, after rehearsing the conversation with another manager. Don't do the meeting alone, but don't gang up on the employee. Only the direct manager should have the conversation with another manager taking notes.

4. What do you do if you are in a small company, with no other managers? Call your attorney to join you for an interview with the problem employee.

5. One of the best tools for an employer is an Employee Assistance Plan (EAP). This gives all employees an 800 number to call for advice and direction on just about any issue. Employees and their household members may use EAPs to help manage issues in their personal lives. EAP counselors typically provide assessment, support and referrals to additional resources such as specialists for a limited number of program-paid counseling sessions. The issues for which EAPs provide support vary, but examples include: substance abuse, emotional distress, major life events, including births, accidents and deaths, health care concerns, financial or non-work-related legal concerns, family/personal relationship issues, work relationship issues or concerns about aging parents. These are all the stresses of daily life that can explode into the workplace.

6. EAPs are not expensive when compared to the total benefit package and can be as low as a couple of hundred dollars per year per employee. Your benefits insurance broker is your starting point for doing more research. Don't purchase an EAP just for fear of the distraught and gun-toting employee; a plan will improve productivity in your company by reducing attendance problems and helping employees to focus more on work rather than outside problems. But when you have an EAP in place, it may just prevent an employee from getting to the extreme position of picking up that gun. You may never know if the EAP prevents this, but I know EAPs do work. We had one at our company and the employees raved about it. This benefit sounds

almost too good to be true. Trust me ... it will help your company. Your job, once you purchase the plan, is to promote its usage by your crew.

7. Most companies, like Steven's, have grown, and each office expansion adds more confusion rather than coherence. The layout of your office significantly affects your office productivity. Lay out your office carefully; get the help of an office designer. This layout service is often made available for free by office furniture companies hoping to sell their wares. When you do this layout, design with security in mind. Consider natural barriers to entry: a door with a buzzer system for controlled entry and one central entry point to the office. Employees should have a clear view of the entry doors.

8. Call your alarm provider and install panic buttons under the desks of the receptionist, the office manager and all senior managers in your place. These are now wireless and easy to place anywhere.

9. Set up a confidential phone line that allows an employee to leave an anonymous message concerning the potential of violence. You'll waste time on prank calls where one employee complains about another, but if you do prevent one incident, it is worth it. Take each call seriously. Also, Steve should place a locked mailbox outside his office where employees may leave a private note.

10. Within your company, never allow a manager to fire someone without getting a second opinion. Never. If a manager comes upon a situation where an employee deserves to be fired, such as theft or sabotage, suspend the employee and schedule a meeting for the next day. This allows for cooler heads to prevail, setting up an organized conversation. In an on-the-spot firing, shouting matches often occur, leading to situations that can lead to disgruntled employees and so on.

11. When you plan to fire an employee, you should discuss what his reaction may be with his immediate supervisor. In 30 years of

management, other than economic lay-offs, I only fired one person who didn't expect it; and that was because he thought the rules did not apply to him. His reaction was unpredictable. Otherwise I was able to predict the response in every other case. This prevented many problems from occurring.

12. When you do fire an employee, you should decide if the employee is allowed back on the property. In most cases, this will be okay. But if you feel uncomfortable with someone returning, tell him that at the termination time. Send a memo detailing this to all employees and advise them to call the police if the employee tries to come into your company facilities. Be sure to send this to your branch locations as well.

13. Adding insult to injury, literally, half of Steven's office went on workers' compensation, very legitimately, claiming stress, post-traumatic stress syndrome, inability to sleep, and fear of going into the office. Then OSHA came in and levied a fine for an unsafe workplace. It is impossible for Steve to prepare for this aspect of the situation, other than to prevent the violence in the first place. Consequently, a strong follow-up program for these employees will not only help them to deal with these problems but also help prepare them to confront or prevent future incidents of violence.

Several types of assistance can be incorporated into the post-incident response. For example, Steven might bring in trauma-crisis counseling, critical-incident stress debriefing or employee assistance programs. Certified employee assistance professionals, psychologists, psychiatrists, clinical nurse specialists or social workers may be used.

Chapter 54

The Five-Minute Solution to Lowering Workers' Comp Costs

5ive minute consultant™ **Problem**

You own Grandma Ethel's Apple Pie Emporium, where you bake thousands of pies daily for local restaurants, delivering on your own trucks. You have 74 employees, from office staff to bakers and truck drivers. Your workers' comp rate last year was $2.15 per hundred dollars of payroll, but this year it ballooned to $4.90 a hundred, an actual increase of $81,400. How could this happen in one year? What should Ethel do now?

Possible Outcomes

- Ethel shrugs her shoulders and accepts the higher overhead. C'mon Ethel, you can do more than this.
- She called Mike, her insurance broker, who told her that she had four serious accidents last year, and the new rate would be in effect for at least three years.
- Ethel only recalled two accidents. She asked her bakery manager, Lester, and he only remembered two as well.
- Ethel has really never been aware of the make-up of this bill. Her accountant always said the bill was low and presented no problems. This year he raised the storm warning flags.
- Ethel is confused. How can she understand her bill, and more importantly, what can she do to reduce it?

What Did Ethel Find Out About Her Workers' Comp Bill?

1. Some basic definitions helped Ethel:
   a. Employee classification—each employee position is given a classification that sets the rate per hundred dollars of gross wages. Classifications vary based on the risks of the job. For instance an apple cutter would have a higher rate than a file clerk based on the history of all apple cutters and all file clerks. Forty-four states use a standard classification created by the National Council on Compensation Insurance (NCCI.com). The exceptions are California, Delaware, New Jersey, New York, Pennsylvania and Texas;
   b. Reserve—the amount of money that Ethel's insurance company predicts a given accident will cost, including medical bills, lost salary and future earnings reductions;
   c. Claim closure—the process of working with the insurance adjuster from the carrier to close an accident or change the reserves for a given situation;

d. Mod—or modification rate. Because of the four accidents on the books, Ethel's mod is 1.6. This means her rate is 1.6 time higher than the standard rate across all of her classifications; and

e. Loss control—the granddaddy of all terms; this is safety and accident prevention. If you have fewer accidents, or less severe accidents, your comp bill is lower. See Chapter 54 for more info on safety and loss control.

2. A workers' comp bill is always created on an estimate of payroll and verified by audit at the end of the year. Your actual payroll will control the bill. But what about the employee classifications? Many companies work with their insurance brokers or insurance specialists to reclassify their employees to lower rates. The auditor may agree or disagree; be prepared to justify your changes.

3. Let's say you have Lester listed as the bakery manager; the auditor may see Lester as working in the hot bakery and subject to a higher rate. But if Lester spends most of his time teaching employees and doing other office work, I would list him as an office person. Since Lester is highly paid, a reduction in his category is big savings. Did the auditor change Lester's job class last year and now you feel the increase? Ethel should be aware of any changes in her classes.

4. Do you have employees in multiple states, maybe in a branch office, or your drivers regularly travel in an adjacent state? You may have to use the rates in both states and pro-rate the hours of these employees. Rates for the exact same class will vary by state, based on how rich their benefits are. Can you shop the rates for the best deals by state? Yes, if the auditor agrees with your backup details of how much time is spent in each state.

5. Ethel should have semi-annual meetings with her whole company discussing workers' comp. Many workers feel that a claim doesn't hurt Ethel's as the state is paying if you are in a state-managed fund, or the insurance company is paying. Ethel needs to teach her

crew that workers' comp claims deeply impact Ethel's by increasing Ethel's costs, leaving less for capital expenditures and salaries.

6. Every television show seems to have an ad by an injury attorney urging people hurt at work to call for their share of the jackpot. Ethel can't wait until an accident occurs to counter this. Ethel must get brochures from her insurance carrier or broker geared to the reading level of her employees, in languages her employees are comfortable with and which are easily readable, describing what comp is. The attorneys who specialize in working with employees will have language professionals and the easy-to-read brochures.

What Steps Should Ethel Take to Decrease Her Comp Insurance Costs?

1. First step … hire people with the physical skills to do the job. (*See Chapter 67.*)

2. The biggest part of Ethel's increase came from a whopping increase in her reserve for the four accidents. The reserve is created by Alan Adjuster soon after the initial accident report, based on medical reports, conversations with the claimant, and Alan's experiences. If Alan feels the claimant will be out of work for three months and incur a certain level of medical bills, this becomes the reserve which sits on Ethel's policy for three years.

3. Why three years? Because accidents usually trend. If you have no accidents, your mod may be .8, which is a 20 percent discount to the published rate. But if you show four accidents, which is above the average for companies like Ethel's, then the mod will be higher, based on the premise that Ethel is running her business unsafely.

4. Next, Ethel asked Alan for a copy of their accident reports and the reserve calculation. Ethel and Lester only remembered two accidents, yet there were reserves for four. Two workers with minor accidents and who were back to work in two days, had big reserves. Only a small fraction of the reserve had been paid out.

5. This is where Ethel has to take charge. Once a reserve is established, it doesn't go away on its own. Some insurance companies do review the reserve, but it is up to Ethel and her broker to stay on top of this. Ethel called Alan Adjuster, explaining these two men were out of work two days and sent in payroll records as proof. Alan called the doctors who filled out the initial reports and found the injuries were not as serious as first thought. The reserves on these cases were cut down to actual expenses paid, which was a tiny fraction of the original reserve.

6. This left two accidents on the record. One, where a worker broke his leg, is still pending. The other, where the worker claimed he hurt his back lifting a bushel of apples, seems phony, bringing up the question of malingering or fraud.

7. There, I said it. The "F" word in workers' comp. Proven fraud only accounts for about 5 percent of all cases, while "exaggeration" occurs in about 25 percent of cases.

8. After an injury you want to do two things:

   a. Make sure your employee is getting the best care and is comfortable; and

   b. Get the employee back to part-time and then full-time work ASAP.

9. Contact the employee's family immediately, telling them about the accident and which medical facility the employee is going to. Let them know you are here to help. If the employee is in overnight, stop by the next morning on your way to work. Let him know you care. Keep in touch with the family continually. You are not doing this just for the sake of workers' comp, but it does help an employee to realize that he shouldn't take advantage of you with an exaggerated claim.

10. What can Ethel—and every other business—do?

    a. Have an active program of light-duty work available. An employee still at work, even at 25 or 50 percent, is a ton better than sitting at-home watching the attorney commercials. Keep a list of 10 or 15 tasks on-hand; have your managers write wish lists of jobs they would like accomplished but never have time to do;

b. Prepare a letter describing each task. When an injury is not serious, send this letter with each person who visits a doctor asking the doctor which tasks the employee may undertake during rehab. Walk-in clinics and emergency rooms are used to this and will fill it out. Train your supervisors that this letter goes with each person and must be faxed back by the doctor that day; and

c. Some companies send a supervisor along with every initial doctor visit just to go over this format.

11. In some states, employees are permitted to select their own doctors and change doctors as often as wanted, which leads to doctor-shopping. In other states, employees are allowed to select their own doctors but have to stick to the same one. Still other states allow employers to prepare a list and employees must choose from a doctor on that list. Finally, some states let employers choose a specific doctor. Check with your carrier or attorney for your state.

12. Many companies hire a medical review officer (MRO) to go over their employees' injuries. This is a doctor who will review all injuries quickly. The biggest advantage of an MRO is being able to speak with the injured person's doctor directly, explaining the light-duty program. If, after getting a green light for light duty, an employee chooses not to work, the benefit is reduced, the reserve goes down, and you save.

13. Be sure to go over your light-duty program with your comp carrier. The carrier should know that you have work available that will fit just about anyone; you'll even set up a work-from-home program as needed. Employees want to feel they are still a part of your company, and light-duty does this. If you treat an injured employee poorly, you will get back the same results, which will severely impact workers' comp in the future.

Chapter 57

The Five-Minute Solution to Buying Season Tickets

Problem

You have worked for years growing your business, Uncle Les' Umpire Supply Company, where you manufacture and distribute supplies, rule books and instructional videos to baseball umpires and referees in other sports. You are a sports junkie; that's obvious. You have some spare cash and have always wanted to buy season tickets to the New York Mets. Four seats run the range from $5,556 to $128,280, with 21 price points in between. You think this is a better investment than advertising, as you will get prime face time with customers by inviting them to the games.

Possible Outcomes

- You end up spending about $35 a ticket, or $140 a game. With parking and food, you are looking at $200 a game for 81 games. (It could be more if the Mets make the playoffs.) You spend quality time with key customers, have fun, and feel this is the best investment you have made in a while.

- You love the game, but about a third of your customers cancel at the last minute and leave you with open seats. You're angry you wasted this money.

- You offer seats to key employees but this bites you in the tail when Jim complains that John got seats to a better game. Then Joe's game was rained out and he wants another date, but you don't have any left.

- You get really upset when you invite a key customer to a big game, and he gives the tickets to his cousin.

How Could Umpire Supply Have Handled This Better?

1. The only way to tell if advertising (or any promotion) works is to measure its success rate after the fact. So, my initial suggestion is to start small.

2. Buy a 20-game package. Set up 12 games with key customers, four games for your employees, and four games for your family. This is one of the perks of owning a business, so enjoy it.

3. At the end of the 12 customer games, ask yourself if it was a success. Did customers appreciate the offer? Did they show up and were they enjoyable to be with for three or four hours? Did you discuss business, and was it a successful conversation?

4. Here's the big one: Did you set a business objective before the game, and did you achieve it? The objective can be to generate more sales, or it can be to resolve a previous problem, or to learn

about a competitor's programs.

5. The most basic objective, to spend fun time with a customer, should happen automatically. Don't offer the tickets to someone who doesn't like baseball! They may feel obligated to go, and then they will be grumpy.

6. Maybe you are better off with buying limited ticket packages to three different sports rather than a whole season of baseball. Since you sell supplies for all sports this would have a better reach. Whether a major league game or a local college basketball team, you want to appeal to what your customers' likes are, not your own (though I don't see how anyone would not love a Mets game).

7. After the first season, follow the sales of the customers involved. Did they go up? Or did problems decrease? If so, expand next season.

8. Since Uncle Les' Umpire Supply is in the sports business, odds are you received tickets to games from your vendors. Use these as your starting sample. Take customers with you and see if you gain sales.

9. When you invite people and give them the tickets, there is the risk that they will give them away. Tell your guests that if they can't make it to please let you know in advance so you can make alternate plans. It's good to have a few names of people who will go to a game on a moment's notice.

10. The same is true for you. When taking someone to a game, don't change plans and send your shipping clerk. Your customer was expecting you. Be there.

Is There a Better Way to Handle Working with Season Tickets?

1. Start early. Order your tickets early in the ticket selling time period. You'll get better seats. Target your key customers early. Give a couple of dates to your first customer and ask which one works for him; then your next customer, and down the line. This takes a lot

of time and coordination. When customers pick the games they want, there is a stronger chance they will actually show up. Follow up one month before the game and again a week before the game.

2. Ask your customer how many tickets they want: one, two or three, and who they would bring with them. If a spouse is coming, you might want to invite yours. If he wants to bring two kids, then you're going by yourself.

3. Sometimes the customer is greedy and will want all four and then you lose your face time, which is the goal. If you give all four, you are giving a gift, which you hope will be remembered. It's in poor taste for the customer to do this, but it will happen. It is really galling to then find out he brought one of his customers! But do remember this for next year and offer this guy a Tuesday night game that you didn't want to go to anyway.

4. Don't bring your order pad or copies of the invoices with which you have a problem. It is fine to mention these things and then follow up with a call after the game.

5. Bring plenty of cash to the game. Some customers will expect you to pick up every expense, from beers to souvenirs. Others will reciprocate and buy your dinner. Remember which ones are the good guys.

6. Drinking at a sporting event is always an issue. Your company may have a no drinking policy when with a client. If so, follow it. Realistically, having a beer at a game is part of our culture, but you should be careful. When you have one too many, your customer may look at you as a problem, not a drinking buddy. If your customer has too many, definitely drive him home, no questions asked. You may have liability if you bought the beers and later there is an accident.

7. Do you go out for dinner before the game? Or after the game if it was an afternoon contest? Up to you, your time availability and your budget. If the customer volunteers to take you out, it

is polite to go.

8. Here's the tough call of this chapter. Your customer asks for four tickets. You give them. Then you see the tickets offered on a ticket reselling website—at a price above face value, because they are good seats. Since I am writing this book, I should give you the perfect response. There is none. If you call the customer on this, he may be so embarrassed that he stops doing business with you. He may laugh it off, and then you may be so angry you don't want to do business with him. He may apologize, but you are still hurt. So, the best answer is: do nothing. There are some things you just don't want to know.

9. Sports tickets are considered business entertainment and are only tax deductible for 50 percent of the face value of the ticket if you attend the game with your client. Same for the food at the ballpark. Be sure to keep a log of the business conversation that took place. If you donate unused tickets to a registered charity you can deduct the full value. If you give all four tickets away, the most you can deduct is $25 per ticket, the maximum of a gift. If you bought tickets from a scalper you can't claim half of what you actually paid, just the face value.

10. Giving tickets to your employees can be a can of worms, but it doesn't need to be. Give the tickets as a reward for outstanding members of your team. Let everyone know what your standards are for earning tickets: maybe perfect attendance for six months, fewer customer complaints or returns, or an increase in sales of a specified item. Give all four tickets to the employee that earns them. If you go with the employee it usually is awkward and you definitely get stuck paying for the parking and food. Don't give two tickets to two different people for the same game. It is tempting to spread the tickets throughout your company, but this will cause more headaches than it is worth.

11. Confirm your employee is going to use the tickets. Employees shouldn't give tickets to another person or put them up for sale.

Make this cause for discipline within your employee handbook. Set your policy that rain-outs or rescheduled games go back to the company to redistribute the tickets.

12. Reserve about 20 percent of the tickets you buy for your staff. Give them games that don't interfere with work schedules, or give them the time off with pay as part of the gift.

13. For whichever sport you pick, decide which games you want to go to with your kids or your best friend. Give yourself a little present. You deserve it.

Chapter 58

The Five-Minute Solution to Setting Up a Sales Team

Problem

Your company, Penny's Body Parts, manufactures replacement car and truck body parts for late-model cars. You are 20 percent less expensive than buying from dealers; your customers say your parts fit better, have better paint quality and your service can't be beat. Does it get better than this? No. But your sales are down due to the recession. You decide to hire two salespeople to get the word out about Penny's, but you've never employed salespeople before. How do you set them up?

Possible Outcomes

- You hire Ellen and Charles; both with sales experience. Sales grow and both quickly pay back more than their salaries.

- Both salespeople start well, but being rookies in your industry presents problems. They don't know how to structure a sales call to body shops. After two months, sales are not growing.

- Ellen grows sales in the eastern territory, but Charles doesn't seem to have connected in the west. Is it okay to ask Charles to work with Ellen and pick up some tips from her? Do you have to pay Ellen more? Will Charles be upset?

- Accidentally, you discover that Charles has not called on Brian's Auto Parts for two months. Is this happening with other accounts? Is this why his sales curve is not growing?

- You give up ... the cost of two people is eating more cash flow than is being generated. Do you keep both? One? Neither?

What to Do About Ellen and Charles

1. Is two months enough time to evaluate the sales program? If you started a new paint line where it takes time to train the employees and retool the plant, you may budget a year or two to get a return on your investment. But, new salespeople are not a depreciable asset. Most entrepreneurs would like to see a salesperson turning positive within three months. In tough economic times, investments need quicker returns.

2. Keep Ellen? She has been a success. Give her the entire territory? If something works, don't fix it. Yes, keep her and let Charles go. Ellen will need to shuffle her time use. She'll only get to see the more important accounts, because she will be traveling more. The smaller accounts she has tried to cultivate won't see her; will they think Penny's is unreliable as they pulled Ellen after two months?

3. This needs a well-written letter, both to Ellen's and Charles' customers; a different letter to each. For the customers that

Ellen is not going to see, praise her and explain that she is gaining a larger territory. Give the customers a contact in the office, someone they can call for their needs. In Charles' territory, simply explain that a seasoned pro is coming to service them. After two months, not many customers will have an attachment to Charles. Again, tell them about the office based service representative that will help them.

4. As Ellen continues to succeed, you begin to think about building a sales organization to continue the growth. You have been selling in a 50-mile radius around your plant. How can you build a real sales team?

How to Start a Sales Team That Works!

1. Decide to build a sales organization just like you would any other major change to your business. Lay out the costs and the benefits. Actually, the benefits are easy; your profits will increase more than the costs associated with building the sales team. Let's look at the costs:

   a. **The cost of recruitment.** Are you going to use a professional or do the search yourself? A recruiter will generally charge from one-quarter to one-third of a year's base pay. The advantage is less demanding on your time and a quicker start to your program because of their pre-screened candidates.

   b. **Payroll and benefits for six months.** Give yourself a range on salary. You will pay more for an experienced person and it is worth it in this case as you don't know much about teaching and managing salespeople.

   c. **The sales expenses.** Don't start out giving a company car. Pay your team the IRS rate for mileage. This sounds high, but it is better than buying or leasing cars for a program to which you are only committing six months. Since you are in the automotive industry, the salespeople's cars have to be in top condition, always clean and presentable. Make that a prerequisite of hiring. Pay for car washes as needed.

d. **Communication is key.** Smartphones and laptops should be in your budget.

e. **The cost of collateral material.** Do you need new selling brochures? How about upgrading your website and web-based order program? If Ellen is successful in her presentations, yet the customers have a hard time ordering, have you really succeeded?

f. **The cost of training.** Ellen and Charles have sold computers and were good at it, but they have to learn your products. How long will this take? Who is going to do the teaching? You should plan on a month in house. If they haven't learned your line by then, start with new candidates.

g. **Set up an information system.** Your salespeople need to access your customer history, accounts receivable and inventory. You don't need to be elaborate here. A weekly printout will work, but online is better.

2. Early on, Penny decided that she wants company-paid salespeople, which brings up the program's most important employee issue: salary versus commission; or part of each? A higher percentage of earnings in salary will bring in more stable salespeople, but fewer risk takers. Higher commission percentage will bring in shooting stars, which can be extremely successful, or burn out. (*See Chapter 66 for the solution to manufacturers' reps versus company-paid reps.*)

3. Starting out without any established territories, it is rough to expect a commission person to invest a month in the factory and office when they are not earning. Also, since Penny has no idea on how to structure a commission program, she is better off with a salary to start, and promising to create an incentive program within a year. But, she can still create and pay some incentives right now:

a. A specific bonus, say $200, for every new account that does over $10K in its first six months.

b. Or, $500 for the same new account doing over $25K. In this case a salesperson would get a total of $700 for bringing in 25K in business, a 2.8-percent cost.

c. How about a bonus for every new account in a certain geographic area, to optimize a delivery route? This would be a small bonus, of say, $50.

d. If a customer has bought before, but has been dormant for 24 months, Ellen should earn the new customer bonuses.

4. For the base salary pay a salesperson what a good foreman in your company makes, including the foreman's overtime. You can expect a salesperson to put in at least a 50-hour week. If they don't, they will not be top performers. If a salaried salesperson works through a weekend, say at a regional trade show, it is appropriate to add a something extra to that week's pay.

5. Miscellaneous expenses include meals with customers, tolls and some office supplies. I would rather give a salesperson an advance of $500 on his expense money than give a company credit card.

6. One way to learn about current salary structures is to call a professional recruiting firm. Describe your job opportunity and ask him what he would recommend. A good recruiter will gladly share that info with the hope that you retain them for the search.

7. Define your strong points and look to the sales role to augment your areas of weakness. For instance, if you sell to small companies, and have not succeeded in large chains, target a person with that experience. Do you sell to business owners or to purchasing agents? Are your customers old or young? Match the salesperson to the buying audience. Are language skills important to reach a diverse customer base? If so, you'll pay more for a multi-lingual person, but that should pay you dividends.

8. If you are a regional business local travel is easy. In a larger geography, make sure the person is comfortable being away from home. Check his driver's license history through your insurance carrier. When he is driving his car, on your business, your insurance company approval is required.

9. Is this hire different than any other hire? No. Use good judgment. Even though you have not hired a salesperson before, do the same multiple interviews, check references and do the same gut-feel check you would for any key employee.

10. Call a half-dozen good customers and ask them who are the best salespeople that call on them. Ask them to pass your name to anyone who might be looking for a new career.

11. Do your competitors have sales people? Are they good salespeople working at a weak company? Again, ask a good customer to specifically pass your name to these special folks.

Chapter 59

The Five-Minute Solution to Employees Getting Sick and Other Disasters

5ive minute consultant™

Problem

You own Arthur's Segway tours and Rentals. In Boston, you have about 200 Segway Personal Transporters which you rent, mainly to tourists. Your business is successful, with not a problem in view. Your busiest time of the year is always the week of July 4. On July 1, you take your team of 30 tour guides out for a well-deserved dinner at Ranger's Steak House. The next morning, 23 people call in sick.

Possible Outcomes

- You call Ranger's and find out it has been closed by the Health Department.
- You call the other seven guides, explain what happened, ask them to come in early and be prepared to spend a long couple of days.
- You end up renting only 60 Segways daily for the next three days, which places a major crimp in your cash flow. You had counted on this big week to make a payment on your bank note.
- You are busy turning away customers and one of those turned away is the travel reporter from the *Boston Globe*. An article appears on July 4 stating that Arthur's is unreliable. When everyone returns to work, your business is off 50 percent.
- How could you have possibly gone from "not a problem in view" to laying off of half your tour guides and falling behind on payments?

What Can Arthur Do When the Twenty-Three Call in Sick?

1. Take a deep breath and count to ten. Call your competitors, explain what has happened and ask if you can borrow some employees. Some will laugh at you and try to take advantage of the situation; hopefully one or two will work with you. Maybe you can switch some reservations to the friendly competitors.

2. Call your past employees to come back for a couple of days. You may have to swallow your pride a little here. Ten come in for two days each.

3. Can Segway's regional office send experienced riders to teach the tourists? This will cost a bundle, but it's better than canceling pre-paid reservations.

4. Call a local TV station, explain what happened, and maybe it will run a feature story, where you plead for experienced riders to help a local business.

5. Call local temp employment companies and check to see if they have people that can help you.

6. Is it too late to think about the emergency procedures book you were going to work on last winter, when there was no business? You bet it is.

What Can Arthur Do to Protect His Business?

1. Don't go back to Ranger's. Ever.

2. Arthur might say he will never take his whole company out for dinner together again, but this is such a long-shot, that he is over-reacting. The morale value of being together far outweighs the miniscule chance of mass food poisoning.

3. Maintain a cordial relationship with your competitors. Yes, they take business away from you every day, but you do this to them as well. You don't have to like a competitor, just be able to speak with them. After all, if you or they get into trouble, it affects your entire industry!

4. Look into technology before you need it. Segways have an option of a GPS display screen and earphones that deliver self-guided tour information. Does your industry have a technology that you decided not to use because it added to your costs? Think beyond day-to-day costs and imagine what would happen if you took your crew to Ranger's.

5. Do you have a slow time? In your daydreaming, think of what could happen and how you would react. Have a plan for:

   a. Losing power. How would you process payments without your computer?

      • You need a battery back-up for your key functions.

      • On-site diesel or gas electric generator should be part of your business infrastructure.

      • Have your electrician wire a hook-up to your main electric feed line, where a portable, truck-mounted generator can supply your needs.

b. Losing water. Do you need water in your business?

- Will a couple of five gallon bottles let you flush the toilets?

- Will your water work without electricity? If not, definitely get that generator.

- Is water a key item in your business? A used tanker truck may find a home in your parking lot.

- If you own a restaurant, it's time to close the door.

c. A drunk driver drives through your front door.

- Have the name of a local glass company that will do emergency repairs or a board-up.

d. A major vendor recalls one of your key components for a safety problem.

- Always try to split vendor purchases with the 80/20 rule.

- Even though it costs, keep as much inventory on-hand as you can.

e. A major weather event hits your area.

- Have a decision tree written detailing who is in charge of closing or staying open; who does what when you can't open and who starts the rebuilding process.

f. You have a fire or a flood.

- There are companies that specialize in reopening businesses. Keep one name on your speed-dial. Google "disaster recovery companies." They should inspect your place before they are needed, so they know the layout and your most important needs.

- Here is a great primer from the U.S. Food And Drug Administration (FDA) on what to do after an emergency: http://www.fda.gov/Food/FoodDefense/Emergencies/FloodsHurricanesPowerOutages/ucm112713.htm

g. Your computer system crashes.

- Have both on-site and off-site continuous backup.
- Keep a local data center service on retainer where you can transfer your computer operations when in need. Even a very small business should have a separate computer that can run your basics.

h. Never be in a position that you can't make a sale!

- Keep a cash box to do cash sales, make change and stay in business!

i. Twenty-three people call in sick.

- Come on, you know that one by now. But really, what if there is a major flu epidemic in your area? Do you have face masks and germicidal soap? What about plans to deliver your products to customers who don't want to travel?

6. Keep a list of short-term employers; maybe the unemployment office or a temporary staffing company can do the trick. Waive your standard requirements, such as drug testing for people from a staffing service. Prescreen the temp agencies and learn which have people that fit Arthur's.

7. Make sure you have every employee's phone number. Many companies won't hire someone without a phone, in case of an emergency like this.

8. You can't get insurance for going to Ranger's, but check with your broker about business interruption insurance that pays when fire or flood visit you.

9. Can you sue Ranger's for impacting your business? You might get some publicity, but don't waste your time. You won't win money damages.

10. Have an emergency kit in your office, home and the trunk of your car with:

a. Flashlight and candles (*Don't* use candles where there may be a gas leak!);

b. Matches and flares;

c. Plastic and leather gloves, reflective vest and a loud whistle;

d. A manually cranked a.m./f.m./weather radio;

e. Bottled water and water purification tablets;

f. First Aid kit, blanket, sterile water, food energy bars, sunscreen, basic disinfectant, mild pain killers like aspirin, and a First Aid manual;

g. A basic tool kit, pens, pencils, paper, a hand crank generator for your phone;

h. Hygiene items—toilet paper and other personal needs items;

i. A portable camera to record damage; and

j. The ultimate fix-up item—-Duct Tape.

11. Here is a great web-site on emergency preparation from the U.S. Small Business Administration: http://www.sba.gov/content/preparing-emergency-can-determine-your-success

12. The federal government and many state and local agencies help companies with special loans and programs following a disaster. Eating at Ranger's won't qualify, but most natural disasters can qualify you for assistance. If your problem is designated a disaster area, there will be press releases and tons of information about it. Keep your ears peeled.

13. Know how to call-forward your business phone lines to any phone.

14. Train your crew annually on emergency procedures for your company.

Chapter 60

The Five-Minute Solution to the Unchecked Increase of Monthly Bills

5ive minute consultant™ Problem

You are Roye, the business manager and husband of the famous Lainee Gee, a singer and producer of big-stage shows. You have about 100 people on the payroll from stagehands to performers. You pay the bills, usually from a hotel room on the road. Your recently hired bookkeeper, Maya, called and said, "Roye, our cell phone bill is ridiculous; last month it was $17,000. What's going on?"

What Happened With This Bill?

- Since the company travels a lot, each person has a company cell phone. The troupe has been on the road quite a bit, but you have an unlimited calling plan, so that should have not made a difference.

- Was there a mistake on your bill? You know how it is with these computerized billing statements covering so many phones. You call Maya; it takes her exactly two minutes to explain the bill is correct.

- You remember changing phone carriers last year, which saved about $3K each month. You ask Maya to check, and yes, that did drop the bill last year, but it has steadily crept up since then.

- The troupe is very successful financially. You go over every bill from the theaters, the costume rentals companies and all the local expenses in each city where you perform. How did this fall under your usually keen radar?

How Did This Bill (and Others) Go Through Roye's Checkbook Without a Question?

1. We all do it. We scrutinize the bills that we don't know. But the regular bills just flow. You paid it last month; it looks the same, so pay it again this month. And if you don't pay it promptly, there is a whopper of a late charge and a finance charge.

2. In this case, Maya found out that the cell phone bill had been increasing an average of 5 percent a month since Roye put in the new carrier. Maya spent time analyzing the phone bill and found that 20 of the users accounted for 70 percent of costs. They were calling out of the country, which ran up huge costs.

3. Roye talked with the people and intended to really yell at them, but was he surprised! When the new plan started, he sent an

email to everyone stating they could call anywhere on their new flat rate plan. People then started calling overseas to family and friends. Roye, on reflection, realized it was his fault for not giving clear instructions. As soon as he told these folks that the overseas calling was costing the troupe a ton of money, they immediately stopped. They had no intention of purposely costing the company extra money.

4. The problem's cause was twofold:

   a. Roye's instructions were based on the fact that he knew it was a national calling plan, but didn't make this clear to his company.

   b. More importantly, the phone bill was one of the basic bills, and Roye approved them each month out of habit.

5. Roye realized he had to learn a new way to pay bills. Since he was always on the road, his office assistant emailed him a summary list of the bills, showing the total amounts. He said yes or no to the entire list, and it was always yes.

6. He asked Maya to help him. She had experience running a gymnastics and sports company.

What Did Maya Teach Roye? Could This Help Everyone Who Pays Bills?

1. Bill paying is not a chore to be relegated down the line. It is one of the core functions of leadership to make sure that every dollar expended is in the best interests of the organization.

2. You cannot assume that an invoice from a customer is correct. At our company we found that about 5 percent of the invoices that we paid every ten days were incorrect, almost always in the vendor's favor. I don't remember a single case of intentional error. But there sure were mistakes, by vendors and by our purchasing agents.

3. Start with a purchase order system, either computerized or hand-

written. Key points that must be on every purchase order:

a. Who placed the order;

b. Whether it's confirming a phone or electronic order;

c. Quote or order program reference;

d. Vendor information;

e. Order and due dates;

f. Item description;

g. Item accounting information;

h. Quantity ordered;

i. Price per unit of measure;

j. Packing and shipping info;

k. Freight costs;

l. If it's a taxable item; and

m. Payment terms.

4. Using the original PO or a copy, the receiving person notes the quantity received and any discrepancy from the order amount, including broken or defective materials.

5. Do not allow your purchase order writers to fill in the pricing after the invoice is received. If unsure of the price, why are they ordering the material or service? The pricing negotiation has to be conducted prior to ordering the goods, not after receiving.

6. After the invoice is received, the accounting department matches all the paperwork, verifying the price, quantity and confirming all other details, the most common of which will be price discrepancies. Maybe your vendor raised its prices since the last purchase, you ordered different quantities, or heaven forbid ... there is a mistake by your vendor. Just because you wrote the price on your purchase order, the vendor's computer program doesn't have to agree.

7. When a discrepancy is found, the invoice package goes back to the purchasing person at your company for resolution within three

days. If it sits on someone's desk, you lose your payment discount terms and credibility if you complain long after the fact.

8. What about the fine print that says the company's pricing overrides your purchase order? Well, my fine print can kick your fine print. Every purchase order has a page of it and so does an invoice. Copy yours from POs you receive; you don't need a lawyer. Buy a preprinted pad of POs at any office supply store and you'll have a good starting point. If the pricing comes down to whose fine print is finer, you should be looking for a new vendor. Now relationships become important. Maybe there will be a price increase for the next order, or you'll change the quantity next time to earn free shipping. There is give and take here, on both sides. (*See Chapter 4 on selecting good vendors*)

9. Once all the paperwork is set, the check is ready to process. Whether you approve the paperwork or sign the check, you should review each packet completely. Your team will understand quickly that they have to get it right the first time, which will save you big dollars in the long run. You should process all bills promptly, even if you don't have the cash flow to cut the checks. You have no bargaining power when a bill is past due.

10. Let's go back to these recurring bills where you have no purchase order for verification. Prepare a simple spreadsheet with the name of the bill and record the amounts for the last eighteen months. You will easily see any trends or single month problems. Your electric bill may go up in the summer with air conditioning, or your gas bill will go up in the winter when heating. One simple sheet for each vendor; you'll see last year in the same month, seasonal trends and the occasional spike, which will need research prior to payment.

11. Yes, it really is this simple. A spreadsheet, some timely homework and a top-down commitment to getting the best pricing and terms from vendors will save you time, dollars and stress.

Chapter 61

The Five-Minute Solution to the Air Conditioning War

(Note: If you are in San Diego, Calif.,
you don't need to read this chapter.)

5ive minute consultant

Problem

David Kay is the accounting department manager at a very large company. He has 70 people working for him, all in cubicles in one large office. The office has 4 zones for heating and air conditioning, and never once have all 70 people ever been comfortable. In fact, the biggest single complaint that David gets is people are too hot or cold. He has received petitions, delegations, complaint letters and angry calls. He's put locks on the controls, but the next morning they were pried off. How does David regain control of this unruly mob?

Possible Outcomes

- He appoints a blue-ribbon commission of senior employees to resolve this issue on their own. The only thing they resolve is that David has left them out in the cold.

- David meets each section in the office and earnestly tries to make peace. Does the "cold war" sound familiar?

- David lets people move their desks from the north wall to the south, but then those same folks complain that the sun is too strong and close the blinds, setting off another feud.

- Before this becomes a hot war, David calls his friend Sandy, who gives him great advice. The problem is solved and David is forever in Sandy's debt. Here's how.

What Advice Does Sandy Have for David?

1. A comfortable working temperature improves productivity. That's the good news. But, there is no reliable measurement of comfortable. It depends entirely on the person. One may be fine at 71 degrees while the next person will be chilled. There is no government standard, but the General Services Administration (GSA), with energy conservation in mind, sets 72 degrees for the summer and 68 degrees for the winter.

2. If you let the summer indoor temp get into the 80s, and people faint or have the beginnings of heat stroke, OSHA can come on the scene and cite you for hazardous work conditions. You don't want this. If the air conditioner breaks for a day or two, you won't get in trouble, but if you consistently allow 85-degree temperatures, one of your folks will surely complain.

3. Sandy tells David that he will never make everyone happy, but that he should try for the best he can. Most large rooms have warm and cool sides based on the windows. Try moving people's work stations as much as the work process allows.

4. The next step is to bring in your HVAC vendor and have the air flow balanced, which should be done every year. Based on changing building usage, the volume of air on each branch of the system will need adjusted. Some folks will complain about too strong an air flow, which feels drafty. Make sure this is corrected; otherwise people will start taping cardboard over vents, which will upset the balance of the rest of the system. Also, change your air filters by following the manufacturer's recommendations—twice every year at a minimum.

5. Check the humidity level, maintaining between 25 and 45 percent. The lower side is better. Too low (below 20 percent) will make the room feel colder as well as cause people to develop sore throats, which may lead to other illnesses.

6. What about letting people have small personal fans or heaters at their desks? Sandy tells David that this may help, but to be sure and speak with the building engineer first. Heaters place an extreme load on the electrical panel, causing breakers to flip. She also tells David that in many areas, heaters are banned as a fire hazard in an office situation. They can fall over easily and can ignite a carpet or papers. If David allows fans and heaters, his electric bill will be in for a big spike!

7. Sandy also explains that women will feel colder due to wearing skirts. Open-toed shoes also can lead to colder feet. Sandy advises David to relax the dress code during the heat of the summer. Business casual for the summer can include proper length shorts and casual shirts for both women and men. David does not want to join the fashion police and measure the length of clothes. He insists his people remember this is a business first.

8. David also learns that his highest priority should be employees with allergies to pollen, fragrances or other air/dust-related situations. Sandy also tells him that menopausal women can have huge swings in temperature on a daily basis.

9. Some of David's employees have complained of smells. He learns

that his system takes in fresh outside air as well as having air returns inside the building. If there is an air return near a kitchen or lunchroom, the smell of fresh coffee all day long will make people go to the break room more often. David's company is smoke-free, but allows smoking outside. If the air intake is near the smoking area, second-hand smoke will waft in. Also, make sure that bathroom vents are never near an air intake.

10. Air intakes can also let disturbing noises into the area. The noise may not be obvious, but can have a negative impact on productivity.

11. David should make sure the thermostats are not accessible. The control freaks will be moving it three times a day and absolutely no one will be happy.

David Calls Hastings Architectural to Learn More About Building Design

1. The first question Al Hastings asks is if David's company owns or leases the building. If leased, would the landlord participate in the cost of renovations? If owned, what is their budget, and what length of payback do they expect? Dave tells him they own the building, and it has not been renovated since it was built 20 years ago. The owner tells Dave to prepare a budget for his review.

2. Dave learns the company's HVAC system is very inefficient and they could save at least $40,000 annually with a more energy-efficient unit. The local utility will give them a $10K grant and there will be accelerated depreciation for tax purposes, giving this a six-year payback.

3. The more efficient unit will mean lower motor speeds for the fans, reducing the drafts in the office and more even heating and cooling. David is all in favor of this.

4. The next point discussed is the glass in their windows. Being so old, the windows are extremely inefficient compared to today's higher technology offerings. David learns that low-E glass reduces

heat gain in the summer and reduces heat loss in the winter. There are different formulas for the type of glass depending on the climate the location is in. This aspect of the renovation becomes a super money saver for David's building.

5. The glass itself should be double-paned insulating glass, which further reduces heat transfer and reduces exterior noise, and picking the correct colors of the glass can reduce solar heat gain by 70 percent, but still let in plenty of light. This will significantly reduce the air conditioning load.

6. The glass on the south side of the building can stop a lot of heat and light. David can get a glass that lets in more heat and light on the north side. This will help balance the heating and lighting load of the building, reducing temperature differences in his office, and further saving money.

7. David can install blinds or sunscreens on the south and west sides that will close automatically as the sun reaches its peak intensity. This will prevent people from jumping up to open and close the blinds. Solar films can be applied to the existing windows for a much lower cost, but will not be as energy-efficient at a total glass replacement.

8. Lastly, the metal framing of the windows can be made with special thermal-break aluminum that prevents the transfer of heat during winter and summer. All told these three changes, used in completely changing the window system will cost about $150K, but save over $20K per year in energy costs, over and above the changes from changing the HVAC unit. Along with the tax breaks, this will create a six-year payback as well.

9. The last thing David learns is to replace his lights with more energy-efficient lighting, which will also reduce the generated heat. There are huge rebates from utility companies and tax credits for this as well.

10. All-in-all, David is a winner doing this renovation. It is about $300,000 with a six-year payback, but the biggest win is creating a happy and productive staff.

Chapter 62

The Five-Minute Solution to a Lay-off at Leaping Lou's Liquors

Problem

You own Leaping Lou's Liquors, a wholesale distributor of liquor, beer, wine and snack foods to retail stores. You run 23 daily truck delivery routes. You've treated your employees like family for 20 years and never had a lay-off. The recession finally has caught up with Lou's, and for the last six months sales have decreased by 18 percent. You have eliminated all overtime, encouraged extended vacations and frozen new hires. Still, when you are in the warehouse, you see there is no work to do. The trucks are all back by 1:30 p.m. each day. What should you do?

Possible Outcomes

- You do nothing and hope times will improve. They don't. You realize you are about 20 percent overstaffed.

- You have finished every cost-cutting trick in the book and even invented new ones, but it still comes down to too many workers for the times.

- You have two choices: reduce everyone's hours to 32 per week, which will upset all, or reduce headcount. You have 105 employees, and that means laying off 20.

- There are rumors in the plant about a big shake-up coming. You have to act soon.

How to Decide Between an Hours Reduction or a Lay-off

1. The hours reduction may be better if:

   a. You expect the time period to be less than 12 weeks;

   b. If your pay is on the high side of normal for your region;

   c. You have a highly technical or well-trained workforce and you need all your people to run your business; and

   d. You are large enough to be covered by the WARN Act.

2. The lay-off is better if:

   a. You have employees who are easily hired and trained;

   b. You want to close a shift or department completely;

   c. You are not sure when your business will pick up;

   d. You have a labor contract that requires negotiating an hours reduction but not a lay-off; and/or

   e. You know a laid-off employee can collect benefits, while a worker cut to 32 hours can't.

3. A lay-off reduces benefits costs where a reduction in hours will still have Lou paying medical and other insurances, for smaller

overall savings.

4. Because Lou has never done a lay-off he has a lot of soul-searching to do. "What is best for his employees" has always been his motto. But if he doesn't do something soon, he will endanger the whole company.

5. Lou is leaning toward the lay-off. He calls his favorite five-minute consultant to learn about the WARN Act. Here are some details:

   a. The <u>W</u>orker <u>A</u>djustment and <u>R</u>etraining <u>N</u>otification (WARN) Act is a federal law that requires workers be given a 60-day advance notice of a mass lay-off. The purpose is for employees to begin training for new jobs and to plan their finances. Some states have different rules. Check with your attorney;

   b. The act applies to employers of 100 or more, where people have worked more than 20 hours per week, and at least six months in the last 12. So far, Lou is covered and will have to take WARN into consideration;

   c. The final criterion is if a covered employer lays off at least 33 percent of the workforce, or more than 50 workers at once, then the act takes effect. Lou, planning to lay off 20 percent of his workforce, is not subject to the act. If he were, he would be required to send all workers a letter, 60 days before the layoff date, stating the layoff is coming, who will be affected, and the phone number of an executive at the company they can call for more info. Also, Lou would be required to report this to his local unemployment office, who would immediately step in to help relocate workers;

   d. A couple of other points—is "bumping" available? This would come into play if Lou was going to close his second shift. Would higher-seniority workers have the right to bump lower- seniority workers on the first shift? If bumping is allowed, it must be stated in the letter. Lou also has to say if this is a permanent or temporary layoff;

e. The exceptions to the WARN Act are if the layoff is due to a natural disaster, or a totally unpredictable business situation;

f. If an employer doesn't follow the act, he is absolutely liable to pay his workers for the 60 days with their benefits.

6. After talking with his key managers, his accountant and lawyer, Lou decides the layoff is the route to take, based on the savings on benefits and to keep morale high for the 85 people who are staying.

Let's Walk Lou Through the Exact Steps He Should Take for the Layoff

1. Read your employee manual. What does it say about layoffs? A good manual will cover this, and the best comment is: "In the event of a layoff, management has the sole right of decision. We will take into consideration work effort, attitude, cooperation and seniority." If your manual or an employment contract states that seniority is the sole criteria, you have little choice.

2. Some decisions have to be made before the layoff:

a. Who? Lou must work very closely with his supervisory team. These folks know the workforce best and really should make the decisions in concert with Lou. Be careful not to discriminate against older employees or folks from one of the protected groups, such as race or religion. The layoff size is critical as you don't want to do a second round. If Lou is not sure if it should be 16 or 20 people, go with the 20 now. In a couple of weeks he can call back a few people if necessary. If Lou does a second round of layoffs, even at a small number, this will significantly hurt morale more than the first round. People will never be sure that there won't be a third round or more;

b. When? Do it as soon as possible. Except if near a holiday or near the year-end when people will qualify for a year of profit-sharing or other benefit. Nothing is tackier than laying people off two weeks before Christmas. Don't do it on a Friday as your remaining folks will have all weekend to be upset. Mid-week is best, so that you can meet with everyone staying during the next couple of days;

c. Will there be a severance package (based on the person, seniority, or job title)? No need for this if you are expecting a temporary layoff; if a permanent one, give this some thought. A good number is a week of salary per year of seniority, up to a given maximum of say, eight weeks of pay.

d. Benefits? How long will you continue benefits? If you can afford it, I recommend keeping only medical insurance for up to 90 days. This says you care about the people and their families. Be sure to send the Consolidated Omnibus Budget Reconciliation Act (COBRA) letters on the first day of the layoff and state that you will pick up the payments for the first 90 days.

e. Are you going to hire a job outsourcing company? Even though Lou isn't required to do so, he should contact the local unemployment office and set up a meeting for the laid-off folks to learn about unemployment insurance. Lou can also hire a consultant to give tips on job hunting, resume writing and interview skills.

3. Plan the announcement. I recommend you tell the whole company at once and then meet individually with the ones being let go. Write out what you are going to say. Under no circumstances should you say, "This hurts me more than it hurts you." You still have a job, and they don't. Don't justify the layoff, or try to blame governments or other agencies for bad policies.

4. Don't give false hopes by saying you hope to bring everyone back shortly. Be realistic in this discussion. Will there be a callback list if another current employee leaves? There should be and you can say this, but make no promises.

5. Keep the announcement short and to the point. Once you say there will be layoffs, nobody is really listening to the rest of what you say; they are all thinking about whether they are on the list or how their workload is going to be increased. Give the laid-off people a letter, detailing the points discussed, including any severance or benefits package. Even though you said this in your talk, people really were not listening.

6. Immediately after the announcement meet with the folks who are leaving. Stress that it is not personal to them, but a business decision you had to make. Expect some to be really upset. Let them vent. Be sensitive to their comments, but do not express agreement with them that the lay-off is wrong or they should have been retained. Your final decision is non-negotiable. Never be alone when telling an individual; always have a note-taker with you. Don't let it turn into a debate. You decision is firm. If you feel someone will be so upset that violence may occur, have another supervisor just outside your door.

7. Employees may ask to speak with someone higher up the ladder. Let the employee have access to one level up in this case. Your supervisor should be able to handle this. In Lou's case, there is no one else. Don't allow a conversation that says "you should have laid off someone else and not me." This can only go downhill. People will tell Lou about their personal problems and debts, and how the layoff will causer further problems. Listen politely, but do not change your mind. If you feel strongly that this person should stay, call them back to work in two weeks. If you let one person change your mind today, every other employee will try to do the same.

8. Each state has different laws. Check with your attorney and ask if you have to give final paychecks on the day of the layoff. What about accrued vacation or sick days? That may have to be paid as well.

9. Place on hold all new equipment purchases for the time being, maybe 30-60 days. If you just took delivery of a new car, don't

drive it to work. Don't hire a family member. In short, don't do anything ostentatious.

10. This will be a tough day for you and your management team. Accept it … it goes with the territory. The folks who are staying will appreciate that you have taken decisive action to maintain the health of Lou's, and that you have noticed how the ones who are staying deserve to stay. Some may be upset that their friends have been laid off. Let them grumble for just a day and then go forward. Don't allow them to make a case for bringing someone back.

11. When you meet with the remaining workforce, discuss each person's workload and what is now expected of them. Emphasize that now is time to improve their skills to make the increased workload doable. Offer whatever training help they need.

Chapter 63

The Five-Minute Solution to the Company Truck Traffic Accident

Problem

On Tuesday afternoon, at 2 o'clock, you get a call from your truck driver, Tracy, that he has been in an accident. He tells you he is not hurt badly, but the paramedics want him to get checked out at the hospital. He tells you that Carl, the owner of the other car involved, was taken to the hospital.

Possible Outcomes

- Carl is only shaken up and gets released from the hospital; Tracy has a bump on his head, and your insurance will cover all of the costs. The odds of it being this simple are about the same as you throwing a perfect game in the World Series.

- Carl has a broken leg and collar bone; Tracy will be out of work for two weeks getting physical therapy for a stiff back, and you receive a $3,000 clean-up bill from the city sanitation department for cleaning up the mess your truck dumped during rush hour.

- In addition, Irma, your insurance agent, calls you and asks who Tracy is, as he isn't listed on your insurance. She tells you Tracy was found guilty of DWI two months before you hired him.

- Tracy files a workers' compensation claim and is advised by his cousin, Lou the Lawyer, that he should not go back to work for at least six months and should sue you for not maintaining the truck he was driving when he had the accident.

- Okay, you get the drift … start buying aspirin by the caseload.

What to Do After You Get the Phone Call from Tracy

1. Your first call is to Irma. This is the reason you have a local agent and not an 800 number to a call center four states away. Give the facts as you know them. She should arrange for an immediate clean-up crew and a tow truck. Ask to get an insurance investigator to the scene and to the hospital as soon as possible.

2. If Irma can't help you with a clean-up crew or tow truck, get everyone you can to the accident site with brooms, shovels and trash bags or cans. You want this cleaned up as quickly as possible to avoid financial charges and to keep you off the six o'clock news as the source of the largest traffic jam in two years.

3. Go to the accident site yourself. Check with the police, and super-

vise the clean-up and the towing of your truck. Take plenty of pictures of your truck, Carl's car and the area around the accident. Look for signs that may have not been placed correctly, burned-out traffic lights, or parked cars blocking the road.

4. Get the names of every witness you can. Many people will try to avoid getting involved. Use your charm and be polite. If a person won't give you his name, write down his license plate number.

5. Next, go to the hospital to check on Tracy. Let him know you are there for him. Tell him in no uncertain terms that he is to speak to no one other than the police or the medical staff about the accident. If he has not yet called his family, help him with that. If Tracy will be at the hospital overnight and has children, offer to cover babysitting costs. Ask Tracy about the accident. Make good notes, but do not record the conversation.

6. Back at your office, make plans for tomorrow's deliveries, deciding on a rental truck and if you need a temporary worker to do Tracy's job. Contact your customers who will be impacted by your lack of a truck.

7. Confirm all that you know about the accident with Irma. Fill out your own accident report paperwork for OSHA records. Contact vendors if you need product that was lost or damaged in the accident.

8. Call Tracy to get an update on his status. Remind him that you are there to help him and that he shouldn't speak with anyone about the accident.

9. Listen to Irma's advice. This is an ordinary occurrence to her and she will know how to handle it.

Let's Try to Prevent the Problem or Reduce Its Impact

1. You should ask Irma to check the driving histories of any prospective employees who might drive your company's vehicles or drive their own vehicles on your behalf before hiring them. If they have DWIs or other traffic convictions, don't hire them. If they drive

their own vehicles, make sure they are insured up to a specific amount set by you and Irma.

2. Enforce a sharp policy of no phone calls and no texting while company vehicles are moving. Insist that seatbelts be worn at all times. How will you do this if you are not in the truck? If a driver calls in, you can tell he is moving by the road noise; when he returns, write up a warning. On the second offense, give him a day's suspension. If a driver has an accident and the police report shows no seatbelt use, suspend him for a week or longer when he returns to work.

3. Drivers must inspect every truck for safety daily using a standard checklist. You can find one by visiting www.fiveminuteconsultant.com. If your trucks carry inventory or heavy loads, have a supervisor confirm each load is secured properly and balanced. Have a supervisor accompany each driver four times a year.

4. Hold monthly driver meetings. In addition to your business needs, go over:

    a. What to do in the event of an accident, such as speaking only with police and medical personnel:

       • Call the police;
       • Get all drivers' and passengers' contact and insurance information;
       • Call the office;
       • Clean up road debris.

    b. Safety rules; and

    c. The importance of completing driver logs and inspection forms

    In addition, have Irma attend the meetings once a year and review safety. Also remind drivers that driving safety also covers forklifts and yard trucks. Seatbelts are a must in every case.

5. Have Irma review each employee's driving record every year. Make sure your employee manual states that a conviction of DWI or DUI is cause for termination or job change.

6. Understand federal and state driving laws. For a complete list of U.S. regulations, visit www.fiveminuteconsultant.com. Visit your state government website for local regulations and follow them. If you or your employee violates them and has an accident, all you can do is … you know it … open your checkbook.

7. You should strongly consider putting GPS-based vehicle-tracking systems in your trucks. (To locate one of these, visit www.fiveminuteconsultant.com.) These record speed and driving conditions. Monitor the results and, if employees speed, then discipline them accordingly. By the way, these systems really help you in scheduling and in answering questions about when a delivery can be expected. They quickly pay for themselves in customer service.

8. Place speed governors on all trucks. Set the maximum speed based on the type and size of the truck and the types of loads it carries. This also improves your gas mileage.

9. If Tracy is injured in a vehicle accident, get him back to work as soon as possible. Even if he sits in the office and does filing or answers the phone, it is better than him sitting at home watching daytime TV, where all of the ads are for lawyers urging him to sue you. Let him go to physical therapy, if needed, and come to the office part-time. Light-duty work, even with no productivity, is much cheaper than a workers' compensation claim.

10. Have a prepared list called "What to do in the event of an accident," and follow it. (Visit www.fiveminuteconsultant.com for a sample.) With this you won't waste time figuring out what to do and you won't skip important items. Have Irma help you write this based on your industry and location.

Chapter 64

The Five-Minute Solution to the Employee Who Asks to Work Through Her Vacation

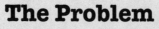 ## The Problem

You own Big Mark's Merchandising, a distributor of household goods, with 63 people on your payroll. Beatrice Bookkeeper comes to you in early June, asking if she can work through her two-week vacation scheduled for the end of July. With her husband out of work, you know she needs the money. Your employee manual is silent on this. Do you let her work?

Possible Outcomes

- You tell Beatrice no, because you don't have the budget to pay her. You based her payroll on 52 weeks of salary, and now you would end up paying her 54 weeks, increasing your expense by 3.8 percent. If you let Beatrice do this, you would have to allow others, and your bottom line just can't afford this. Beatrice is not happy with your decision.

- You tell Beatrice okay, but to keep quiet about it. She is the best bookkeeper you have ever had and you know that the other people trained to do her job won't do it as well as she does. You naively think that no one else will ask to be paid. Boy, were you ever wrong.

- You meet Beatrice half-way, letting her work through one week only. You really feel that employees need to take time to relax and be with family, but wonder if her family would be better off with the extra income. Beatrice is still not happy with this option.

- During the one week Beatrice is off, Arnold, the accounts receivable guy who is filling in for Beatrice, asks you a question about a disbursement account he is not familiar with. Neither are you, but you make a note to ask Beatrice about it when she returns on Monday.

What to Do When Beatrice Asks the Question

1. Since you have said no in the past, but are considering it this time, take an hour to think about it. Big Mark's can afford to pay the extra for Beatrice, but you are worried about the precedent. You know that if you allow it, others will definitely ask. You know that many of your people work second, part-time jobs, and that some work during vacation time at their second jobs.

2. You want to be compassionate, but there is a slight alarm bell ringing in the back of your head about the cost.

3. You know that people who come back from vacation are more enthusiastic about work and seem to be sharper.

4. You wonder if the extra income is the reason for Beatrice's question. Does she feel that no one else can do her job? Is she worried that sharing information with her replacement will reduce your dependence on her? In tough economic times, is she worried about a layoff during her absence, or maybe you realize you can survive without her?

5. So you compromise in your mind, and offer Beatrice one week of extra work and tell yourself that she really deserves your help. If anyone else asks, you are going to say she is working on a special project for you.

6. The one thought that doesn't enter your mind is that Beatrice is doing something underhanded.

Some Things for Mark to Consider Before Going Forward

1. The request to work through vacation will come up in every company, more so in tough economic times.

2. You should have a written policy covering this, and then stick to it. Your policy can say just about anything, as long as you implement evenly throughout the company.

3. Can you afford to add one full week to your labor costs? It will increase your workers' comp costs and all other wage-related costs including pension.

4. At my company I did allow a small amount of vacation to be worked. Here is the formula I used: People with one week of vacation could not work through it. People with two or more weeks of vacation could work one week. The policy also stated that this benefit could be withdrawn at any time, based on the economic needs of the company. There were a couple of years where we did just that and no one complained.

5. How do you run your company? Do people work late, on weekends, or do extra work from home? If so, granting this request would be one extra way to say thank you. Does your current vacation package include a 'use-it-or lose-it' program? If so, paying for people's unused time is more logical than having everyone take off two weeks in December. Do you pay for unused vacation? That is the same as Beatrice's request, just framed differently.

6. Another variation is to let your lower-paid employees have this option, but not the ones on the higher side of the scale. This allows you to help the people who may need it the most and not impact your financials as strongly. Make this distinction at the time an employee is hired or promoted.

7. At Big Mark's Merchandising, everyone is required to take his vacation. Studies have shown that people are better employees after they return from a vacation. No doubt about it. This starts a couple of weeks before vacation as people think about the good times to come, and wears off after about six weeks back at the job.

8. There is another part to the policy. No one who handles financial transactions, either from the sales desk or in the accounting department, should work through their vacations. Tell this to new applicants up front and there will be no problem. Why? All businesses have to be cognizant that there are opportunities for employees to become "silent partners" without your being aware of the partnership. All companies should have a second person be able to step in to every financial position and should do so once a year. This is one of the best fraud deterrent systems you can put in place. This means everyone in accounting, without exception.

9. All employees, at every company, think they are indispensable. Many keep their job knowledge to themselves, not sharing their skills. In making vacation schedules, be sure to have an effective cross-training program so that at least two people know every job at your company. This even goes for your job! You will gain more from this than just about any other program you can im-

plement at your company. Yes, it does feel redundant, but I promise you it is worth it. You never know when an employee will leave, get sick or win the lottery. Cross-training gives everyone a good feeling ... people get to learn a new job and change their point of view of work. If a rookie can do a job quickly, then why did the guy on vacation take so long? This is how you can identify and work with your employees who want to learn and grow at Big Mark's Merchandising.

10. Now that you have made up your mind, update your employee manual.

Chapter 65

The Five-Minute Solution to Changing a Company Name

Problem

Your dad started Carl Johns Family Planning Service 40 years ago. At that time, family planning had a different connotation than today. Dad was a financial advisor to growing families, helping plan retirement and estates. Now, you, Carl Johns' son, Carl Jr., are taking the reins of the business and feel it's an appropriate time for a name change. How do you pick a new name and make sure your clients know who you are?

Possible Outcomes

- Carl does not change the name and pro-life groups continue picketing;
- The name is changed to Carl Jr.'s Family Financial Planning. Three weeks after all the paperwork is done, and thousands spent on printing, Carl receives a cease and desist letter from Carl's Jr.™, a West Coast chain of restaurants;
- For his next choice, Carl consults with a corporate naming service. They quote $30,000 to research a new name and company tagline. Their service includes three weeks of in-depth study of his industry and five consumer focus groups. Wisely, Carl feels this is overkill for his company; and
- Carl feels like a ship-wrecked sailor alone on a tropical island. What can he do?

What Steps Should Carl Take to Get a New Name?

1. He calls his friend, Diana, who has great experience with this. She tells him the following traits make for a great name:

   a. The name has to be memorable and easy to recall. It should be pronounceable and roll off the tongue easily;

   b. It has to be easy to spell so look-ups in the phone book and on-line are simple. Don't change "C" to "Q" or "K." Don't be cutesy or silly. People want to find your business—make it easy.

   c. Carl needs a positive connotation in the name. Avoid words like: old, gray and mare. Use vibrant words. Mom is a friendlier word than mother. (See a great list of positive words at the end of this chapter.) Financial Services in a firm's name is stronger than Financial Company.

   d. What your business does should be in your name. If you say, "Carl Johns' Services," no one will call you. By inserting "Financial Planning," you are immediately recognizable. If you have millions in your ad budget, you can have an obscure name that the public will learn. (Think Xerox).

e. Your name and then your logo should impart, where possible, a visible image with which customers can associate. Carl's name should contain the word "financial" in one form or another. The typeface should look financial, not like puffed-up balloons.

f. Keep the name as short as possible. This makes for easier look-ups and better domain names. Avoid clichés and obscure Latin phrases that few people will understand.

2. Using a personal name connotes a family business. This is good in many situations and gives the customer an expectation of dealing with an owner. Family names demonstrate a strong sense of pride in the business, which is a plus in hands-on, local and personal businesses. Family names don't translate well if you are thinking of an international plan. If you are planning to sell the business in the future, avoid a family name.

3. Don't create a committee to help you create your name. Ask only one or two trusted people to help you brainstorm. With a committee you will be trying to please everyone, and you will get a plain vanilla name.

4. Next step—what is the expected geographic reach of your company? A plumber working in just one town can say, "Mayberry Plumbing," but if you plan on growing, avoid a geographic reference.

5. Check your potential name for ethnic or language implications. A made-up word may be a real word in Spanish or Chinese, and according to Murphy's Law, it will be a very negative word. There are services that will research this, but Carl can do this for free. Drop a note to the embassy of some major countries (I suggest France, Spain, Germany, China and Japan— for addresses go to: http://www.embassyworld.com/Foreign_Embassies_In_The_USA/) asking if your

name translates appropriately in their language. Easier yet, contact the foreign language department at a local college or high school.

6. Carl is based in an area containing many mountains. Taking a cue from this, he has decided on Mountain Top Financial Services. He figures his logo will be a family standing on top of a mountain. But is he selling insurance or mutual funds, or giving advice? He needs a tagline that will always follow his name.

7. "Financial Planning for Everyone," "Financial Planning for Serious Investors" or "Professional Financial Planning" are choices. A tagline helps explain your business in a couple of words. This is as important as the name when the name doesn't specifically describe the business. Keep it short and extremely descriptive. When you answer the phone, the customer should hear: "Mountain top Financial Services—We do financial planning—Can I help you?"

8. Let's look at these three tagline choices:

   a. "Financial Planning for Everyone"—Does Carl plan on servicing families with a certain minimum net worth? Will he take on people who want to save $30 a week from their paycheck? Probably not, but this tagline invites low net worth families to come in.

   b. "Financial Planning for Serious Investors"—invites the higher dollar families, but what if a family wants their funds invested conservatively and not constantly traded? This tagline would turn off these families.

   c. "Professional Financial Planning" might work; it says, "we are pros at we do, and what we do is financial planning." Though it doesn't qualify the minimum net worth of clients, Carl feels that can be cleared up with a few questions during the initial phone interview and can be expanded upon in a blurb in his webpage and in advertising.

9. Carl now has a potential name and a tagline. His next step is to go online and search for all iterations of this name and tagline. Unless he sees this being used in his state already, he is ready to speak

with his lawyer, Abigail. Abigail will research similar names in Carl's state, and any bordering states where Carl plans to do business. She will explain that the business name needs to be registered with the Secretary of State. This will give Carl the exclusive use of the name, but only within his state.

10. Carl asks Abigail about copyrighting his name. She tells him a trademark is more what he needs. A copyright is for something specifically created, from a book to a song to an article in a magazine. Carl can copyright a brochure about his company, but that doesn't protect him from someone in another state from using the exact same name.

11. Carl can trademark his name, which will protect him in the United States. Get Abigail to do this, or she may refer Carl to a lawyer specializing in intellectual property. This will end up costing about $4000.

12. Carl now has everything set, except ...

How Does He Position His Company in the Marketplace?

1. Changing a name has costs. Everything has to be reprinted and re-programmed. It is a great chance to redesign color schemes, letterhead, and the big one ... update the website. Schedule a turnover day where everything is changed. It may be three months out; that's okay—you only get one chance to do this right.

2. You may need to reregister with the state, the IRS, any regulatory bodies that cover your industry and local and county business authorities.

3. Your vendors may require a new credit application. Banks will require new declarations; you must change your credit cards.

4. In the Internet age, many people think the Yellow Pages are obsolete. They are far from correct. List your old name for a couple of years as well as the new name. Old habits die hard and people will remember your dad's company name for a long time. Take that as a compliment to your dad.

5. It is a good time to change your communications channels as well. Start a monthly broadcast email, with the first issue being your name change. Two good companies for this are Vertical Response (verticalresponse.com) and Constant Contact (constantcontact.com). Vertical Response has a free program for non-profit organizations that can't be beat! Update your Facebook, Twitter and LinkedIn sites.

6. Send a personal letter to all of your customers. Whether you have 100 or 10,000, send each one a note showing both the old and the new name. Talk about the company's growth and the improvements all customers will see.

7. Follow this with a second letter 30 days later. Your customers will need a second and maybe a third notice to firmly place Mountain Top in their minds.

8. Throw yourself a party. Have an open house and invite clients, vendors and potential customers. It is one of the times that an imprinted paperweight or mouse pad will really pay benefits.

9. Extend a personal invitation to every media outlet that has a business reporter. If you are in a large media market, you might want a special open house just for media. Stress that you are an established company with a new name and even stronger approach to customer service.

10. Send a press release to every magazine, journal and blogger that covers your industry, all the way from national to local coverage.

11. Arrange to sponsor a charity event that gets good press coverage. You are not going to buy naming rights to a major league baseball stadium, but how about a Little League field, or a charity golf event? Where do your current and potential customers hang out? Upscale events would probably help Mountain Top. How about sponsoring a local theater company for a season?

12. Lastly, make sure that you are reinvigorated. Don't let this change become a chore; make it a celebration of the new you and the new company.

How to Speak Positive

Here are some words, phrases and terms you can use to speak positively when promoting your business.

A1	Astounding	Breezy	Complete
Able	Attraction	Brief	Compliment
Absolute	Attractive	Bright	Conclusive
Absolutely	Auspicious	Brilliant	Concrete
Absorbing	Award	Brimming	Confidence
Abundance	Authentic	Buy	Confident
Ace	Awesome	Care	Connoisseur
Active	Bargain	Caring	Consummate
Admirable	Beaming	Celebrate	Content
Adore	Beats	Certain	Continue
Advance	Beautiful	Charitable	Convinced
Advancement	Benevolent	Charming	Cool
Affirmative	Best	Cheer	Courageous
Agree	Better	Cheerful	Courteous
Alert	Betterment	Chic	Coy
Alive	Bewitching	Choice	Creamy
Amazing	Bits	Clean	Creative
Ample	Blooming	Clear	Crisp
Appealing	Blossom	Clever	Cuddly
Approval	Boost	Collaborate	Cute
Apt	Bounce	Collaboration	Daring
Aroma	Bountiful	Colorful	Darling
Assertive	Brainy	Comfy	Dazzling
Assured	Brave	Compassionate	Debonair
Astonishing	Breakthrough	Competent	Decisive

Delicate	Endless	Famed	Friendly
Delicious	Energizing	Famous	Fruitful
Delightful	Energy	Fancy	Full
Deluxe	Engrossing	Fanciful	Fun
Dependable	Enhance	Fantastic	Gain
Desire	Enjoy	Fashionable	Gallant
Diamond	Enlightened	Fascinating	Galore
Difference	Enormous	Fab	Generous
Dimple	Ensure	Fast	Genius
Direct	Enticing	Favorable	Gentle
Discerning	Essence	Favorite	Genuine
Distinguished	Essential	Fertile	Giggle
Drool	Exactly	Fetching	Glad
Dreamy	Excellent	Finest	Glamorous
Dynamic	Exceptional	Finesse	Gleam
Easy	Exciting	First	Glitter
Economy	Exclusive	Fitting	Glorious
Ecstatic	Exhilaration	Fizz	Glowing
Effective	Exotic	Flair	Go-ahead
Effervescent	Expert	Flattering	Golden
Efficient	Explicate	Flip	Goodness
Elated	Exquisite	Flourishing	Gorgeous
Elegant	Extol	Foolproof	Graceful
Eloquent	Extra	Forever	Gracious
Eminent	Exuberant	Fortunate	Grand
Emphatic	Eye-Catching	Fragrance	Grandiose
Empowering	Fabled	Free	Gratified
Enchanting	Fair	Freshness	Great

Grow	Incredible	Keenest	Merry
Growth	Indelible	Kind	Mighty
Guaranteed	Independent	Kissable	Miracle
Handy	Indisputable	Know-how	Modern
Handsome	Infinite	Knowing	Money-making
Happy	Ingenious	Leads	More
Healthy	Initiative	Legend	Mouthwatering
Heartwarming	Innovative	Leisure	Multi
Heavenly	Innovator	Lifelong	Munchy
Helpful	Insightful	Light	Natural
Hero	Inspiration	Lingering	Need
Heroic	Inspire	Lively	New
Holiday	Instant	Logical	Nice
Home	Integrated	Longest	Noble
Honest	Integrity	Lovely	Notable
Honesty	Intelligent	Lucky	Nutritious
Hope	Interesting	Luscious	O.K.
Hopeful	Intriguing	Luxurious	Optimist
Humorous	Inventive	Magic	Optimistic
Ideal	Invigorating	Magical	Opulent
Imagine	Invincible	Magnanimous	Original
Imaginative	Inviting	Magnificent	Outlasts
Immaculate	Irrefutable	Marvelous	Outrageous
Impactful	Irresistible	Matchless	Outstanding
Improve	Jewel	Magnifies it	Overjoyed
Impressive	Joy	Maxi	Overwhelming
Incontestable	Jubilant	Mellow	Palate
Increase	Juicy	Memorable	Palatial

Paradise	Premier	Recommendation	Select
Pamper	Premium	Refined	Sensitive
Passionate	Prestige	Refreshing	Sensational
Peace	Priceless	Relax	Serene
Peaceful	Pride	Reliable	Service
Peach	Prime	Remarkable	Sexy
Peak	Princely	Renowned	Shapely
Pearl	Progress	Reputation	Share
Perfect	Prominent	Resolute	Sharp
Permanent	Promote	Resourceful	Sheer
Phenomenal	Promotion	Resplendent	Shimmer
Pick-me-up	Prize	Responsive	Shy
Pizzazz	Promising	Rest	Silent
Pleasure	Propitious	Rewarding	Silver
Pleased	Prosperous	Rich	Simple
Pleases	Protection	Right	Sincere
Plentiful	Proud	Riveting	Singular
Plenty	Pure	Robust	Sizzling
Plum	Quality	Rosy	Skillful
Plump	Quantity	Royal	Slick
Plus	Quenching	Safety	Smart
Popular	Quick	Save	Smashing
Positive	Quiet	Satisfaction	Smiles
Power	Radiant	Satisfactory	Solar
Powerful	Rational	Scores	Smooth
Precious	Ravishing	Secure	Soft
Precise	Real	Seductive	Sound
Prefer	Reap		Sparkling

Smooth	Supersonic	True	Welcome
Soft	Supreme	Trust	Whiz
Soul	Sure	Ultimate	Whole
Sound	Survivor	Ultra	Whopper
Sparkling	Sweet	Unbeatable	Winner
Special	Swell	Unblemished	Wise
Spectacular	Symphony	Unceasing	Wonderful
Speed	Tan	Undeniably	Worth
Spice	Tangy	Unending	Wondrous
Spicy	Targeted	Undoubtedly	Wow!
Splendid	Tasty	Unique	Youthful
Spotless	Tempting	Unquestionably	Yule
Spruce	Terrific	Unrivalled	Young
Stalwart	Thoroughbred	Unsurpassed	Yummy
Star	Thoughtful	Useful	Zap
Stellar	Thrilling	Valiant	Zeal
Strong	Thriving	Valued	Zen
Stunning	Together	Valuable	Zest
Stupendous	Togetherness	Vanish	Zip
Stylish	Torrid	Varied	Zoom
Subtle	Totally	Versatile	
Success	Traditional	Victor	
Succulent	Transformation	Visionary	
Sun	Treat	Vivacious	
Sunny	Treasure	Vivid	
Super	Tremendous	Warm	
Superb	Trendy	Wealth	
Superlative	Triumph	Wee	

Chapter 66

The Five-Minute Solution to Setting Up a Manufacturer's Rep Sales Team

Problem

You own Mike's Polar Bear Manufacturing, which manufactures insulated and energy-efficient storage facilities for refrigerated and frozen food. Your sales have been from referrals and a well-executed web advertising program. You want to start selling into a new market niche: pharmaceuticals. You ask your vice president of sales, Mike Jr., to set up a sales force to sell the drug makers and distributors. He is trying to figure out whether to hire company sales people or create a network of manufacturer's reps.

Possible Outcomes

- Junior budgets for eight salespeople across the country and plans $70K for salary, $30K for benefits, $60K for expenses and $20K for overhead for each. With gross margin of 30 percent, each salesperson has to generate $600,000 to break even.

- Five million in annual sales is a big increase. To do this you need a large investment in new equipment and additional warehousing.

- Junior looks at hiring manufacturer rep firms. The start-up will cost $60K to bring the reps to the office for three days, train on your products and give them sales literature. Also, you would hire two customer service people for the office to handle the reps' inquiries and do their follow-up, but you probably would need these for the company-paid people as well. Your total investment is around $250K, plus most of Junior's time for the first year. You figure your break-even is about $1 million in new sales.

- Mike and Junior decide to go the route of manufacturer's reps. Now what? How do you hire the reps? How do you set their commission? How much time do you invest in each rep organization?

How Should Junior Create the Rep Program?

1. Don't try to reinvent the whole program. There are tons of companies doing this very successfully. It is just a matter of doing homework and fitting the details to Mike's philosophies of business and the intricacies of Mike's products.

2. Start by going to pharmaceutical trade shows. Approach vendors and ask them how they sell to the trade and, if they use reps, would they share a name with you? Some won't, but you will get some good starting points. Junior might think of kicking off his product sales at a trade show, but should he wait? If he doesn't have the reps in place, how will he service the leads? On the other hand, if he has lots of leads, will more reps want to come on board?

If Junior is a gambler, he will set up a booth and start selling. If conservative, he'll wait.

3. At trade shows, there will always be a bulletin board for reps wanted. Put up a notice. Place ads for "reps wanted" in a couple of trade magazines. These should draw plenty of resumes and line-cards. Ask the editors if they have a list of reps for their industry. Many do. What's a line card, you say? It is a listing of the lines that a rep carries. Junior wants a firm with complimentary lines to his, with no more than twelve lines. Some rep firms will have booths at the show, showcasing all of their lines. Many shows use color-coded name tags to represent reps.

4. Before starting the rep hunt, Junior should have a good grasp of the geographic locations of his potential customers and key on reps for those areas first. On each rep's line card Junior should find out the coverage for each principal company. They will not always be uniform. You want to make sure the area you are discussing for the rep is one in which they already have coverage.

5. Mike's has a great website. Place a banner ad on this site, talking about your new push into pharmaceuticals, asking reps to apply.

6. Since Junior is new to this, he needs to ask questions, and the best people to ask are the reps with whom he is potentially interested in working. Explain to them that you are new and want to learn; a good rep will work with you. Junior needs to know:

   a. What commission do they expect? The answer usually will depend on the amount of time and effort the rep has to invest. If the rep is only bringing in qualified leads, the commission should be on the low side, maybe 5 percent. If the rep needs to hand-hold the buyer through ordering and installation of cold rooms, then a higher commission, upwards of 15 percent, would be appropriate.

   b. Do the reps expect to be paid at the time of invoice or after the customer has paid the invoice? Junior should go for the later choice where possible.

    c. How much training time will the rep commit to Mike's?

    d. How often should Junior travel with each rep?

    e. What support does the rep need to be successful with Mike's?

How Does Junior Actually Get Started?

1. Junior needs to define the actual scope of the work the rep is expected to do. This includes:

    a. Generating leads for the in-house sales team;

    b. Promptly following up on leads that come into Mike's;

    c. Will the rep call on existing customers for parts and service orders? Most reps will say this is the responsibility of the in-house sales team. If Junior wants the rep to handle this, his commission costs will be higher; and

    d. Reports to the office. Most reps hate sending in call reports. It will be tough for Junior to get these unless he makes it extremely simple and accessible through the Internet. I would recommend that Junior not worry about this at start up.

2. Next, define the sales goals for each rep territory. Clearly lay this out to the rep in advance. Is it simply a dollar figure or a certain number of installations per year?

3. Does the rep have the skills and tools to close an order, or does Junior need to be there for the final order?

4. Is the rep expected to assist accounts-receivable in collection of past due monies? Does the rep have the authority to settle disputes? Will you give enough training for them to be effective in dispute resolution?

5. Is the rep responsible for and getting paid for on-going and repeat customers? Or is Mike's goal for the reps only to bring in initial orders? I recommend that the reps have ongoing responsibility. The commission you pay on a parts order is small compared to the

goodwill you create when the customer has a friendly rep that will help him.

6. What information are you sending the rep? Too much and it gets ignored, too little and the rep isn't effective. Reps should get a copy of every lead, quote, invoice and personal correspondence to the customer–and promptly. A quote mailed out at the end of the month doesn't do anything but waste paper. All correspondence should be emailed to the rep on the same day it is sent to the customer.

7. What is Junior going to do for the reps when the home office of a customer is in one territory and the "ship to" of the cold room is in another's territory? How is the commission to be split? This must be defined up front. Junior can't wait until a sale is made and then worry about it. A 50/50 split is the most common answer.

8. Will reps in different parts of the country have different commission rates? Reps that cover large geographic areas have higher travel expenses. Is Junior going to pay more under these circumstances? Probably an extra one percent is due.

9. A well-written contract is required. Definitions needed include:

   a. The payment or commission amount; the payment date; if rates are different on various parts of your product line; how chargebacks are handled; and whether the rep forfeits commission if the customer is a slow or no pay;

   b. A clear statement on the ability of the house or the rep to cut commissions in order to close a sale;

   c. For tax purposes, a statement that the rep is an independent contractor;

   d. The term of the contract and what happens at the end of the term–whether the rep is going to get paid for pending orders or only invoiced orders;

   e. A clear definition of your product and a non-compete clause to your product;

f. A description of what is trade and confidential information and how the rep will handle during and at the end of the relationship;

g. Most reps will balk at daily or weekly reports, but Junior can expect quarterly and annual sales forecasts to help with production and investment planning;

h. The extent of customer service work expected; and

i. How direct expenses are reimbursed, if any. Normally, the only expenses Junior should pay are for the rep to attend a sales meeting at Junior's office. Also, will Junior share in any expenses at trade shows where the rep has a booth? If Junior has a booth at a show, is the rep expected to be there, and who covers these expenses?

10. It comes down to money. Let's say a good rep grosses $250,000 a year, with about $100,000 in expenses. So, if a rep can earn $25,000 on your line, expect about 10 percent of a rep's time.

11. There are some good websites to visit with listing of reps in thousands of industries:

    a. Replocate.com;

    b. Rephunter.com;

    c. MRPusa.com;

    d. Greatrep.com;

    e. Salesagentusa.com.

Chapter 67

The Five-Minute Solution to Sending Employees for Pre-Employment Physicals

 **Problem:**

You own Groucho's Marks A Million Markers, a manufacturer of white boards, blackboards and different types of marking pens. When hiring for the plant, you tell applicants they need to lift 60 pounds. But your workers' comp rate is going up, and you discover that most claims come from new hires. How do you go about setting up a pre-employment physical program that is cost-effective and meets legal standards?

Possible Solutions

- You bring a 60-pound box of markers into the personnel office and ask applicants to lift it. If they can, you go ahead with the interview. After six months, your workers' comp mod goes up as two new hires hurt their backs.

- You make the skinny applicants lift the box ten times in one minute. Last week, two applicants couldn't do it, you didn't hire them, and this week an investigator from the Equal Employment Opportunity Commission (EEOC) came in and asked why you had two Hispanic men lift the box, but other applicants didn't have to. OOPS! Do not pass go; do plan to pay out a lot of money.

- Your attorney tells you to test everyone at a proper medical clinic. This will cost about $200 per applicant. You tell him with your turnover, this would cost way too much.

- Duh! You wake up in the middle of the night and realize how much you will save in reduced turnover and insurance if you hired better. The next morning you start your homework on pre-employment physicals.

What Did Groucho Learn About Pre-Employment Physicals?

1. They are legal and very helpful if done correctly. Basic steps are:

    a. Each job must have a written job description, detailing the physical requirements, such as the weight to be lifted, the time standing or walking and all other physical requirements, called Bona Fide Occupational Qualifications (BOQs); and

    b. Work with your workers' comp carrier to help writing the BOQs.

2. Groucho needs to find a local medical group to do the testing. Google "pre-employment physicals in (your state or city)" and you will get ads and info about providers in your area. Your comp carrier should also make good recommendations.

3. If Groucho decides to hire someone, he offers a "conditional offer of employment," usually in writing, and stating the conditions, which, if met, will result in a permanent job offer. If Groucho does drug or aptitude testing, that must be done prior to the conditional offer of employment and the physical test. The physical test has to be the last test, and if the employee does pass the test, the offer of employment cannot be rescinded. If you are not drug testing, this is a good time to start. (*See Chapter 20.*)

4. Groucho also learns that many people feel pre-employment physicals don't give the correct information. People may not tell the doctor their back hurts after lift testing in order to get the job. By itself, a physical won't tell you the success of an employee, but it may prevent a failure. The doctor is only going to tell you yes or no—not any details of the test or why the applicant didn't pass. Don't ask; you don't really want to know.

Groucho Has Made Up His Mind to Start Physicals ... Now What?

1. If Groucho has more than 15 employees he is covered under Federal discrimination rulings. Some states set the floor lower. It shouldn't matter how big your company is. Don't even think about discriminating because you are small and can get away with it. It will come back to bite you in many ways.

2. Set the BOQs. Ask your present employees how much they lift and how often. Ask how long they stand and how much bending and reaching. Look at your previous injury reports and see how injuries occurred and if an employee's strength or stamina had an impact on the accident.

3. Be sure to write BOQs for hearing and vision. A flashing light for a fire or an alarm bell for tornadoes has to be seen and/or heard. If your employees need to wear a respiratory mask around hazardous materials for safety purposes, then a pulmonary test

should be part of the pre-employment physical. If your work environment requires a lot of heavy lifting, and all you are hiring are former wrestlers, it is time to rethink your plant. Adding overhead cranes or more forklifts will make you more productive and reduce injuries. It will also allow you to hire folks of a "smaller" size, opening your workforce to women. This will be the best thing to happen to your workforce and also might protect you from future discrimination actions.

4. Avoid generic BOQ forms. One size doesn't fill all in this respect. Make your BOQs right for your company. It's worth it.

5. Shop around for testing. It shouldn't run more than $200. Some states require an MD perform the test, other states allow a physical therapist, or nurse. Check with your attorney. A cheap testing service that doesn't give reliable results is not worth it. The cost is really an investment in improving productivity and lowering your workers' comp costs. One study I read showed that pre-employment physicals reduced a company's comp costs by 78 percent in two years. Now, this study was written by a testing firm, so I am sure they picked the best result they had, but it is solid logic that by hiring physically capable people you will have fewer on-the-job injuries. Don't think about making applicants pay for the test.

6. You cannot ask for any genetic or family history in the physical. You're right, family history does play a large part in medical history, but not so in specific job performance. You cannot gather genetic information either. Both family and genetic history can lead to discrimination claims based on race or national origin.

7. You'll also need to think about reasonable accommodations for handicapped people. A guy in a wheelchair can't load a truck, but if he is applying for a position in the dispatch office, his chair should not be considered a problem. If the door to the office is only 28 inches wide, and should be 36 inches, and the guy is fully qualified for the job otherwise, you'll need to widen the door

frame. If the door is encased in solid concrete and changing the concrete can hurt your building structurally, then this is not a reasonable accommodation. But realistically that is a one-in-a-hundred shot, and you are going to change the door. In my company, I had extremely good success hiring people with handicaps. The big difference was in attitude. They so appreciated being given the opportunity; and this showed in every part of their work.

8. If the testing location does send you a medical report, you must keep that in a locked location separate from the employee's regular personnel file. Limit access to this file to the most senior executives.

9. If you have drivers that cross state lines or drive a certain size truck, in addition to pre-employment physicals, you need a Department of Transportation (DOT) physical which includes a urine test for drugs. It is a grey area if the DOT test has to be performed prior to the pre-employment test, or if they can be given simultaneously. Check with your attorney.

10. Back injuries come from improper lifting technique more than just the amount lifted. By teaching proper techniques Groucho will have safer employees. Go to http://www.ergodoc.com/liftpdf.pdf for a great brochure.

Chapter 68

The Five-Minute Solution to Preventing Accidents at Work

 Problem

You are the owner of Liz and John's Musical Theatre, with a 350-seat auditorium and a production area for building sets for yours and other theatre groups. In fact, this is the primary source of your income. You employ 20 actors and musicians and 25 people in the set production area. Also many local folks volunteer, both in set production and in the theatre. Last year you had four accidents, none of which, fortunately, was serious. You want to work more safely and set a goal of zero accidents for this year. What should Liz and John do?

Possible Outcomes

- John hangs up big signs that say "SAFETY FIRST" and tells everyone to work safely. John is sure this will help, but Liz doesn't care for this plan.

- Liz wants to bring in a safety consultant to train their crews. John doesn't want to spend the bucks with a supporting actor from the Five-Minute Consultant. They can't agree and end up doing nothing.

- John appoints their chief carpenter, Three Finger George, as safety director. Liz sees the irony in this. George feels since he toughed out his accident that everyone else should, too.

- After the second accident of the season, their insurance broker suggests Liz and John bring in a consultant, Tony A. Ward, a noted safety specialist for theatres.

What Did Tony Do to Help Liz and John?

1. Before Tony arrived, he reviewed their safety record on the OSHA 300 form. This is the log of every accident or job-related illness which is the starting point for all accident prevention, as it tells you where and how accidents did take place. If you are not filling this out, go to www.osha.gov for blank forms and instructions. Tony saw that the accidents occurred in the carpentry shop of the set building unit.

2. Tony spent three hours touring the production shop, the theatre and the offices. He came back to Liz and John with a clipboard full of ideas. Tony told Liz that the single biggest cause of accidents is clutter on floors which causes trips and falls.

   He pointed out the carpentry shop as an example with cutoff pieces of lumber, sawdust, extension cords and open paint cans scattered around. The electrical shop was nowhere nearly as bad.

3. Tony suggested he spend time with all the foremen and some extra time with George, the chief carpenter. He also wanted

time with Liz and John to ensure their total commitment to a safety program and explained that no safety program ever works without the complete cooperation and backing of company leadership.

4. In the morning he explained the budget needed for safety, which includes:

   a. Five- to ten-minute clean up periods, three to four times per day. If workers clear their messes as they are created, this would not be necessary. Tony explained it will take constant reminding from the foremen and John to achieve this.

   b. New electrical lines run so that all extension cords are eliminated. These are a trip hazard as well as a fire hazard. Take away all portable electric heaters in the office. They are an extreme fire hazard. Beef up the heating system to compensate, carpet the floors and add insulation where needed.

   c. A vacuum system around each saw and sander to eliminating 99 percent of the sawdust, a major slip hazard along with being a fire hazard.

   d. First aid kits and eye wash stations be set up in the shop. Most importantly, people had to be trained to use these properly. Tony recommended that John contact the Red Cross (redcross.org) to set up a first-aid training class at the theatre. Wearing medical gloves must be mandatory when treating an employee for a cut.

   e. Personal protective gear (PPE) for all people in the shop. This includes approved safety glasses, work gloves, steel toe shoes and respirators for the carpenters and painters.

5. Tony pointed out other potential OSHA violations and explained all doorways must be kept clear; electrical panels must be openable and not covered with scenery or props; paint thinner and chemicals must be in leak-proof containers and properly identified; walking lanes must be clearly marked and kept litter-free;

employees should not smoke anywhere in the facility; and an evacuation plan needs to be visible in the building. He objected strongly to the practice of using compressed air lines to blow sawdust from people's clothes and hair as this is one of the biggest causes of eye injuries.

6. Tony told Liz his observations were common in 95 percent of the businesses with whom he consulted. He mentioned that generally, in companies with more than a hundred folks, there was usually a full-time person assigned to safety, but in their size company, he rarely saw a full-time safety professional. He said John needs to appoint Frank Foreman as safety leader in the plant. Let him attend OSHA on-line webinars, take some courses and learn about safety. He suggested committing about 25 percent of John's time to safety.

7. The most important thing, Tony said, was to give Frank an adequate budget and the full authority he needed to improve safety at Liz and John's. He also needs the complete authority to enforce wearing safety gear, up to and including termination of a repeat offender who flaunts or violates the rules.

What Else Did Frank Foreman Learn from Tony?

1. It is tough to ask volunteers to abide by strict safety rules. If they are hurt at your place, it goes on your OSHA log and workers' comp rate. If volunteers won't follow the rules, they have to become ushers in the balcony.

2. Frank learned that every accident can be prevented or mitigated. If an owner or leader tells an OSHA rep that a certain type of accident can't be prevented, odds are the OSHA rep will close that part of the factory. They are right to do so. Frank may have to redesign part of the shop to change work flow. This expense is still better than having increased risk of a serious accident.

3. Frank's goal has to be zero tolerance of an unsafe situation. This includes instituting a lock-out/tag-out program for the shop. This means that whenever people are working to repair a machine or device that has the potential to harm someone, a physical lock has to be placed on the electrical panel controlling this device so it can't be turned on accidentally. Most mechanics will say this is unnecessary, as they work around live electricity all the time. Frank has to stay tough on his enforcement of this rule in the scenery shop.

4. There are thousands of safety rules from OSHA and your state agency as well. Tony told Frank not to learn each one, but to concentrate on what he sees in their place. For instance, Tony advised rules be established for the prop guns and knives. Each gun and knife must be inspected by at least two people before every performance and they must ensure that blanks are loaded and the knife blades are blunt and dull. These are the type of rules that are unique for Liz and John's; every company in the U.S. has something that makes them unique as well.

5. According to the Department of Labor, sprains and strains are the most common workplace injury. Tony supplied Frank with information on how to lift correctly. (Visit www.fiveminuteconsultant.com for details.) Clutter is the major cause of tripping, which leads to sprains. Unless you have the proper storage space, don't save everything on the off chance you will need it five years from now.

6. Tony laid out an incident form and accident report for Frank to use. What's the difference between an accident and an incident?

    a. An accident is any time an employee is injured enough to require first aid. It includes every situation, even though there may not be a trip to the doctor. A bruise, a small cut or a scrape qualify.

    b. An incident is a close call to an accident. Something happened, maybe just a trip and stumble, or a box fell from an overhead storage rack.

7. The accident report is filled out within one hour by the supervisor of the area where the accident took place. The report shows all relevant info, a diagram of how the accident took place; statements from witnesses, if available; preventive strategies suggested by the supervisor; and what the supervisor thinks is the root cause of the problem. The root cause is not "Bill was not looking where he was going," but that something was out of its normal place, creating a tripping hazard. Every incident needs to be investigated, with an eye for preventing escalation to an accident. Look at incidents as a tool for education of employees.

8. Next, Tony taught Frank about forming an active safety committee. This should be about four or five people, one from every major department in the theatre. Their roles include:

   a. Meeting once a month to discuss any new equipment or procedures at Liz and John's and its impact on safety;

   b. Being the safety ambassadors throughout the theatre; and

   c. Meeting immediately after any accident or incident, reviewing the root cause of the accident and making changes to prevent this from happening again. This is, by far, the most important role of the committee.

9. Only by tracking every incident can you see where an accident will likely occur and take preventative action. The other foremen and supervisors are going to complain about the paperwork. Don't give in. They'll soon realize it is easier to run a safe shop than to argue with you.

10. A prevented accident is better than a small accident. Don't accept a one-stitch cut as a minor incident. It only means the worker was lucky not to get a ten-stitcher. A one-stitcher will not impact your workers' comp when you handle as a first-aid case at the local walk-in clinic. The safety committee has to find out if the injured

worker was wearing her gloves, was careless or lucky not to get a more serious injury. The goal is prevention, as every accident can be prevented.

11. Besides the worker's comp savings, why is safety so important? The obvious answer is so people don't get hurt. But there is a less obvious answer as well: good safety improves your product and your profits. If you have a safe working regimen you will find that:

    a. You have fewer rejects on your product line, because procedures are followed that improve safety as well as making your product better;

    b. Employees are happier knowing they are working for a company that cares about their safety. Happy employees make better products. Honest; and

    c. An accident seriously hurts morale and productivity.

Chapter 69

The Five-Minute Solution to Running Your Business as If It Were a Unionized Shop

(Note: This case is different than others in this book. This is a true recount of my own experience operating a glass fabrication company.)

Problem

Chuck owned our company and together we ran it. We had three locations, our home office in New York and two satellite plants, one in Connecticut and one in New Jersey. Our New York plant, with about 150 employees on three shifts was unionized. Our other two plants, with about 40 folks each, were not. We operated under two distinctly different plans for payroll, vacations, retirement, hiring and terminations. Were there advantages to each? Can you benefit from our experiences?

Possible Outcomes

- All three plants ran smoothly. We never had any problems. So, this chapter is unnecessary. Yup.

- We had our share of problems in each location and used our brilliant minds to easily solve them with no repercussions. Would you like to buy a bridge?

- The different status of the plants caused problems in sharing workers and ideas. But we learned from each situation. Or we thought we did.

- The unionized plant ran the best because of stricter guidelines and rules. Two strikes and the unknowns were a small price to pay. Small?

- The unionized main plant was our smoothest operating plant from a personnel level. We had fewer problems with hiring, education, maintaining discipline and, when necessary, terminations. Our other plants ran on-time and with excellent quality because they were more flexible with the ability to utilize their team.

- Was it even-steven because of the differences? No. It's like comparing apples and kumquats. Each operating type had advantages; let's go over these advantages and teach you what we learned.

The Advantages of a Unionized Facility

1. We were in a construction-related business, fabricating glass into insulating glass for energy savings, manufacturing safety and blast-resistant glass for commercial and residential usage, and making glass furniture, such as high-end glass table tops. The New York area is a union-friendly environment for construction. Did our being affiliated with the glass union help us here? In our early years (1960-1990) it did. As unions in general began to lose influence, the positive impact faded.

2. The contracts made us plan better. We had many three-year contracts and went to five-year contracts in the 1990s, which

stretched our predictions on labor and benefit costs. How many companies without labor contracts think about labor costs four years out? This made us better managers as we had an outline to follow. We avoided the annual angst concerning wage increases, bonuses and changes to benefits. The union workers generally had stronger benefits, but lower raises, which led to disparities. In good times we were very generous with our non-union workers, but held back when the business climate was weak.

3. We had a two-tier contract, with one group of skilled folks at $32 an hour total cost (in 2005) and a semi-skilled group at $18 per hour. This caused divisions in the company which at times were uncomfortable, but allowed us to control costs better. With the raises for each subsequent year defined, along with the increases for the benefits programs, our labor costs were predictable. The only variable was actual headcount and hours worked. We didn't have these strong delineations in our satellite plants and this caused more payroll questions.

4. Very few union members asked for raises during the term of the contract. We did give occasional merit raises and promotions. In our non-union companies, even though we had a defined time at the end of the fiscal year for considering raises, a greater number of folks came to us mid-year asking for special consideration. People expected us to give them raises when they were needed, whereas the union folks understood the rules.

5. We had to keep close parity between the union and non-union people so that the union organizers would not have a leg up going to our non-union plants.

6. We had fewer personnel problems in the unionized New York plant. There was a defined progressive discipline system in the union contract, which ended with submission to an arbitrator. In 22 years we went to arbitration once, and came away with a confusing split decision. Whenever we wanted to discipline a union member our managers were very well prepared and documented the situation.

This was not true for our non-union people. We followed our employee manual, but didn't pay as much attention to correct procedure or documentation.

7. We were better managers under the union relationship. The union shop steward, our full-time employee, oversaw the day-to-day contract ins and outs, and didn't allow us to cut corners. Above the shop steward was a union business agent (BA) who would visit the plant once a week for a couple of hours. Instead of complaining to our managers about something, the employees would complain to the BA, and if he felt the complaint had merit, he would bring it to management's attention. He carried the respect of the workers and, more often than not, the BA would tell the person to forget it. We worked with many different BAs over the years and only had one who would stir up the employees rather than working with us. Before we fired an employee we would discuss the situation with the BA and get his advice; once there was agreement, we never had a complaint about a firing. That one time we went to arbitration was a case of misunderstanding on wages, and both we and the union were sure we were right. The arbitrator cut the baby in half. On the whole, the BAs with whom we worked were among the best people I have known and worked hard to help both the employees and our company.

8. The union provided us with skilled workers when we couldn't promote from within. Our union affiliation made it easy for us to deliver to union job sites without having to hire Teamster drivers. In the long run, the union knew that their success hinged upon ours. We were the largest glass industry employer in the New York area, and while some small competitors went out of business during slow periods, the union worked with us to ensure our business health.

9. Contract negotiations were always tough. People were never happy with the final numbers, but that is what a negotiation is; a meeting in the middle. Time commitment is a given during negotiation periods. But, it was still easier to meet a dozen times every three years

than to work with individual employees every year. Our managers did employee reviews without having to set raises, making the reviews more honest and helpful to the managers and employees.

Were There Problems? How Were They Solved?

1. Even though we became better managers, the union concept was not easy. The employees felt the union was more important than the company mainly because their benefits were administered by the union. We paid 100 percent of the costs, but all the interaction was the union's responsibility. If we had a do-over, we should have administered the benefits. We would have needed another person in our personnel office; it would have been worth it.

2. We had two strikes in 22 years, both lasting four days. Neither one changed the offers on the table, so both failed economically. But they succeeded in causing lasting ill-will on both sides. Could they have been avoided? No. The times, a few rabble-rousers and a union leader trying to make a name for himself were all factors. There were wounds from both strikes that took years to heal. Our non-union plants kept working, and in fact sent workers to the main plant to help. Unfortunately, a couple of these employees' cars were vandalized.

3. We spent $20K per year on a law firm specializing in labor relations. We could not have done this on our own. The laws and regulations are immense and complicated. Our only significant use of the firm was for the incident of failed arbitration. If there had been more problems, we would have ended up needing an in-house attorney. For the most part, this was money that could have been better spent on salaries or capital improvements.

4. We fed the BA any changes in advance, so that he could answer questions from the employees. If we had left him in the dark and caused him embarrassment, it would not have been good for us.

Fortunately, the BAs were quite proper in handling confidential situations. If they were not, it would have caused problems.

5. We sold the company in 2004 to an international conglomerate. We were a squeaky-clean company with no debt and no problems. The biggest hurdle in the sale was the existing union contract. The acquiring company spent more time on this than any other part of the deal. They had to meet with union leadership many times and sign a new labor contract in order to complete the sale. The union was extremely cooperative; if they had not been, the sale could have been scuttled.

6. If I had a magic wand, would I have kept us affiliated with the union? No. Not because of any actual problems; on the whole, it helped us more than it hurt us. But this was because we had good cooperation. I know of many companies that have been hurt or closed because of intransigence from union leaderships. And having this hang over our heads was always a worry. All business owners plan for today and tomorrow. Today was rarely a problem with our union, and we were fortunate that tomorrow wasn't either. But this could have changed on a whim from the national union headquarters, or an election of a local president. This inability to handle our future was not worth the advantages we gained.

Chapter 70

The Five-Minute Solution to the Guy Who Makes a Pass at You

Problem

You are Molly, the owner of Acme Internet Marketing Co. You and your husband started the company ten years ago. Unfortunately, your husband left you and the company three years ago. Now, you are legally separated. Last weekend, while you were attending the wedding of one of your graphic designers, you were approached by Mike from the sales office with amorous intentions. Maybe a little too much champagne? Or should you take this seriously? What would the impact be on Acme if you dated an employee?

Possible Outcomes

- Even though Mike is a great guy, single and suave, Molly knows this can only be a problem and has to squash all ideas of a relationship. Since you are working 70 hours a week anyway, you have no time for romance.

- Molly is flattered by the attention. Mike said he had been trying to get his nerve up to ask her out. Molly never considered dating someone in the company, but starts to rethink this position.

- Molly starts seeing Mike, and the office gossip hits like a ton of bricks. Productivity falls off because of all the talk about the romance. A month later, the dating ends, and the gossip goes into overdrive. Mike, who is a great employee, resigns.

- The romance goes on for three months, then stops. A month later the salary reviews are handed out. Mike and Molly have a wall-busting argument; Mike is not satisfied with his raise and says it was promised to him. He files a sexual harassment claim with the Equal Employment Opportunity Commission (EEOC). Was Mike truly denied his due raise or was he taking advantage of the circumstances?

Oops! What Does Molly Do Now?

1. She calls her friend and attorney, Clarice Darro, who has experience in this area of law. They meet, go over the facts, the complaint and the possible paths Molly can take.

2. You know the old expression, "There is good news and bad news; which do you want first?" In this case Clarice couldn't come up with any good news. She explains the basics of a sexual harassment case that Mike will make.

   a. Mike says he was promised a certain wage increase. His work output didn't change during or after the breakup; he will claim his work was well received.

   b. When the wage increases for the year were announced and his was low, he says says the lower amount was because he broke up the relationship.

    c. Mike and his attorney will present evidence establishing that Molly's reason for a lower raise was merely an excuse; more likely than not the end of the sexual relationship was the cause for retaliation and discrimination under the laws of sexual harassment.

    d. If this is indeed true, Molly should bring her checkbook to the hearing, for she will most definitely have a large payment coming out of it.

3. Clarice then tells Molly what she needs to make a successful defense.

    a. Molly will have to present evidence that establishes that the lower increase was not due to the change in their relationship, but was due to legitimate business needs. Evidence demonstrating Mike's reduced performance or poor work skills could establish that the decision was legitimate and unrelated to the end of their relationship.

    b. Are there employee reviews that would support Molly's decision? Do they show the change in Mike's quality or quantity of work? Are there communications from customers commenting on Mike? Do they support the downturn in Mike's work?

    c. Are other employees willing to comment on Mike's work? This is often hard to get as Mike may still be friends with your team.

4. Clarice goes on to list the damages that Molly could pay:

    a. Back pay, including lost wages and benefits. By the time the case actually goes to trial, this could be a couple of years;

    b. Mike's attorney fees, which may be higher than Clarice's fees to Molly;

    c. Expert witness fees that Mike's team incurs;

    d. Compensatory damages covering emotional pay and suffering. There is no way to predict what a jury would set this at … but it can be a whopper;

    e. Punitive damages; just keep the checkbook open; and/or

f. Court costs, imposed by the judge.

5. Holy cow ... this could be in the millions of dollars. Suddenly Molly is scared. She now realizes what a huge mistake she made by accepting Mike's advances. Mike is asking for one year's salary and his legal fees. Clarice advises Molly to pay it. It is cheap compared to the potential liabilities. Mike also wants a written apology from Molly. Molly has a tough time with this and still doesn't feel she did anything wrong. Clarice drafts the apology anyway and convinces Molly to sign.

How Does Molly or Any Other Employer Prevent This from Happening?

1. If you are a supervisor or an owner, the simple answer is: Don't. Unless you get married, the odds are you will end up in trouble.

2. Train your supervisors, and again, train your supervisors, and then next year, train your supervisors. You cannot repeat the rules too often. The rules are:

    a. No sexual jokes, teasing remarks;

    b. No suggestive looks, gestures or ogling;

    c. No touching or cornering;

    d. No pressure for dates or romantic relationships;

    e. No pressure for sexual favors; and/or

    f. No unwanted phone calls, letters, cards, emails or any other communications.

3. In "Quid Pro Quo" sexual harassment, one suggestive remark or intimation that sexual favors will help an employee is enough to get a company in trouble. If you get sued from this position, you have little defense if the remark was overheard by another person.

4. In a "hostile environment" case, there is a higher threshold for proof as most of the actions are indirect. It doesn't matter if you as the owner didn't do the harassing. If one of your managers did, the company is liable, and you will sign the check, not the offending manager!

5. What if a salesman comes into your shop and says something to your secretary, then she complains to you? If you do nothing about it, and the dumb-bunny salesman does it again, you are liable for a hostile environment claim.

6. What exact steps should Molly take for Acme Internet Marketing?

    a. Have a strict policy against sexual harassment in your company. Make sure the policy is followed by all. Make the policy real and enforceable.

    b. Make sure every employee knows the policy and has a channel directly to you to make a confidential complaint. Investigate every complaint within 24 hours and take serious action if the complaint is valid.

    c. Make sure there is no retaliation for making a complaint.

    d. Would these steps have helped Molly? No. She created her own problem, but they would help a guilty supervisor.

    e. Show real consistency in your employee relations. Don't wink at one situation and react strongly at another.

7. What about Molly? She is going to write a check to Mike, to her attorney, to his attorney and to the court for fees. She is also going to become unflappable at work when it comes to romantic interests.

8. Can an employer ever win a case? Yes, but it is not easy. Juries consistently award for the plaintiff in harassment cases, and they tend to punish companies through their financial awards. Clearly the best defense is to prevent in the first place, and this takes a solid plan and actions that follow through with creating an environment that does not tolerate any forms of sexual harassment.

9. There's a small voice that is telling me that many office romances start and stop, some ending up with marriage, others with hurt feelings, and none of these cause lawsuits. What gives? When two people are on an equal level and cannot influence the other's work career, then c'est la vie. In our current litigious society, being careful is better than anything else.

Chapter 71

The Five-Minute Solution to Suddenly Becoming a Business Owner

Problem

You are Sadie and suddenly become the sole owner of Sadie and Max's Importing. Your husband, Max, passed away in a tragic accident and leaves you the business, which imports and warehouses holiday decorations and employs 25. Max was a hands-on owner. While Max had great office and warehouse managers, none could step up and make the business decisions that Max made. As Sadie and Max's first bookkeeper you know the business, but haven't been active in the business recently. You're 45 years old with twins just getting out of college. Max left you financially comfortable. What happens to Sadie and the company?

Possible Solutions

- You decide to run the business. On your first day the managers brief you on many small situations. You realize that Max wasn't a good teacher or delegator and your work is cut out for you. By noon your headache is as big as the Empire State Building.

- You try giving the managers more authority and encourage them to make decisions. They don't succeed. Max hired them because they were good followers, not leaders.

- Two weeks later you decide this is not for you, meet with your attorney and accountant, and start plans to sell the business. In the meantime, you still have to run the business and keep it viable for sale. You now buy aspirin by the case.

- You have dinner with your best friend, and she tells you it is not about the future of Max's. It is about what you want to do with your life. What should Sadie do now?

Let's Look at Sadie's Path to Her Decision

1. Her friend is right. The decision is not about Sadie and Max's, but is about Sadie. Sadie knows that whatever her personal decision is, she has to continue running Max's until the decision is implemented for the 25 families there.

2. Sadie should spend time with her children, lawyer, accountant, financial planner, a competitor or two of Sadie and Max's, and the two managers at the business. Sadie should be open with each group, getting their input.

3. If her children want to come into the business, the decision is made. She keeps it going and starts to train them. But, it turns out they want to go forward and get master's degrees, one in biology and one in art.

4. Sadie's financial advisor and lawyer discuss the tax implications

of selling the business. Sadie and Max's value is about $3 million plus inventory. Sadie would end up paying $1 million to Uncle Sam and live nicely on the remaining $2 million. The advisor's projections for the business are obvious; if Sadie runs the business well, the value goes up; if she fails, the value can go to nothing. A big gamble, but it still comes down to Sadie's goals.

5. Sadie next speaks with two friendly competitors. She learns a lot, including that:

   a. The industry is growing. Consumers are putting up more and more decorations in homes and businesses. The advent of LED Christmas lights has encouraged homeowners to replace their old incandescent bulbs;

   b. Selling prices are lower than last year, driven by the super-sized discounters and Internet sales;

   c. The scariest issue is the sourcing. Most goods come from China, where costs are rising due to currency valuations and political needs to raise wages. Finding new Asian sources is not easy and will require Sadie to visit factories. Sadie occasionally traveled with Max on his buying trips, but is nervous about handling the negotiations; Sadie feels she will be at a strong disadvantage as a female; and

   d. She also learns that small importers are slowing being rolled into larger companies to achieve greater buying power.

6. The most important meeting for Sadie is with her two managers. She's worked with them for a month. She wants to know if and how they could grow; if they have the "fire in their belly" to grow and what they think of the future of Max's. Also, find out how they feel about a sale, Sadie staying on, or their reactions to working for an experienced general manager (GM)?

7. After these conversations, Sadie feels that while neither of the two could become a GM, she trusts them and both would work well with a new GM, if he knew the industry. Sadie decides that a GM

from another industry would not work, as she doesn't know enough to be the teacher, and she doubts the two managers have good teaching skills.

8. Sadie is a strong person, but has never had to make this big a business decision. She sees her choices as:

   a. Sell the business;

   b. Stay on and give her all to managing and growing the business; or

   c. Bring in a pro to run the business with her.

What Should Sadie Do?
How Does She Proceed?

1. It all goes back to this question: What does Sadie want from her life now that she has lost Max? She doesn't want to sit at home, the kids don't need her now, and she had been contemplating going back to work. She knows she has the skills to run the financial parts of Max's and she easily converses with customers.

2. Sadie decides not to sell the business. Since she doesn't want the overseas travel schedule, Sadie decides to hire an experienced GM and stay on as president.

3. Sadie now has to decide her own roles and those she wants the GM to handle. She is looking for the yin to her yang, someone whose pluses balance her minuses.

4. What must she do as the owner? She can't delegate these duties:

   a. Hiring and managing the GM and shaping his duties;

   b. Long-term budgeting and goal setting; and

   c. Tax and estate planning.

5. Each of these duties can be covered in their own chapters. Let's look at the most important one: the hiring and managing of the GM. What does Sadie want in this person?

   a. The GM must have experience in importing, customs, international finance and travel and the conventions of dealing with Asian businesses and people. How about language skills? Helpful, but not a necessity.

    b. Is Sadie more comfortable with a woman or a man? This is not a discriminatory situation. If twins with identical skills walked in, who would Sadie be more comfortable sharing so much of her life with?

6. How does Sadie find this person? An ad in the local paper won't cut it. She needs an ad in trade magazines and on trade websites specific to import/export or recommendations from friendly competitors, vendors and customers. But how can she write an ad when she isn't really sure what she wants in a GM? In this specific search her best bet is a professional head hunter with experience in Sadie's imports industry.

7. A good placement person will meet with Sadie personally, helping define the position, the financial package and the goals of the job. If the head hunter doesn't have a clear picture he can't fill the job! Expect to pay from 35 to 60 percent of the first year's salary. This is negotiable based on the salary level and the agency you choose. Make sure you get a "warranty"—if the GM doesn't last a minimum amount of time, you get a new search for free. At a minimum get 90 days, but you should be able to negotiate this to 180.

8. The placement agency should bring you a half-dozen candidates they have pre-screened to your standards. After your first interviews, if you didn't connect with a candidate, don't hesitate to ask for another panel of applicants. Chemistry with the person is the single most important quality Sadie is looking for.

9. Sadie should hold second interviews with candidates where she's comfortable. This will be the real in-depth conversation, lasting a full day and evening. Some tips for Sadie are:

    a. Bring in your current paperwork and ask the candidate for his opinions;

b. Open up your computer programs and ask the candidate to browse and ask questions, allowing you to see his computer skills. Does he look at customers first, or the general ledger? Is he interested in vendors or banking relationships? This subtly lets you know his interests;

c. Take him to lunch and see how he is in a social situation. Encourager him to order first; does he order a drink? Talk about his family at lunch or dinner. If a move is involved, talk about how this disruption will affect him;

d. Back at the office, bring in the history of some serious problems you have and discuss what he would do. You don't have to make up scenarios to test candidates; use real life from Sadie and Max's; and

e. Invite your two managers to spend time with the candidate and let them ask questions about situations they face. Get their opinions afterwards.

10. Reference-checking is important at this level. Even though the head hunter will have done this, you should ask the candidate for references and specify that you want their supervisor(s), not their assistants or their friends.

11. Keep the reference phone call conversational and personal. The agency will have confirmed employment dates, salaries and such. Ask about problem-solving ability, leadership experiences, work ethics and reaction to stressful situations.

12. If all you get is name, rank and serial number on the reference call, get back with the candidate and ask him to call his previous supervisor and say it is okay to speak with you. Even still, some companies will have a hard and fast rule about not giving references. References are easier to get from smaller, privately-held companies than larger public companies.

13. Do not take the best candidate the agency brings to you if you are not completely sure about hiring. Don't settle for "I hope he can

do the job." You want the feeling of, "I can't wait for her to start leading my team!"

14. Sadie should set up "stop signs' three months after hiring the GM, then six months, and another at twelve. She has to evaluate first her ongoing role and enjoyment and then the business success under the GM's leadership. Sadie must remember her initial goal: What does she want to do with her life?